D0929614

Markets, States, and Public Policy

# Markets, States, and Public Policy

## Privatization in Britain and France

Nikolaos Zahariadis

Ann Arbor

THE UNIVERSITY OF MICHIGAN PRESS

Copyright © by the University of Michigan 1995
All rights reserved
Published in the United States of America by
The University of Michigan Press
Manufactured in the United States of America
⊖ Printed on acid-free paper

1998   1997   1996   1995      4   3   2   1

*A CIP catalog record for this book is available from the British Library.*

Library of Congress Cataloging-in-Publication Data

Zahariadis, Nikolaos, 1961–
    Markets, states, and public policy : privatization in Britain and
France / Nikolaos Zahariadis.
        p.   cm.
    A revision of the author's thesis (doctoral)—University of
Georgia, 1992.
    Includes index.
    ISBN 0-472-10542-6 (alk. paper)
        1. Privatization—Great Britain. 2. Privatization—France.
    3. Industrial policy—Great Britain. 4. Industrial policy—France.
    I. Title.
    HD4148.Z34   1995
    338.941—dc20                                      94-46259
                                                           CIP

*To Ellen, for being there*

# Contents

# Acknowledgments

Just like so many other things in education, books are more than just products; they are journeys. The purpose is not so much in the final destination but in getting there. So I think it appropriate to present this work in the form of a journey. Inspiration came from "Ithaki," a poem by C. P. Cavafy who was a Greek poet from the turn of this century. He was in turn inspired by the work of yet another Greek, Homer's *Odyssey*. The translation of his verses is my own. The book is accordingly divided into four parts. Part 1 explains the purpose of the journey, details preparations for departure, and charts in broad terms the course to be followed. Parts 2 and 3 narrate the actual journey into two different ports. Part 4 describes the moment of arrival by reflecting upon the journey and by preparing for possible future ones.

The study first took shape as a dissertation, which I submitted to the University of Georgia in 1992. It subsequently went through numerous revisions to end up in its present form. I am intellectually indebted to Christopher S. Allen of the University of Georgia, who read tirelessly the entire manuscript during the various stages of the writing process. He has been a mentor, a colleague, and a friend. Hal Rainey, Martin Hillenbrand, Gary Green, Paul Sabatier, and Gary Bertsch also gave me constructive criticism. The library staff and Serge Schoen of the French Embassy in Washington, DC, were very helpful in making hard-to-find material available to me. Unless otherwise noted, all translations from the French are my own. During the formative stages of the process, I also received help from Asterios Kefalas, Euel Elliott, Al Cohan, Rick Travis, Ernie Morgan, Don Rodgers, Rod Whitlock, and Ahmed Liman. Peggy Bales at the Center for Global Policy Studies of the University of Georgia deserves special thanks for secretarial support. I would also like to thank the political science editor at the University of Michigan Press, Malcolm Litchfield, and two anonymous reviewers for many helpful comments and suggests. They certainly helped make this a better manuscript. My gratitude also extends to my parents for their emotional support throughout the various journeys in my life. Finally, my deepest gratitude is reserved for my wife, Ellen. Her devotion and patience have served as happy reminders that there is more to life than academia.

# Abbreviations

| | |
|---|---|
| BG | British Gas |
| BIMP | Banque Industriel et Immobilière Privée |
| BNOC | British National Oil Corporation |
| BNP | Banque Nationale de Paris |
| BOAC | British Overseas Airways Corporation |
| BP | British Petroleum |
| BR | British Rail |
| BRP | Bureau des Recherches de Pétrole |
| BT | British Telecom |
| BTC | British Transport Corporation |
| BTP | Banque du bâtiment en des Travaux Publics |
| BTUC | British Telecommunications Union Committee |
| CEO | chief executive officer |
| CFP | Compagnie Française de Pétroles |
| CGCT | Compagnie Générale des Constructions Téléphoniques |
| CGE | Compagnie Générale d'Electricité |
| CIC | Credit Industriel et Commercial |
| CII | Compagnie Internationale pour l'Informatique |
| CL | Crédit Lyonnais |
| CNCL | Commission Nationale des Communications et Libertés |
| DGT | Direction Générale des Télécommunications |
| DOI | Department of Industry |
| DOT | Department of Transport |
| DRG | Direction de la Réglementation Générale |
| DTI | Department of Trade and Industry |
| ECMT | European Conference of Ministers of Transport |
| EFL | external financing limit |
| ENST | Ecole Nationale Supérieure des Télécommunications |
| ERAP | Entreprise de Recherches et d'Activités Pétrolières |
| EU | European Union |
| FO | Force Ouvrière |
| FT | France Télécom |
| GDP | gross domestic product |

| | |
|---|---|
| IMF | International Monetary Fund |
| ITU | International Telecommunciations Union |
| LPTB | London Passenger Transport Board |
| MP | Member of Parliament |
| NOA | National Oil Account |
| NUR | National Union of Railwaymen |
| OECD | Organization for Economic Cooperation and Development |
| PO | Post Office |
| POEU | Post Office Engineering Union |
| PRT | Petroleum Revenue Tax |
| PSBR | Public Sector Borrowing Requirement |
| PSO | public service obligation |
| POUNC | Post Office Users National Council |
| PUK | Pechiney-Ugine-Kuhlmann |
| RAP | Régie Autonome des Pétroles |
| RPR | Rassemblement pour la République |
| SG | Société Générale |
| SNCF | Société Nationale des Chemins de fer Français |
| SNEA | Société Nationale Elf Aquitaine |
| SNPA | Société Nationale des Pétroles d'Aquitaine |
| SOE | state-owned enterprise |
| SOGENAL | Société Générale Alsacienne |
| TF1 | Télévision Française 1 |
| TGV | Train à Grande Vitesse |
| TUC | Trades Union Congress |
| UAP | Union des Assurances de Paris |
| UDF | Union pour la Démocratie Française |
| UNIR | Union Nationale pour l'Initiative et la Responsabilité |
| UPOW | Union of Post Office Workers |
| VANS | value-added network services |

# Part 1
# The Purpose

When you set out on your way to Ithaki
wish the journey to be long
full of adventure, full of discovery.

# CHAPTER 1

## To Sell or Not to Sell

In a memorable phrase, Adam Smith contends that "no two characters seem more inconsistent than those of trader and sovereign."[1] After considerable experimentation with state ownership, many governments are now taking Smith's assertion seriously. They are embracing policies designed to sell state-owned enterprises (SOEs)[2] as part of a general package of reforms aimed at redefining the appropriate economic role of the state. Paving the way, British Prime Minister Margaret Thatcher announced in 1979 a modest, at best, program that gradually became a tidal wave of privatization. Seven years later, French Prime Minister Jacques Chirac sought to reverse the growth of his nation's public sector. In both countries, governments have announced and implemented the most ambitious privatization programs to date in the industrialized West.

This trend is by no means confined to developed countries. Privatization has spread like wildfire in the underdeveloped countries of Africa, the stagnant economies of Latin America, and even the impressive "tigers" of Asia.[3] Even more remarkable is the trend among countries of the former Soviet bloc. Indeed, the push toward privatization is global. By the early 1990s, roughly $250 billion worth of state assets had been sold worldwide,[4] and in 1991 alone, $53.3 billion more was added to the total.[5] As one analyst astutely observed, "something is in the wind—something that has too much substance to be regarded as ephemeral."[6] These profound changes in policy raise an interesting question: Why do countries privatize?

Despite the global popularity of privatization, very little systematic attention has been paid to its underlying motivations. Analysts offer conflicting and sometimes "mystical" explanations. A member of the Prime Minister's Policy Unit on Privatization in Britain, for instance, characterizes the process as an "act of faith."[7] An analyst claims that privatization is part of a broader "myth" that "borrows aspects of neo-liberalism."[8] Another maintains that the policy has several rationales,[9] but the goals obviously differ across countries.[10] Finally, in a widely read article, Kay and Thompson contend that privatization is a policy in search of a rationale.[11] For all the hype about privatization, there is considerable analytical confusion, and the puzzling question remains unanswered: Why do countries privatize?

Conflicting claims, the conspicuous absence of theoretically grounded analyses—particularly those with a cross-national focus—and the plethora of advice on how to privatize suggest that many analysts are content with assuming the role of objective implementation experts. However, as the Nobel laureate George Stigler reminds us, "until we understand *why* our society adopts its policies, we will be poorly equipped to give useful advice on how to change these policies."[12] This book takes Stigler's advice seriously and aims to illuminate the dynamics of the policy-making process by identifying the factors that explain the shift away from state ownership in two European countries, Britain and France. The decision to transfer state assets to private hands has a profound impact on theories of political economy. If the corporation is, as Lindblom argues,[13] an instrument of political control, state corporations can be viewed as tools of state control. Does privatization aim to more clearly demarcate the boundaries of the public and private sectors in favor of the latter, or does it simply seek to alter the means of state control? Is it, as its proponents advocate, designed to roll back the state, or does it back its role?

Still, privatization involves much more than that. It helps redefine the appropriate economic role of the state and delves to the core of capitalism itself. As Sir Peter Parker, the former chair of the British Railways Board, astutely observed: "What is at stake is more than the credibility and respectability of public enterprise itself... there is also the credibility and respectability of the mixed economy."[14] Does privatization indicate the end of the entrepreneurial state? Is it a vindication of Adam Smith's claim that the characters of sovereign and trader are incompatible? Answers to these questions have profound implications for the future of mixed economy and will undoubtedly inform debates on the configuration of the single European market.

**What is Privatization?**

Interpreted broadly, privatization encompasses a wide range of policies aimed at changing the relationship between public and private sectors in favor of the latter. Indeed, one author characterizes privatization as "an umbrella term for many, different policies loosely linked by the way in which they are taken to mean a strengthening of the market at the expense of the state."[15]

This definition, however, is too broad to be useful in comparative research. Transferring responsibility can take numerous forms that differ across sectors and across countries. To avoid conceptual confusion, I adopt a narrow definition. Privatization is defined here as the transfer of the central government's ownership rights in commercial entities to private investors. I have chosen this definition for three reasons. First, this form includes a fairly tight set of similar questions and actors in contrast to the diversity of other forms. Second, this type is the most widely practiced, most ambitious, and most visible form of privatization. Third, it alleviates problems of issue equivalence.[16] Privatization often takes different forms in different countries. For analytical purposes, this is the most commonly used definition and the most appropriate to the countries under investigation, Britain and France.

There are several noteworthy features of my definition. First, it pays explicit attention to two crucial components of the term. It specifies what the focus of the transaction is and to whom responsibility is shifting.[17] Second, it keeps privatization conceptually distinct from other policies, such as deregulation. As two analysts astutely observed, "there is no logical connection between privatisation and competition" although the two "have been seen by some observers as intimately linked phenomena."[18] Indeed, as I will later show, the two are distinct options, and one may be pursued at the expense of the other. Third, the definition refers only to commercial activities commonly associated with manufacturing and infrastructural industries—such as oil, steel, telecommunications, or rail—and explicitly excludes the mass media and welfare-related services—such as health, housing, or education. Finally, the definition involves actions taken by the central or national government in its capacity as the sole or majority shareholder. Here I exclude privatization at the local level because the latter usually takes a different form, namely contracting out, and involves a different set of actors and questions.

Two final points need clarification. First, commercial entities here refer to parent corporations or commercially operated organizations, such as telecommunications authorities, and exclude subsidiaries. What makes privatization in the 1980s and 1990s unique is the call for selling parent corporations. Managers of French SOEs, for example, have been selling subsidiaries as part of their strategy to rationalize their portfolios since the early 1960s.[19] Second, with a few exceptions, privatization involves a transfer of at least majority ownership. Because these sales constitute integral parts of privatization policies, the definition here has been broadened to include partial divestiture as well.

### The Argument in Brief

The goals of this book are to identify factors that explain privatization across sectors within the same country and to show how variations in these factors also help explain differences in privatization across countries. The theoretical lens adopted in this study is a slight modification of Kingdon's agenda-setting model.[20] His work is situated within the broader "multiple streams" approach, which attempts to explain policy-making at the national level by employing the logic of timing and the structure of garbage cans.[21] In his formulation,

Kingdon conceptualizes the policy process as consisting of three unrelated streams: policies, problems, and politics. Specific policies are more likely to be adopted when the streams are coupled or joined together in specific ways during critical moments in time referred to as policy windows. Two features of this model merit special notice at the outset. First, the effects of each stream or factor—I use the terms interchangeably—are not additive. Each factor by itself is not likely to have an impact; rather, policy outputs depend heavily on coupling all three streams at an opportune time. Second, timing is conditioned by the structural elements of each stream and the institutional arrangements within which coupling takes place. In this way, both serendipity and institutional structure affect the final outcome. Although the multiple streams approach can conceivably be extended to cover the entire policy process, it is used here to explain only policy formation.[22] Thus, Kingdon's model is broadened here to cover not only agenda setting—that is, the process by which issues become the focus of the government's attention—but also decision making—that is, an authoritative choice among a limited universe of alternatives. Based on his work, I argue that privatization is brought about by coupling three factors in critical moments in time: the availability of alternatives generated in policy communities, high government borrowing needs, and the ideology and strategy of the governing party or coalition. More explicitly, I argue the following four points.

1. *The availability of alternatives generated in policy communities affects the likelihood of privatization. Such availability is conditioned by two elements: technical feasibility and value acceptability.* The policy stream includes a variety of ideas generated by specialists in policy communities—networks that include legislators, bureaucrats, business executives, union leaders, consumer groups, and researchers interested in a specific policy area (for example, telecommunications)—which are tried out in various ways, such as hearings, papers, or private conversations. Some ideas survive the period of "softening up" largely intact, others are combined into new proposals, and still others fade away. While the number of ideas floating in this primordial soup is quite large, only a few ever receive serious consideration. There are two selection criteria: technical feasibility[23] and value acceptability. An option that appears easier to implement stands a better chance of surviving this process; hence it is more likely to be adopted.[24] Moreover, proposals that do not conform to the values of most specialists are less likely to be adopted.

Whether an issue is raised or a solution adopted is heavily influenced by the option's "competition." Some solutions are available in certain instances and contexts but not in others. In this light, an examination of previous debates on the scope and mission of the public sector is an essential prerequisite to fully understanding the form that current solutions take. Precedent is important because the form of current alternatives is at least partially conditioned by the consequences of previous policies.[25] In general, the list of competing options relevant to privatization includes (1) default—current practice; (2) recapitalization—injecting private funds without changing ownership; (3) liberalization—removing statutory barriers to entry; and (4) internal reorganization—changing the legal status of an SOE or restructuring it internally without transferring ownership rights. The task is to show where privatization falls on this list and why it may float above others.

One reason for privatization's appeal is technical feasibility—that is, the extent to which the option can be implemented. Of particular interest here is the perception of policymakers that a possible sale can attract private interest. Asset valuation is an important consideration. Entities that already operate as commercial SOEs are more likely to encounter fewer valuation problems and consequently are likelier candidates for privatization than are others that operate as government departments. In addition, profitability and a strong demand growth make some SOEs more attractive than others to private investors. Another reason for considering privatization is value acceptability. If privatization is compatible with the values and interests of most community specialists, it stands a greater chance of being adopted. Consensus includes constant bargaining among interested groups, but it is also affected by their sense of equity and efficiency, which are subject to wide cross-national variations.

*2. Public finances affect the likelihood of privatization.* The second stream is that of problems. Why do policymakers pay attention to some problems and not others? The answer lies in the way officials learn about conditions and how these conditions are defined. Conditions can be identified in one of three ways. First, indicators (for example, a program's cost) may be used to assess the existence and magnitude of a condition. Sufficient change in a condition can then be used to catch official attention. Second, dramatic events or crises can occasionally call attention to a problem. Plane crashes, for example, serve as powerful stimulants for increased air safety. Finally, feedback from existing programs can bring conditions to the fore. In this context, precedent, or the success or failure of previous policies, may bring attention to certain conditions and help define them as problems.

Budgetary constraints are an important problem affecting the likelihood of privatization. Rising government borrowing needs create pressures to curb public expenditures, particularly in times of increased hostility among the electorate toward raising taxes. Privatization is viewed as a policy that, at least in the short term, reduces the need to borrow funds. Other things being equal, higher borrowing needs make privatization more likely.

*3. Parties matter!* Turnover of key policymakers in the broader political stream means that new issues will be raised and consequently different options may be adopted. In this sense, the ideological complexion of the governing party or coalition makes a difference because an influx of officials who are predisposed against "big" government is likely to propel issues such as privatization into high prominence. At this point, a distinction should be made between the Anglo-American preference for limited government and the continental European tradition of an activist state.[26] Against this broad background, parties differ ideologically within specific national contexts. It follows that depending on electoral success, some policymakers are more inclined than others to adopt privatization measures.

Ideology is obviously important, but the usual conservative-socialist dichotomy is too simplistic to serve as a guide here. Even though Britain's Thatcher or Major and France's Chirac or Ballabur can be labeled conservatives, for they are certainly not socialists, they differ markedly on their views over the appropriate economic role of the state. How can the effects of ideology be understood? Inspired by Castles's work,[27] I argue that close identification with state ownership colors a party's view of the role and limits of the sovereign entrepreneur. When times are good, politicians cherish the affiliation of a successful economic strategy with their party. They strengthen and promote this identification as much as possible to enhance their electoral success. This is particularly true of highly visible policies, such as nationalization, which run through the very core of party ideology and are espoused with considerable fervor. De Gaulle and his partisan successors in France and, to a lesser extent, the Conservatives in Britain are two examples. In periods of economic crisis, however, dissociating the party from the policy becomes problematic because past legacies cannot be easily overcome. A possible reversal of policy requires action on two fronts. Politicians must not only dispel the voters' perception of their lack of responsibility for failures, but they must also convince their own supporters that reversing course is to the latter's benefit. Consequently, parties intimately involved in nationalizing and running SOEs are less likely to endorse privatization. In case they do, the scope of privatization will be limited. In addition, the likelihood and form of privatization are influenced by political strategy—that is, the ability of the opposition to offer credible ownership and funding alternatives.

*4. Specific policies are more likely to be adopted when all three streams are coupled. This process differs across countries making privatization, in some instances, a policy in search of a rationale.* An important feature of the multiple streams approach is coupling. The impact of each factor is conditional upon its specific combination with the effects of the others. The effects of the aforementioned factors, in other words, are not additive; rather, policy outputs depend heavily upon coupling the streams at critical moments in time, labeled policy windows. Policies, in this case privatization, are more likely to be adopted when all three streams are coupled. A viable proposal worked out in the policy stream stands a greater chance of being adopted "when all three elements—problems, proposals, and political receptivity—are coupled into a single package."[28] When windows open, operationalized here as opened by election outcomes, specialists in policy communities try to take advantage of the political climate by attaching a problem to their pet solution. Timing is an important ingredient of successful coupling. The particular problem-solution sequence of coupling—whether policies are espoused first and then given a rationale or vice versa—differs across countries, depending on histori cal circumstances and the degree of fragmentation of political power. Finally, success in one area may also spill over to another. Politicians, for example, find it easier to argue for privatizing an SOE if they can point to previously successful sales. This is because the same coalition of forces can be trans-ferred across sectors within the same country and because of the powerful effects of precedent.

My argument has two theoretical aims. The first of these is to illuminate the dynamics of the policy-formation process. The theory is grounded on Kingdon's model, and my contribution to his work is twofold. First, I broaden the multiple streams approach to the entire policy-formation process, beyond Kingdon's narrow focus on agenda setting. The comparative focus of the study also allows me to examine a model that was developed within a specific national context (United States) and explore some of the limitations of Kingdon's conclusions. The analysis bears the cost of being restricted to one, albeit very important, issue, but it reaps the benefit of generalizing from evidence in several sectors across two countries. Second, I seek to illuminate the features of different countries that not only structure the flow of each stream, but also condition the process of coupling. Conventional perspectives of policy formation assume a problem-solution sequence: solutions are thought to be the result of careful and clear definition of problems. Kingdon, however, claims the reverse often to be the case. Policy entrepreneurs fre-quently espouse solutions first, then seek out problems that policies might conceivably solve. The approach's attention to timing enables me to address this paradox by specifying the conditions under which one sequence might be more likely than the other.

The second theoretical aim of my argument is to show that privatization in and of itself is a concern in political economy. Privatization involves a politically forged decision to shape the configuration of markets by foregoing direct control (ownership) in favor of indirect control (hybrid or proxy owner-ship and regulation). Far from rolling back the frontiers of the state, the findings suggest that political influence is likely to continue not because privatization has been derailed from its original objectives, but because main-taining some form of political influence was part of its original design. Still, the decision to sell involves more than just a political debate on SOE inefficiency. The ability of SOEs in certain countries to deliver the goods and services they promised as well as to provide a public service—at a substantial cost, to be sure—supply a rationale for maintaining some or perhaps adjusting the ownership composition of others. These ideas pose a challenge to reformulate the state versus market debate in search of novel forms of economic organization that will ultimately serve the public interest.

## Research Design

Why do countries privatize? Concentrating on industrialized democracies, I draw mainly from the experience of Thatcher's and Major's Britain and Mitterrand's France.[29] Although governments in both countries have implemented large-scale privatization programs, the specific form differs dramatically between them. The choice of countries follows the logic of a "most similar systems" design.[30] Its purpose is to find a pair with as many similarities as possible, thereby controlling for the effects of theoretically important factors, and explain cross-national differences on the basis of a few experimental variables. It follows that the case studies must show variation in the independent as well as the dependent variables. The selection of Britain and France is well suited to the argument outlined previously for three reasons. First, the values of the three streams in each country—for example, the ideological complexion of governing parties—vary considerably over time, allowing me to examine the effects of a variety of combinations that might affect the final outcome. Second, there is sufficient cross-national variation in the streams at any given time to permit a comparative analysis—for example, the availability of alternative solutions in policy communities varies considerably. Third, coupling takes place against sharply contrasting historical traditions and institutional rules, illuminating the conditions under which the three streams might be coupled successfully and pointing to possible variations in the problem-solution sequence.

Furthermore, the two countries conveniently hold constant four variables that are often cited in the literature as important factors affecting a state's economic policy. First, the size and openness of a country's economy affect that state's response to external factors. Small economies, for example, tend to be more open, in that such economies have high ratios of trade relative to GNP and are therefore more vulnerable to the international environment. As a result, their policies favor institutional flexibility and adaptation to "changes imposed from abroad."[31] In contrast, large states are accustomed to "rule making" rather than "rule taking," although the former is becoming increasingly difficult to accomplish in an interdependent world.[32] By selecting two midsize economies with similar levels of openness, I seek to control for the effect of world markets on differences in privatization.

Second, a country's level of economic development also affects policy.

Countries at the early stages of development tend to bestow upon the state a more active economic role. In many developing countries, for example, SOEs commonly have been used as substitutes for a nascent and feeble private sector, as tools for asserting national independence, or as instruments for capturing oligopolistic rents.[33] Moreover, developing countries tend to be more susceptible to pressures from international organizations. For instance, loans and expert advice from the International Monetary Fund (IMF) and the World Bank have acted as catalysts for bringing about privatization in developing countries.[34] By selecting two countries with high levels of economic development, I seek to control for the degree of external pressure to illuminate the domestic aspects of the privatization decision.

Third, the size and scope of the public sector affect the propensity to privatize. It is clearly difficult to privatize extensively if there is little to sell. Consequently, the selection must include countries with comparable levels of state ownership. Table 1.1 provides percentages illustrating the extent of state ownership by industry in a number of industrialized nations in the Organization for Economic Cooperation and Development (OECD) for the late 1980s. What is striking about the data is the extreme diversity across countries. State presence seems strongest in France, with 100 percent state ownership in six of the eleven sectors, and weakest in the United States, with no 100 percent presence in any sector and 0 percent in eight sectors. Moreover, SOEs seem to be more prevalent in infrastructural sectors—such as rail, post, and electricity—and less prevalent in competitive sectors—such as steel, automobiles, and shipbuilding. Comparing privatization in France with the United States is bound to reveal differences attributable strictly to the lack of SOEs in some sectors. By selecting Britain and France, I can control for the effects of size and scope of the public sector.

Fourth and finally, both Britain and France have unitary structures of administrative power. This fact eliminates problems in intergovernmental relations concerning the articulation and implementation of privatization.[35] Several authors, for example, have noted the importance of regional German governments (*Länder*) in shaping patterns of state ownership and minimizing the role of the central government.[36] In unitary systems, the state does not normally encounter such counterbalancing opposition from subnational governments.

Explanations that stay exclusively on a systemic level, however, overlook a crucial component. Policies can vary considerably, not only across countries, but also across sectors or industries within the same country.[37] A complete explanation would therefore have to take into account factors that explain why privatization affected enterprises in some sectors but not in others. To take into consideration all possible outcomes, the theoretical analysis should include eight cases (four sectors in two countries): one sector in

**TABLE 1.1.   Percentage of State Ownership in Industry, Selected OECD Countries, Late 1980s**

| Country | Post | Telecomm. | Electricity | Gas | Oil | Coal | Rail | Air | Automobiles | Steel | Shipbuilding |
|---------|------|-----------|-------------|-----|-----|------|------|-----|-------------|-------|--------------|
| U.S.A.  | 90   | 0         | 25          | 0   | 0   | 0    | 25   | 0   | 0           | 0     | 0            |
| Japan   | 100  | 33        | 0           | 0   | n.a.| 0    | 25   | 0   | 0           | 0     | 0            |
| Germany | 100  | 100       | 75          | 50  | 25  | 50   | 100  | 100 | 25          | 0     | 25           |
| France  | 100  | 100       | 100         | 100 | n.a.| 100  | 100  | 75  | 50          | 75    | 0            |
| Italy   | 100  | 100       | 75          | 100 | n.a.| n.a. | 100  | 100 | 25          | 75    | 75           |
| U.K.    | 100  | 0         | 100         | 25  | 25  | 100  | 100  | 0   | 0           | 75    | 50           |
| Canada  | 100  | 25        | 100         | 0   | 0   | 0    | 75   | 75  | 0           | 0     | 0            |

*Source: Financial Times*, 12 February 1991, 5.

n.a. = not available.

Sector

| Country | 1 | 2 | 3 | 4 |
|---------|---|---|---|---|
| A | P | P | N | N |
| B | P | N | P | N |

Fig. 1.1.   Matrix of privatization outcomes in two countries. P = Privatized;
N = Not privatized.

which both countries privatized, one in which both did not, and two that yield
mixed results (fig. 1.1). Actual sectors in which both Britain and France
privatized are only two: oil and banking.[38] Although there are numerous
sectors in which the British divested but the French did not, there are unfortunately no sectors where the reverse is true. This can be attributed to the
breadth of the British privatization program. To date, major SOEs in Britain
have been sold in all but two sectors—coal and railroads—and they too are
likely to be sold. No SOEs have been privatized in either sector in France.
Because of such peculiarities, I was forced to reduce the number of sectors
to be examined to three (sectors 1, 2, and 4 in fig. 1.1).

Although this exercise dramatically reduces the number of suitable candidates for analysis, the list is still too long. To guide the selection of final
candidates, I used three criteria: importance, breadth, and contrast. More
economically important sectors obviously strengthen the study's implications
for theory and policy. In addition, the sectors should cover as many aspects
of the privatization programs in both countries as possible. Finally, the sectors
should include industries that are structured differently. Selecting sectors that
involve "substantively interesting contrasts" should increase the general-
izability of the study.[39]

Using these three criteria, I selected three sectors: oil, telecommunications,[40] and railroads. They are economically important; taken together, they
capture the key aspects of privatization in Britain and France. Oil is the single
most important source of energy. I also chose to contrast telecommunications
to railroads because in an "information" society, telecommunications can be
regarded as infrastructurally significant as railroads were during industrialization. This is particularly true in developed countries where a shift toward a
service economy means that information-based services are emerging as a
major comparative advantage vis-à-vis developing nations.[41] For this reason,
the sector can be expected to "represent the heartland of the state's control

of industry,"[42] and any attempt to alter the prevailing form of control is certainly of critical economic and political importance. The case of telecommunications takes on added significance in the British case because the privatization of British Telecom (BT) served as the model for selling all public utilities.[43] Moreover, the sale of BT, according to a British official in charge of privatization, served as a catalyst for Thatcher's program as its size and success dispelled skepticism over Conservative commitment to dismantle the entire public sector.[44] I selected oil over banks (the other sector of privatization overlap) partially because oil is a "good-producing" sector, and it contrasts nicely with the other "service-providing" sectors. Moreover, the state maintained substantial oil ownership in both countries, whereas British banks, in contrast to French ones, have traditionally and overwhelmingly been in private hands. Finally, I selected railroads over coal to increase the substantive contrast by examining transport rather than just another source of energy.

Finally, the explanation must also pay attention to the privatization of particular enterprises because state ownership is firm-specific. Here I examine why British National Oil Corporation (BNOC) and Elf Aquitaine were privatized, why British Telecom (BT) was sold but France Télécom (FT) was not, and why parts of British Rail (BR)[45] and Société Nationale des Chemins de fer Français (SNCF) still remain under state ownership. The selection was influenced by cross-national comparability in corporate size and mission.

### Plan of the Book

Why do countries privatize? The central argument of the book is that privatization is brought about by coupling three factors in critical moments in time: the availability of alternatives generated in policy communities, high government borrowing needs, and the ideological complexion and strategy of the governing party or parties. While it is important to clearly spell out what the study will do, it may be equally fruitful to stipulate what it will not cover. I will not address issues of implementation or evaluation; neither will I engage in analyses of issues arising after privatization (for example, regulation) or in prescriptions on whether or when sales should take place.

The book is divided into four parts. The introductory chapter in part 1 supplied a brief overview of the argument. After examining various explanations for privatization, chapter 2 proposes a model for thinking about the process of policy formation that highlights the factors that affect the likelihood of privatization. Part 2 of the book deals with the British experience. Chapter 3 examines events in the problem and politics streams. Chapter 4 analyzes developments in the policy stream across three sectors: oil, telecommunications, and railroads as well as the important process of coupling. Part 3 is devoted to France and similarly divided into two chapters. Chapter 5 looks at the two conceptual variables, the politics and problem streams, while chapter 6 analyzes the French privatization program by focusing on developments in the policy stream. Finally, part 4 is the conclusion, in which chapter 7 addresses the book's theoretical implications for the study of comparative public policy and political economy.

CHAPTER 2

# Perspectives on Privatization

A logical way to begin the search for an explanation of privatization is to look at how others have sought to explain it. I examine three perspectives: rational approaches, the governing-party perspective, and the institutional approach. Each supplies only a few pieces of the puzzle, and none fully answers the question. In a later part of the chapter, I propose a model that gives a more complete understanding of the policy-formation process. It will highlight the factors that affect the likelihood of privatization and will serve as the theoretical guide to the analysis in ensuing chapters.

## Rational Approaches

Rational approaches involve the application of economic assumptions and analytical tools to the study of politics. Focusing on individual behavior, they assume that every person is a rational, self-interested, utility maximizer. Three variants are particularly relevant to privatization: public choice, property rights, and industry structure.

### Public Choice

By focusing on government growth, public choice theorists have been very influential in stimulating the drive toward privatization in Britain and else-where.[1] Although the focus differs from one theorist to the next, explanations arrive at the same two conclusions: (1) public spending is increased by factors outside the control of the governing party; and (2) government—that is, the public provision of goods and services—is inefficient.

Politicians and political parties are thought to be driven by the logic of party competition.[2] Parties compete for individual votes by promising to improve the voter's lot, thereby increasing voter expectations about what government can and should do. Once in office, politicians use a political cost-benefit analysis to formulate public policy. The costs and benefits of most tax-funded programs are either widely distributed among individuals or the costs are distributed and the benefits concentrated. These characteristics of government programs result in the formation of spending coalitions composed of interest groups that include beneficiaries, service or good providers, government administrators, and political activists.[3] In general, groups whose subsidization is cheap or taxation expensive tend to be more politically successful.[4] Operating in a logrolling fashion, spending coalitions push up government budgets containing items that would not be included if voted on individually.

Bureaucratic behavior further reinforces this process. Because rational bureaucrats try to maximize their own interests, budget maximization becomes the overall motivating principle.[5] The bureaucrats' own welfare usually comes in the form of job security or pecuniary benefits, but even selfless bureaucrats acting in the public interest have incentives to inflate the budget. This is so because it is quicker and less painful to improve an agency's effectiveness by expanding its resources, creating a new unit, and staffing it with new people than by firing incompetents or changing attitudes. Thus, agencies tend to inflate their budgets that are submitted to legislatures that share largely similar objectives, particularly when faced with high demand for agency output. For this reason, goods and services tend to be oversupplied by governments; they are supplied in levels twice as high as those provided by private firms. As one author boldly states, the purpose behind privatization "derives from the recognition that the weaknesses of public supply are inherent."[6]

Public choice not only considers the public sector to be inefficient, but also views government growth as increasing by factors beyond any government's control. Pirie summarizes this point well:

> ... neither the resolution of government nor the power it can deploy is sufficient to the task of making substantial reductions in public sector activity, nor in securing any significant savings in the cost of them ... [T]he political forces which operate within and through the state sector of the economy are more powerful than the forces which government can bring to bear upon it.[7]

Using simple yet powerful logic, public choice persuasively explains why a variety of political actors have strong incentives to foster the growth of government. Pointing to the inefficiency of government, it also provides a normative rationale for privatization. Public choice has difficulty explaining the *actual* decision to privatize, however. Why would rational politicians suddenly decide that it is in their interest to *reduce* the size of government? What has caused the collapse of the ubiquitous spending coalitions?

Privatization is a risky and highly controversial issue, making it an unattractive option for risk-averse politicians. As Brittan reminds us, although Conservative planners in Britain considered privatization long before their coming to power in 1979, they were afraid of the formidable technical difficulties involved and the issue's political infeasibility.[8] French officials faced even worse odds. Given the dominant role that the state plays in making economic policy, it is not at all clear why they would favor such a politically risky policy. In short, it is not obvious why rational politicians would not only depart from "politics as usual," but also adopt a policy that may mean political suicide.

Perhaps more plausible would be an explanation stressing the importance of certain pressure groups as part of the winning coalition. If legislators are not likely to press for privatization, then perhaps state managers will. It could be argued that managers on the boards of SOEs can succeed in persuading the government to sell some of its assets. Reality, however, is different from theory. The argument seems to overestimate the actual power of management to single-handedly initiate such a drastic reversal in existing policy in spite of wide political skepticism. Evidence from Britain suggests that managers more often acquiesced and occasionally opposed government plans to privatize. In some cases, particularly those concerning the introduction of competition, the government succumbed to management objections in return for a speedier and more trouble-free process.[9] This means that it is more likely that management played a greater role in shaping rather than initiating privatization.

An even greater difficulty, however, is posed by the very existence of spending coalitions. Public choice theorists argue that government constantly grows. They further stress the importance of interest groups in pressing for more public spending. In this case, there are presumably budget-maximizing groups that intend to reduce the size of government. If the interests of spending coalitions rest with pushing government budgets up, why this sudden change of heart?

So the question remains: what caused the apparent collapse of spending coalitions? For many, it is simply the advent of new leadership, what Dunleavy labels the "heroic" argument.[10] These coalitions collapsed largely because of the personality of wise leaders, such as Thatcher and Chirac, and their ability to forge new coalitions that successfully neutralized the opposition and maximized support for their policies.[11] If this is the case, then public choice also brings into serious doubt previous estimations of the power of budget-maximizing interest groups to foster government growth. Indeed, the "heroic" answer sharply contradicts earlier claims regarding the "myth" of legislative omnipotence. "There cannot be any necessary quality about bureaucratic over-supply and budget-maximization behaviour if a simple change of political will at the helm of representative institutions is enough to make the state apparatus operate in a basically different way."[12] Moreover, by claiming that politicians adopt privatization in the name of the public interest despite widespread opposition, public choice falls victim to the same criticism out of which it grew, namely, the lack of realism in assuming that public officials and civil servants somehow know better and are more dedicated to the public interest than are ordinary citizens.

Although public choice appears persuasive on a normative level, it fails on a positive one. It offers powerful arguments for why governments should privatize, but it has difficulty explaining why they actually do. It is precisely the lack of attention to the role of ideology concerning the public interest that inhibits public choice from providing a full explanation for privatization.

### Property Rights

Scholars who adopt this perspective focus on alternative ownership arrangements as a means of explaining the economic behavior of individuals. Property rights are defined as "the rights of individuals to use resources."[13] Different bundles of ownership rights typically embody different restraints upon such use, and they therefore present decision makers with different opportunities to pursue their individual gain.

Unlike those for public choice, property-rights theorists disagree in theory and practice over the effects of ownership on economic performance. Some argue that the system of property rights under state ownership reduces the extent to which individuals bear the consequences of their decisions.[14] Privatization changes the structure of incentives between the shareholders (principal) and management (agent) by providing managers with stronger incentives to introduce cost-reducing innovations, incur lower operating and production costs, and produce a greater variety of outputs. In addition, even the mere threat of privatization can have beneficial effects: the higher the contestability of ownership—that is, the greater the credibility of the threat of transfer of ownership—the greater the improvements in efficiency are likely to be.[15] Overall, private firms are regarded to be more efficient in meeting well-defined goals because they operate more flexibly than do multipurpose SOEs. This is because SOEs often fall prey to politicians who use them for political purposes, such as maintaining high levels of employment or doing favors for constituents, with little regard to economic imperatives such as profitability. Consequently, it is the status of SOEs as political entities that makes them inefficient.

Others contend that inefficiency, at least in theory, stems from high monitoring costs.[16] This is because performance is monitored at two levels: voters-ministers and ministers-managers. Monitoring is difficult in the first level because it takes place through an imperfect political market that was not set up to address specific issues of industrial performance. It is precisely the weak links between the shareholders at large (voters) and ministers that account for the observed relative inefficiency of SOEs in competitive markets. Beneficial effects of a change in ownership, however, will not be automatic unless the change is accompanied by regulation and competition. Regulation is designed to reduce monitoring costs by restructuring managerial incentives and still promoting the social welfare. Under this scheme, shareholders can better monitor performance by inducing profit-seeking behavior and by enforcing the discipline of capital markets. Moreover, competition decreases information asymmetries by revealing project costs. Ownership matters, so the argument goes, only if factors concerning market structure and regulation are taken into consideration.

The empirical evidence yields mixed results.[17] On the one hand, the two main architects of British privatization, Beesley and Littlechild, argue that ownership matters because profit-oriented private enterprises are more responsive to consumer needs.[18] Therefore, privatization will necessarily yield benefits to consumers by enhancing the quality of services or reducing prices. Moreover, the discipline of capital markets provides efficiency incentives that are uniquely applicable to private firms. Because SOEs do not raise capital in private markets, they have fewer incentives to pursue economic efficiency. In a widely read article, Pryke concludes that the most likely explanation for the poor economic performance of SOEs is state ownership.[19] This is because state ownership destroys the commercial ethic, partly by eliminating the discipline of product and capital markets and partly by inducing the harmful belief that SOEs should maintain unprofitable activities in the name of public service.

Others have presented conflicting evidence. After comparing two Canadian railroad companies, one public and the other private, Caves and Christensen were unable to link poor performance to ownership, concluding that state ownership is not inherently inefficient.[20] Sikorsky points out that in countries where governments do not generally support declining industries, the public sector is efficient.[21] Duch adds that the economic performance of SOEs depends less on ownership and more on political control. Countries in which telecommunications authorities are relatively free of government controls have performed better than the rest.[22]

The explanation for such divergence of opinion rests partially on methodological grounds. There are serious methodological difficulties in isolating the effects of ownership from general macroeconomic conditions, the effects of specific product cycles, and problems stemming from managerial incompetence. Difficulties are further compounded by cross-national differences in legal structures, accounting procedures, and financial controls. SOE access to private capital, for example, differs between Britain and France. Whereas British SOEs have had to borrow from the government strictly within public expenditure limits, French SOEs have been encouraged to borrow in national and international markets to supplement self-generated funds and treasury loans. Without proper qualification, generalizations concerning the discipline of capital markets remain inappropriate.

Moreover, recent experience from leveraged buyouts in the United States suggests that monitoring processes do not necessarily function effectively in private companies.[23] Consequently, even private managers can make decisions that do not maximize shareholder value. Moreover, gains in efficiency can be made by improving monitoring (liberalization or regulation) arrangements, without a necessary change in ownership. Analysts agree that the most that can be said about the comparative performance of SOEs and private firms is that under competitive conditions, private firms tend to be more efficient.[24] The problem, however, is that SOEs rarely operate in competitive markets. The key factor may therefore be that industry structure rather than ownership accounts for a firm's performance.

### Industry Structure

Vernon puts forth the proposition that industry characteristics play an important role in determining the course and form of privatization.[25] Pointing to recent changes in the structure of international markets, he argues that the monopolistic rents that governments hoped to capture by creating SOEs in certain industries have for the most part disappeared. When governments established national oil companies in the 1960s and 1970s, for example, they inadvertently reduced the oligopolistic advantages enjoyed by oil companies in previous decades. A substantial drop in oil revenues caused by the plunge of oil prices in the mid-1980s put the brakes on dreams for high profits and exerted pressure on national oil executives to find ways to reduce costs. In addition, rising budget deficits afflicting most industrialized countries, coupled with increasing numbers of refineries, made the sale of state assets a convenient way to both maximize revenue and curb public spending.[26]

Changes in the basic structure of certain industries brought about by technological innovation have also prompted a reevaluation of the utility of state ownership. By viewing ownership as a restriction on portfolio allocations among investors, Mayer concludes that ownership patterns are not likely to be stable over time.[27] Privatization is more likely to occur in industries that experience high degrees of technological innovation because continued innovation requires substantial investment, and private rather than state ownership permits more efficient gains from investments. In addition, competitive opportunities have opened up in certain areas of the telecommunications industry, largely because of technological advances in transmission services and supply equipment.[28] Although the running of networks, with the exception of long-distance communications, may still be a natural monopoly, there is no reason to expect it in the provision of terminal equipment. Privatization, so the argument goes, is the logical outcome; however, the form that privatization will take depends upon the political muscle of affected interest groups. Thus, to secure political support for privatization from BT's management in 1984, politicians had to make concessions concerning the introduction of competition. This is so not only because securing management's approval is essential to a speedier and politically less troublesome sale, but also because controlling the number of new entrants might enhance the prospects of BT's profitability.

Although this variant goes a long way toward explaining the privatization of several industries, it still does not provide a full explanation. Market and technological changes seem to provide an explanation of the French decision to (partially) privatize Elf, but they do not adequately account for the British decision. Thatcher's government split BNOC and sold one of its parts, Britoil, at the end of 1982. By then world oil prices were falling steadily. The decision to privatize, however, was seriously entertained shortly after Thatcher's advent to power in 1979, when prices were still rising. There were additional, political considerations, quite distinct from industry events, that precipitated the decision. In addition, emphasis on technological innovation says nothing about why the British privatized telecommunications but the French did not. Moreover, it does not explain why the French have not privatized railroads despite considerable technological advances in high-speed rail, but Conservatives committed to privatizing BR in the absence of a comparable level of innovation in Britain.

### The Governing-Party Perspective

Adopting the classical view of politics, some analysts argue that policy outputs are heavily determined by the governing party's ideological proclivities.[29] When new people reach the pinnacles of political authority, they will raise new issues and seek to pass their own legislative program designed to address what they perceive to be the country's pressing problems. As parties move in and out of office, policy outputs will vary, making it more likely that certain policies will be pursued by some parties but not others.

British privatization is commonly explained by reference to Conservative ideology and strategy.[30] Emerging from a major reevaluation of the party's ideological direction, which was prompted by electoral defeat in 1974, Conservative leaders developed a strategy to gain votes by attacking the growing public sector. Although the 1979 Conservative Manifesto devoted little attention to privatization, frustration caused by a sluggish economy and by difficulties in restraining public expenditures had convinced Thatcher that "the nationalized industries were the most persistent area of failure of her [first] administration."[31] Privatization was thus seen as a convenient way of reducing the cash drain on public finances, as an instrument of containing union power, and as a populist way of appealing to a lower-middle-class majority that was leery of supporting the poor and those who did not work hard. Transforming attitudes by creating a new "enterprise culture" based on private ownership and competition further reinforced the drive to sell SOEs.[32]

Ideology was similarly important in precipitating the French program.[33] There were, however, important differences. French officials did not share the same antiunion fervor with their British counterparts. Moreover, with some exceptions, calls for privatization emphasized the need to protect the French state by preventing its further disintegration rather than the need to dismantle the state because of its inherent inefficiency as an economic institution. These differences, the argument maintains, can be attributed to each country's historical experience with nationalization and the political context within which each found itself in the late 1970s and the 1980s.[34] In contrast to Thatcher's privatization, Chirac's program in 1986 was a partial reaction to Mitterrand's massive nationalizations of 1982.

The governing-party perspective provides part of the privatization answer, but the explanation is not without problems, largely because of the way ideology is usually viewed. Parties are divided into either conservative or socialist; conservatives are thought to privatize whereas socialists nationalize. Such a dichotomy, however, is too simplistic to be analytically useful. Certainly, the advent to power of Thatcher and Chirac proved to be a catalyst for privatization. Yet their ideological proclivities were not the same. Chirac attached much greater usefulness and legitimacy to state ownership than did Thatcher. There were consequently differences in the size and scope of privatization that could be attributed to governing parties but cannot be captured by labeling them both as conservative. Moreover, privatization programs have been initiated in other countries under socialist governments, such as Australia and New Zealand under Labour.

In addition, a party's ideology changes over time. Conservatives under Thatcher are quite different from those under Edward Heath in the 1970s or under Winston Churchill in the early 1950s. As I will show in part 2, Churchill accepted the idea of state ownership in certain cases as a necessary tool for industrial reinvigoration. Ironically, although that view was hailed as highly pragmatic at the time,[35] it was later condemned by Thatcher and Sir Keith Joseph as opportunistic and counterproductive. Consequently, generalizations over party preferences must be grounded within a certain historical context. Despite these problems, however, this discussion does not imply that parties are not important. If ideology did not play a major role, should we conclude that had Labour won the election in 1979, still the government would have privatized? Similarly, if parties made no difference, how can we explain Mitterrand's decision to interrupt Chirac's program in 1988, or later sales with a distinct Socialist flavor? The importance of parties must remain, for the time being, a contentious claim.

## The Institutional Approach

Analysts who adopt this perspective seek to explain privatization by calling attention to domestic political structures. By emphasizing the institutional arrangements that bind the state and society, these scholars view policy choice to be the result of regularized patterns of interaction between various political actors.[36] Although they are careful to acknowledge common elements of problem solving, they also maintain that policy-making unfolds according to a national style that is dependent as much on institutional patterns as it is on prevailing elite values. Thus, within a pluralist framework, British government officials generally stress the need for prior consultation with affected groups. In contrast, the French system is said to be characterized by a state that tends to internalize decision making, aided by extraordinary cohesion among members of the political elite.[37] Protest rather than consultation tends to be the mode of input by affected social groups. Finally, important policy decisions may be negotiated directly by political groups and the state in corporatist settings outside governmental forums, such as in Austria, Sweden, or Germany.

Using this approach, Duch sets out to explain why some countries adopt liberalization or privatization measures while others do not.[38] In his examination of telecommunications policy in Britain, France, and Germany, Duch argues that liberalization or privatization is more likely in countries with pluralist styles of interest accommodation, such as Britain. Because of large numbers of fairly small distribution coalitions with relatively open access to policymakers, the chances of success are greatest under pluralism. The absence of a dominant group or coalition and its lack of blocking power ensure that such demands will not be frustrated. In contrast, in countries with statist styles of interest accommodation, such as France, liberalization is less likely. This is because liberalization represents a threat to the state's hold over the economy, and therefore government policymakers and planners, the main actors under statism, have an incentive not to pursue such policies. Finally, corporatist structures are the least responsive to liberalization because he argues: (1) the members of so-called encompassing coalitions, such as major corporations and unions, are also least likely to benefit from increased competition; (2) increased competition threatens the cohesiveness of coalitions; and (3) groups advocating such drastic changes are usually outside the dominant coalition and lack the explicit or implicit designation as "legitimate" representatives of social interests.

Despite its appeal, Duch's explanation suffers from two drawbacks. First, Duch does not differentiate between liberalization and privatization. One alternative must be kept analytically distinct from the other because there is no logical connection between privatization (a change in ownership) and liberalization (a change in market structure).[39] In contrast to liberalization, the logic of privatization conceptually divorces state ownership from state control because governments abandon direct control as providers and assume indirect control as regulators.[40] The second drawback is that Duch's explanation rests on the supposition, rather than the proposition, that institutional arrangements remain constant over time. Certainly, pluralism is commonly used to explain British policy-making, but in the case of privatization, the state has proven to be much more than just a black box or a neutral arena. It made a difference that Thatcherite Conservatives—such as Joseph, Patrick Jenkin, and Norman Tebbit—served at the top of the powerful Department of Industry (now Department of Trade and Industry). They were more sympathetic to privatization than Labour ministers would have been and were certainly influential in shaping the final outcome. Consequently, actors within the state itself played a major role in the policy-formation process. Conversely, the privatization program in France (or its absence in certain sectors) was not strictly the product of a few individuals who occupied the pinnacles of state authority. There were several societal groups that actually supported privatization and others that actively opposed it. Whether the policy was made in the interest of certain groups or at their behest is difficult to determine.[41] The problem is that state interests did not diverge sufficiently from those of certain societal groups. In the absence of such conflict, a statist explanation of the French case remains unconvincing.

The approach's explanatory capability is further weakened because it does not take ideology into explicit consideration. Problems are defined differently by parties of the Left or the Right. All industrialized democracies faced economic difficulties in the 1970s and 1980s. The French Socialists, however, defined their problems differently than did British Conservatives. While Thatcher moved toward privatization, Mitterrand embarked on an ambitious nationalization program. It was only until the Gaullist coalition's advent to power in 1986 that the French began to sell SOEs on a massive scale. As I will show in later chapters, even this program differs considerably from the British program. More importantly, Chirac's privatization was interrupted by the Socialist return to power, but it has since been revived. Explicit attention to ideology can partially account for these variations.

The explanations for privatization so far have been incomplete and inconclusive. The governing-party perspective provides part of the answer, but it does not fully address questions regarding the limits of privatization. Why do governments privatize some sectors and not others? Certainly ideology is important, but there is more to it than that. Although the institutional approach provides a partial remedy to this problem by paying explicit attention to a wider array of domestic structures, it does so at the expense of omitting ideology from the equation. Similarly, rational approaches are also incomplete. Public choice is weak because it provides a normative rationale, but it fails on a positive level to account for the collapse of spending coalitions and the subsequent pursuit of privatization. Although property rights fares somewhat better, it does not take into account political ideology and its influence on shaping the public interest. Finally, industry structure provides a partial explanation of differences on a sectoral level, but it does not adequately capture the political dynamics of events at the national level.

**National Governments and Multiple Streams**

Each perspective has provided only bits and pieces of the answer. It is now time to put the pieces together into a coherent whole. In the next section I outline a framework of policy formation, developed by Kingdon, that combines several factors in a theoretically meaningful way. To better understand its logic, I first describe the original garbage can model upon which Kingdon built his work. Then I explain Kingdon's model to show how the process works.[42] After offering some modifications, I construct a theoretical argument identifying the factors that enhance or impede the likelihood of privatization.

The Original Garbage Can Model

In an insightful article, Cohen, March, and Olsen outline a model that seeks to explain decision making in organizations they term "organized anarchies."[43] These organizations, such as universities, are characterized by three general properties: problematic preferences, unclear technology, and fluid participation. First, it is generally observed that people frequently do not have a clear, well-articulated set of preferences. Decisions, however, are made and may even be facilitated by opaqueness. In contrast to most business firms in which the ultimate goal is clear—namely, to make a profit—organized anarchies operate on the basis of multiple and diverse objectives. As Cohen and his colleagues aptly put it, organized anarchies "can be described better as a collection of ideas than as a coherent structure."[44]

Second, technology—that is, an organization's processes that turn inputs into products—is unclear. Members of an organized anarchy may be well aware of their individual responsibilities, but they exhibit only rudimentary knowledge concerning the way their job fits into the overall mission of the organization. Past experience often guides their actions, making trial-and-error procedures indispensable learning tools. Third, participation in such organizations is fluid. Turnover is high, and participants drift from one decision to the next. Involvement in any one decision varies considerably, and so does the time and effort that participants devote to it.

Under such extreme conditions, theories based on rational behavior are of limited utility. Because problems and preferences are not well known, selecting the alternative that yields the most net benefits becomes an impossible task. Even more so, time limitations and sheer complexity preclude consequential action. Individuals may not necessarily define a problem first and look for a solution later. Quite often the reverse is true: solutions search for problems. In contrast to models that stress rational sorting, the garbage can provides an alternative that is based on temporal order.[45]

The authors postulate four separate streams flowing through an organization: problems, solutions, participants, and choice opportunities. Problems are concerns that individuals inside and outside the organization have. They involve, but are not limited to, such issues as profitability, work satisfaction, career advancement, and promotion. Solutions are people's products; they are answers to questions that may not be generated only when needed. To use the authors' example, a computer is not just a solution to a problem in the payroll department, but also an answer perennially in search of a question. Participants are individuals who take part in decisions. Choice opportunities are occasions when the organization must make a decision. Budgets must be passed, contracts must be signed, people must be hired or fired.

Although these streams are not completely independent of one another, they can be viewed as each having a life of its own. Participants drift in and out of decisions, making some choices more likely than others. Similarly, people generate solutions, not necessarily because they have identified a particular problem, but because the solution happens to answer a problem that fits their values, beliefs, or material well-being. Opportunities arise irrespective of the existence of problems or solutions. Thus, each stream seems to obey its own rules and flows largely independently of the others.

How does the model work? As choice opportunities arise, say a faculty position becomes available in a given department, various participants become involved, each with different time constraints and resources.[46] There are numerous problems to be considered: direction and strength of the department, fund availability, and affirmative action. Concurrently, various solutions will be discussed, such as expanding the pool of potential applicants or focusing on "insider" candidates. Thus, a choice can be viewed, Cohen and his colleagues claim, as a garbage can into which participants dump solutions and problems. Moreover, the mix of garbage in a single can depends on the mix of cans available, on the labels attached to the alternative cans, on what garbage is currently being produced, and on the speed with which garbage is collected and removed from the scene.[47]

To return to the aforementioned example, as time progresses, meetings will be held and various problems and solutions will be considered. Some solutions, such as increasing the number of potential candidates, may be discarded as participants fail to attend. Problems, on the other hand, may be introduced or redefined as new participants, say graduate students, enter the picture. In short, the number of problems or solutions changes constantly as attendance fluctuates. The final outcome may indeed be the selection of a candidate who fits a job description different from the one originally envisaged.

To summarize, the logic and features of the model are as follows. First, the model cannot explain all decisions in all organizations. It is especially relevant to organized anarchies—that is, organizations that meet certain conditions: ambiguity of preferences, ambiguity of technology, and fluidity of participation. Second, running through the organization are four largely separate streams: problems, solutions, participants, and choice opportunities. Finally, outcomes (specific decisions) are heavily dependent upon coupling or joining together in whole or in part the various streams within a given choice context.

At first glance, the model appears to be particularly relevant to the way decisions are made by national governments. First, there is a plethora of participants who drift in and out of government. Legislators come and go, and bureaucrats, especially high-level civil servants, often move from public service to private practice. Moreover, there are nongovernmental actors, such as employer associations, trade unions, and consumer groups, that exercise a significant influence over whether and what form certain decisions will take. In addition, the preferences of these participants are often ambiguous and conflicting. To say that politicians almost never make their objectives crystal clear is hardly novel, but it is true that quite often time constraints force politicians to make decisions without having formulated precise preferences. Finally, the processes of the national government are not well understood by everybody. Jurisdictional boundaries are unclear, and turf battles between different ministries are a common occurrence. Members of parliament often complain of unaccountable ministers, who, in turn, frequently express their frustration with overburdening reporting rules and independent-minded public managers. In fact, the situation is so confusing that "the left hand doesn't know what the right is doing."[48] Thus, it appears that the national government fits the description of organized anarchies fairly well.

Nevertheless, we must not hasten to accept the model at face value. In pure form, the garbage can model suggests that organizational choice depends on specific elements in each of the aforementioned streams as they arrive and depart at different time intervals through organizations. Nonetheless, policymakers at the national government level encounter significant institutional constraints. A number of rules and procedures must be followed. Participation may be limited and occasionally clandestine, and so will be the range of alternatives to be considered. If the model is to be used at the national level, some modifications must be made.

### Kingdon's Multiple Streams Model

Kingdon adapts the garbage can model to the U.S. federal government and uses it to illuminate two predecision processes: agenda setting and alternative specification. Deriving his data mainly from interviews conducted in the period 1976–79, the author concentrates on two broad policy areas: health and transportation. It is noteworthy that although the logic remains the same, Kingdon's model is somewhat modified to fit the conditions and circumstances relevant to policy-making.

Kingdon argues that there are two categories of factors that affect the way agendas are set and alternatives specified: participants and processes. Participants include an array of political forces that could be sources of agenda items and alternatives. Congress, the president, the bureaucracy, and a variety of nongovernmental actors such as interest groups, the media, and the general public are examples of such political actors. Each has a different impact on the processes that Kingdon examines. A visible cluster of actors, which includes the president and prominent members of Congress, exerts the most influence on the way the agenda is shaped. Conversely, a cluster of what he labels "invisible" participants, such as specialists in the policy communities, has a greater effect on what alternatives will be generated and how they will be specified.

After examining the players of the game, Kingdon turns to a description of its rules. He identifies three processes that resemble the streams conceptualized by Cohen and his colleagues: problems, policies, and politics. Each is largely separate from the others, with its own dynamics and rules. At critical points in time, the streams are coupled. The combination of all three streams into a single package dramatically enhances the chances that a subject will receive serious consideration by decision makers.

The first stream that Kingdon discusses is problems. Why do policymakers pay attention to some problems and not others? The answer lies in the way officials learn about conditions and, more important, the way these conditions come to be defined as problems. There are three ways to identify conditions. First, indicators may be used to assess the existence and magnitude of a condition—for example, the cost of a program, infant mortality rates, or highway deaths. These indicators can be monitored either routinely or through special studies. For example, special studies occasionally seek to estimate the number of Americans without health insurance. The indicators then can be used to measure the magnitude of change in the hope of catching official attention. Second, dramatic events or crises can occasionally call attention to a problem. The crash of a Boeing 747 serves as a powerful stimulant for increased air safety. Third, feedback from existing programs can bring conditions to the fore. Letters from constituents and impact evaluation studies are two relevant examples. Of course not all conditions become problems. As Kingdon categorically asserts, problems contain a "perceptual interpretation element."[49] Thus, some conditions come to be defined as problems and consequently receive more attention than others. How is this done? People define conditions as problems by letting their values and beliefs guide their decisions, by placing subjects under one category rather than another, and by comparing conditions in different countries.

Policies constitute the second stream. They include a wide variety of ideas floating around in the "policy primordial soup." These ideas are generated by specialists in policy communities—networks that include bureaucrats, Congressional staff members, academics, and researchers in think tanks who share a common concern in a single policy area such as health or environmental policy—and are tried out in various ways, such as hearings, papers, and conversations. Some ideas survive this initial period basically unchanged, others are combined into new proposals, and some just disappear. While the number of ideas floating around is quite large, only a few ever receive serious consideration. Selection criteria include technical feasibility and value acceptability. Proposals that are or appear difficult to implement have fewer chances of surviving this process. Moreover, proposals that do not conform to the values of policymakers are less likely to be considered for adoption. Proposals to nationalize U.S. railroads, for instance, stand little chance of survival in Washington. Proposals that seem to be financially feasible—in other words, whose cost is relatively low—tend to be met with greater receptivity. Finally, the presence of a viable alternative is an important factor that influences an issue's rise on the agenda—that is, the chances that an issue gains high agenda prominence are increased if a solution can be readily attached to it.

Kingdon labels the third stream politics. It consists of three elements: the national mood, pressure-group campaigns, and administrative or legislative turnover. The national mood refers to the notion that a fairly large number of individuals in a given country tend to think along common lines and that the mood swings from time to time.[50] Government officials sensing changes in this mood through, say, monitoring public opinion polls, act to promote certain items on the agenda or, conversely, to dim the hopes of others. The balance of organized political forces is a factor that heavily influences the process of policy formation. Politicians, Kingdon argues, often view the support or opposition of interest groups as indicators of consensus or dissent in the broader political arena. If, for example, all interest groups voice their support for deregulation, it is likely that government officials will hasten to include the item on the agenda. In case of conflicting views, which is quite frequently the case, politicians formulate an image of the balance of support and opposition. This perception that the balance is tilting one way or another directly affects the chances of the issue's prominence or obscurity. In addition to the aforementioned factors, legislative or administrative turnover frequently affects the agenda in quite dramatic ways. A sudden influx of new members of Congress ideologically predisposed against "big government" is likely to propel the issue of deregulation into high prominence. Moreover, turnover of key personnel in the administration has a significant impact. The advent of a new president or new secretary of the interior signifies potential changes. Certain issues, such as proposals to cut the budget, may receive more attention while others, such as comprehensive national health insurance, may simply be pushed into obscurity. Of the three elements discussed, the combination of the national mood and turnover in government exert the most powerful effects on agendas. In other words, issues will rise on the agenda, even if organized interests strongly oppose them, provided that both national mood and government officials are receptive.

An important feature of Kingdon's argument is coupling. Issues rise on the agenda when these streams are joined together at critical moments in time. He labels these moments *policy windows* and defines them as "opportunit[ies] for advocates of proposals to push their pet solutions, or to push attention to their special problems."[51] Such windows are opened by compelling problems or by events in the political stream. The collapse of Penn Central Station's finances in the early 1970s, for instance, brought attention to the way railroads were funded in the United States. In the political stream, a new administration may be ideologically committed to deregulation. These policy windows are of short duration and may be as predictable as annual budget allocations or as unpredictable as natural catastrophes.

When windows open, policy entrepreneurs, who are individuals willing to invest "time, energy, reputation, [and] money—to promote a position for anticipated future gain in the form of material, purposive or solidary benefits," must immediately seize the opportunity to initiate action.[52] Otherwise, the opportunity is lost and the policy entrepreneurs must wait for the next one to come along. Policy entrepreneurs must not only be persistent, but also skilled at coupling. They must be able to attach problems to their solutions and find receptive politicians to their ideas. An issue's chances of gaining prominence in the agenda are enhanced when problems and solutions or solutions and politics are joined. The issue's chances dramatically increase when all three streams—problems, policies, and politics—are coupled in a single package.

Why do some issues receive prominence and others do not? Kingdon's answer can be summarized as follows. Differentiating between participants and processes, the author argues that the agenda is set by events in the political stream, by compelling problems, and by such visible participants as elected officials. On the other hand, alternative specification is guided by the selection process in the policy stream and the involvement of relatively hidden participants who are specialists in that policy area.

Overall, Kingdon's model is very useful. A number of features increase its appeal, making it highly relevant to the task at hand. First, it is particularly relevant to the policy-formation process at the national level. Cohen and his colleagues make clear that the garbage can model describes decision making well only in organized anarchies. Small businesses are not good candidates for verifying the model's hypotheses or exploring its limitations. National governments, on the other hand, are excellent candidates, making Kingdon's version especially relevant to this study.

Second, the model permits a meaningful synthesis of the various elements of the answer to privatization. Some stress the importance of political parties; others emphasize industry characteristics or the role of state managers. The present model has the advantage of permitting a synthesis of some of these variables in a theoretically meaningful way. It has the additional benefit of linking variables at different levels of analysis—that is, it includes sector-specific variables as well as broader political forces. In this way, I can offer a more complete explanation of why countries privatize. Kingdon makes it abundantly clear that change in policy can be brought about by factors that are relevant to specific sectors and by general developments in the polity. In his view, events in the broader political stream are not exogenous but integral parts of policy-making.[53] Finally, the model acknowledges the importance of feedback from past practice as an indispensable tool for defining problems and formulating solutions. This point directs explicit attention to precedent and highlights its significance in explaining privatization.

## Some Revisions

Kingdon's model is useful because the author is able to adapt the original garbage can model to policy-making at the national level. However, his argument refers to predecision processes in the United States: agenda setting and alternative specification. Are his conclusions generalizable to other countries as well? Staying at the national level, I extend Kingdon's ideas to cover the entire policy-formation process: agenda setting and decision making. Before fleshing out the argument, however, it is necessary to make some revisions.

The logic and structure of Kingdon's model remain the same in all but three respects. First, the model here is used to explain the full policy-formation process of agenda setting and decision making. In this respect, it differs from Kingdon's original application to predecision processes. While agenda setting—that is, the process by which certain issues gain prominence—is conceptualized in the present study as a separate process, alternative specification is not. Kingdon distinguishes between the specification of a narrow list of alternatives from which a choice is to be made and the actual choice itself. I view them as parts of the same process, decision making, defined as the process by which policymakers make an authoritative choice from a limited set of previously generated alternatives. Three reasons serve as the basis for this modification: (1) The garbage can model was originally developed to explain decision making, thus the model should be relevant and useful not only in explaining why issues gain prominence on the agenda, but also why policymakers choose a specific policy alternative and not another; (2) The modification enhances the explanatory capability of the model because the same approach is used to obtain a fuller account of the way policies are formed; and (3) Theories of policy-making do not customarily treat a list of alternatives and the actual choice as separate processes; rather, the two are normally examined as integral parts of the same process. Bearing these reasons in mind, it is reasonable to expect the multiple streams approach, within which Kingdon's work is situated, to be applicable to both agenda setting and decision making.

Second, I do not differentiate between participants and processes. Although the distinction may have proven useful for Kingdon's purposes, it is not crucial to the model itself. In fact, the three streams include the interaction of various actors. Politics, for example, emphasizes the significance of congressional turnover. Bureaucrats tend to be more influential in the generation of policy alternatives. Participants, it seems, are an integral part of the processes themselves. Therefore, an examination of the processes affecting the final policy output without separate attention to participants does not handicap the explanatory capability or alter the logic of the framework in any way.

Third, I combine the three dimensions in the political stream labeled national mood, interest groups, and turnover into one conceptual variable: the ideology and strategy of governing parties. As mentioned earlier, the national mood refers to the notion that a large number of people in a given country think along "certain common lines." Government officials sense this mood and frequently seek to capitalize on it. This is a nebulous definition, however. Of what exactly does the national mood consist, and who are the people involved? Kingdon does not give a precise answer.

Some may argue that public opinion actually captures the essence of the national mood. After all, privatization, the argument might go, was demanded by the public. The evidence, however, yields inconclusive results. Public opinion polls in Britain show that even at the time of privatizing British Telecom and British Gas, the public considered the action to be a bad idea by a margin of 7 percent for the former and 11 percent for the latter.[54] The unfavorable margin increased in the cases of electricity to 34 percent and water to 60 percent. Even fervent advocates of privatization admit that public opinion was manipulated after the fact: "We didn't get public opinion to support it [privatization] until after it was done."[55] Finally, statistical evidence in Britain points to the same conclusion.[56] In France the situation is reversed, partially because privatization was a major theme in Chirac's legislative campaign in 1986. By 1987, 41 percent of voters favored privatization while 27 percent opposed it, according to one poll.[57] The evidence from both countries makes it unclear whether public support for privatization came before or after the fact.

Kingdon warns, however, that the national mood "does not necessarily reside in the mass public."[58] So how can it be operationalized? Moreover, because of mood swings, how do we know when these changes occur? Are they rooted in the outcomes of other policies? For example, the failure of parties to successfully implement their programs may shape this mood, making party politics the main determinant of change. The concept is clearly amorphous and far too imprecise to be empirically useful by itself.

Interest groups and legislative or administrative turnover are similarly combined. Given the decentralized nature of U.S. politics, keeping interest groups and government turnover analytically separate makes sense. Politics in other countries, however, takes place within more centralized confines. Parties play a more important role in shaping policy choice. Members of parties that have the majority of seats in legislative chambers also occupy key posts in the executive branch, thereby centralizing the process. The principal division in British government, for example, is not between the legislative and the executive, but "within the House of Commons separating the majority party in control of both the Commons and Cabinet from the opposition."[59] The French situation is even more skewed. The 1958 constitution substantially modified the relationship between the executive and the legislative by reinforcing the former to the detriment of the latter. In fact, the strict delimitation of parliamentary control gives extensive powers to the governing party or coalition.[60]

Moreover, party discipline ensures that party preferences can often be translated into actual legislation. The net result is that government-sponsored bills are usually approved in parliament with minor modifications. The average proportion of government bills, for example, approved by the House of Commons in Britain during the period 1945–87 is 97 percent![61] Control is equally great in France, where the prerogative to initiate legislation is shared by the prime minister and Parliament. From the beginning of the Fifth Republic in 1959 to October 1985, only an average of 12.5 percent of all laws originated in Parliament.[62] Moreover, during the first Socialist reign in power from 1981 to 1985, only 7 percent of all adopted amendments originated in the opposition. Generally speaking, parties tend to dominate the political stream and exercise considerable control over the shape of policy choices. Consequently, focusing on the ideology and strategy of parties does not bias the expected results.

## Applying the Multiple Streams Model: The Political Economy of Privatization

Having made the theoretical revisions, I can now flesh out the argument. Why do countries privatize? Why do governments choose to privatize SOEs in some sectors and not in others? In brief, I argue that privatization is brought about by coupling three factors in critical moments in time: available alternatives generated in policy communities, high government borrowing needs, and the ideology and strategy of governing parties. Privatization is viewed as a yes-no proposition. If privatization has already taken place in a given sector, the question is what factors account for the change in ownership. If the enterprise continues to operate as an SOE, the question is why privatization was not the final choice.

### The Policy Stream: Alternatives and Policy Communities

Whether an issue is raised or a specific policy adopted is heavily influenced by the option's availability. In other words, what the government does depends upon what it can do. In principle, there are thousands of ideas floating around addressing issues of interest to policymakers. In this study, I am interested in proposals put forth in relation to three sectors: oil, telecommunications, and railroads. Although this first cut decreases the number of potential items, the list still remains prohibitively long. It would be impossible and perhaps unfruitful to examine all alternatives. A useful way of narrowing the list is to address viable alternatives that are only relevant to privatization. This yields four options: (1) default, (2) recapitalization (3) liberalization, and (4) reorganization. The task is to show where privatization lies on the list and what conditions affect the likelihood that privatization will be the final choice.

At this point, I will briefly outline the various alternatives, providing more information about them in the actual case studies. Default simply refers to preserving the status quo. One option that the government has is to continue pouring funds from the treasury into SOEs without disturbing the framework currently in place. This framework differs somewhat across countries and sometimes across sectors. Another competing option is to permit SOEs to diversify their portfolio of funding sources by attracting funds from private investors. Recapitalization can be achieved by borrowing in capital markets through, say, the issue of bonds. As a result, an SOE can increase its capital base without the infusion of public funds. A third option is liberalization, which refers to changes in the domestic structure of a given enterprise's product market. Many SOEs operate as virtual monopolies; this is particularly true of public utilities. Liberalization entails the removal of statutory barriers to entry in a given market to encourage competition without changing the firm's ownership arrangements. The fourth alternative, internal reorganization, is a useful way of shaking up the SOE and making it more responsive to current market or political demands. The classic way to do that is to restructure the SOE along, say, product lines rather than functional departments. Another way is to replace top management and inject a new corporate culture. All these options involve changes in SOEs without transferring ownership. At this point, I shall stress a slight departure from Kingdon. Although he argues against tracing the origins of various solutions, I will briefly examine the effects of past policies to inform current debates on privatization. Precedent is important because it helps shape current proposals.

Whether privatization will rise on the list of alternatives and finally be adopted depends upon two criteria: technical feasibility and value acceptability. The first criterion that privatization must pass is technical feasibility. "Feasibility," Kingdon claims, "is heavily involved with implementation."[63] An option that appears to be easier to implement stands a better chance of being adopted. Of particular interest to this study is the perception of policymakers that a possible sale can attract private interest.

How can technical feasibility be measured? I propose to use three indicators. The first is the ability to value assets. Entities that are already run as commercial enterprises under state ownership are more likely to encounter fewer asset valuation problems and are therefore likelier candidates for privatization than are entities operated as government departments. This observation is particularly relevant to telecommunications authorities because they have traditionally been run in most countries as integral parts of the government bureaucracy. The second indicator is profitability. Private investors will not be willing to invest in companies that are not profitable. By comparing profitability from year to year, I can therefore judge the ability, apart from the willingness, of policymakers to sell a given SOE. Profitability is measured here as the percentage of annual net profit or loss after taxes and depreciation over revenue. I chose net instead of operating profit or loss because I wanted to take into account the enormous allowances for depreciation that are common in capital-intensive industries. Doing so ensures figure comparability across the three sectors under investigation.

The third indicator of technical feasibility is demand growth. SOEs that operate in sectors with strong demand growth are more likely to be sold because private investors are more likely to see growth potential in these SOEs than in SOEs that face stagnant or declining demand. I elected to use demand growth that is industry- rather than enterprise-specific because industry figures are more accurate indicators of growth potential. For example, SOEs can grow in spite of long-term declining demand for the industry due to state assistance or oligopolistic position. Because oligopolies are not as likely to continue after a sale, future corporate prospects may actually be worse than anticipated when looking solely at corporate figures. Besides, in two cases, telecommunications and railroads, corporate growth equals sector growth because of the monopolistic position, until recently, of national carriers. Demand growth is measured here as domestic production plus imports minus exports. This figure gives a complete picture of domestic demand.

Although technical feasibility is a necessary criterion for assessing the chances of privatization, it is far from sufficient. Value acceptability—that is, the degree of consensus among specialists in policy communities—is equally important. Indeed, "policy output is more likely to be evaluated as successful if consensus is achieved by those involved in the process of policy input."[64] Consensus is defined here as acquiescence or active support for a given policy option. Kingdon argues that "proposals that survive in the policy community are compatible with the values of specialists."[65] These values include the specialists' beliefs concerning the appropriate role of government and their conception of efficiency and accountability. There are three policy communities under investigation in this study: oil, telecommunications, and railroads. In addition to differences across countries, I also anticipate differences across policy communities within the same country. Overall, if privatization enjoys agreement by most specialists, it is more likely to be adopted.

Within policy communities, four actors are important: (1) bureaucrats, (2) labor unions, (3) academics and researchers in think tanks, and (4) state managers. Bureaucrats are the civil servants in ministries who exercise public control in the three sectors under investigation. In this group I include civil servants in the ministries of finance because of their support for decreasing the government's borrowing needs and increasing revenues. Unions also play an important role. Given their historical support for nationalization, it will be interesting to see whether and how their opposition was neutralized. Academics and other such experts are also important and prolific producers of policy ideas.

Finally, senior managers of SOEs are important. Kay and Thompson point out that "the clear theme to emerge from the political history of [British] privatisation is that by far the most effective and influential interest groups is the senior management of the potentially privatised industry."[66] Because of the information they possess concerning the company they manage and the market in which it operates, their involvement in privatization is essential, particularly in times of fiscal crisis when funds are scarce and control is tight.

Such situations create financial binds for SOEs whose investment needs do not neatly adhere to government budget plans. Moreover, managers stand to receive personal gains from privatization. Since many of them, it is widely argued, are typically paid less than their counterparts in the private sector, senior managers can expect pecuniary rewards to result from different ownership arrangements. Finally, state managers have a vested interest in resisting liberalization attempts so that they retain market shares and potential profits.

Having said this, it is important to point out that managers will not always view privatization in a favorable light. Some, particularly those seeking a quiet life away from the uncertainty and layoffs of the private sector, are not likely to be strong supporters of disturbances of the status quo. Others may resent privatization on financial grounds, especially when they are asked to hive off profitable subsidiaries. Such asset sales are likely to reduce future income and precipitate financial dependence on public funds. In general, the greater the degree of consensus among specialists in a policy community, the more likely privatization will be.

## Public Finances and Privatization

Rising borrowing needs produce pressures to curb public expenditures, particularly in times of increased hostility among the electorate toward raising taxes. Privatization is viewed as a policy that, at least in the short run, reduces the need to borrow money. It is precisely the widening gap between public revenues and expenses and the inability of governments to control or reverse increasing public expenditures that have made privatization such an attractive option. Other things being equal, higher borrowing needs make privatization more likely.

Selling off parts or whole SOEs yields five benefits.

1. It permits the treasury to take the enterprises off the books so that the general public sector debt can appear smaller.
2. It frees up capital funds that the government would normally pour into the enterprises to cover new investments or operating costs.
3. It saves administrative time spent in ministries drawing up complicated investment plans or mediating into politically costly labor-management disputes.
4. It permits the government to not only shed (in some cases) unprofitable SOEs, but also to raise money. The ability to increase revenue without raising taxes during a period of financial straits is particularly appealing.
5. Because of accounting peculiarities, privatization enables the British

treasury, but not the French, to not only take the enterprises off the books, but also to count the sales as negative expenditures, or positive income.

The benefits must be weighed against costs. Critics point out that the sale of enterprises deprives the treasury of potential future profits. Nevertheless, one point is clear. Privatization is more likely to occur in periods of deteriorating public finances.

Analysts typically use the Public Sector Borrowing Requirement (PSBR) as an indicator of losses. The PSBR represents the amount of funds that SOEs borrow from the British treasury to continue their operations. There are three problems with this indicator. First, there is no direct equivalent to it in France, rendering a comparative inquiry highly problematic. In fact, one study informs that PSBR figures in France are kept confidential.[67] Second, the legal definition of state enterprises varies enormously from country to country.[68] The usual legal form in Britain is the public corporation. In France, however, SOEs take one of several forms, including public enterprise, mixed enterprise, state enterprise, and enterprise of industrial and commercial character. Not all of them are included in official statistics. Since 1974, for example, statistics for French SOEs in national accounts have only included eight large corporations engaged in energy, communications, and transport, effectively excluding most SOEs in manufacturing.[69] Moreover, national French statistics do not normally include figures for subsidiaries, which according to one estimate could actually double the size of the public sector, measured as the number of government-held shares in SOEs.[70] Even in Britain, where PSBR figures are available, figures have traditionally included financial SOEs, such as the Bank of England, but excluded others, such as (now sold) Rolls Royce.[71] Hence, any cross-country comparisons of variations in the PSBR, even if such figures were available, would be misleading. For this reason, I use a proxy indicator: central government deficit over central government outflows (expenditures plus net lending) expressed in percentages. I use ratio rather than absolute figures because I am interested in the burden that the deficit places on government. Other things being equal, the greater the government's borrowing needs, the greater the likelihood of privatization.

### Parties Matter

Kingdon argues convincingly that turnover of key personnel in government is an important factor affecting the agenda. Incumbents in positions of authority bring with them new items they consider important. An influx of new members in the U.S. Congress can create a more receptive political audience for certain items. The election of 1964, for example, produced a large turnover of congressional seats. This turnover enabled the Johnson administration to pass sweeping domestic policy measures including, among others, Medicare and antipoverty programs. The election of Ronald Reagan in 1980 brought a revived concern with "big government," prompting the adoption of numerous deregulation initiatives. In short, partisan politics facilitated by turnover in administration, Congress, and various government agencies affect the agenda. As a congressional staffer pithily observed, "new faces means that new issues will be raised."[72]

The same is argued in this study; parties matter. They affect not only agenda setting, but also decision making. However, how should party politics be understood? Parties differ enormously across countries. What elements of parties are important? Two elements are hypothesized as having an effect on privatization: political ideology and strategy.

Ideology here refers to a fairly coherent set of ideas and beliefs concerning the economic role of the state. On an empirical level, it is commonly examined in the form of a conservative-socialist dichotomy. Conservatives, it is argued, are against heavy state involvement in economic affairs while socialists generally favor it. This dichotomy, however, is too simplistic and perhaps misleading. Privatization is certainly a worldwide phenomenon. Does this mean that party ideology does not play a significant role in precipitating the adoption of privatization? The commonly employed dichotomy might yield a negative answer. Yet, there is considerable anecdotal evidence pointing to the significance of ideology. Moreover, although commonly lumped together as conservative, Thatcher's and Chirac's views on the appropriate role of government differ markedly. Ideology is important, but is there another way of capturing the subtle shades of ideological differences?

Castles's work provides an important point of departure.[73] In seeking to explain why five English-speaking nations—Australia, New Zealand, Canada, the United Kingdom, and the United States—experienced a major reappraisal of the economic role of the state in the 1980s, he argues that the party most closely associated with failures in existing policy finds it most difficult to attack the policy's premises. Because British Labour was largely responsible for the creation of the welfare state in the aftermath of World War II, Conservatives were able to attack it even though they were partly responsible for its maintenance over the years. Similarly, a long Democratic hegemony in Congress made it possible for a Republican president to blame it for failures even if the existing Keynesian pattern was also the artifact of several Republican presidents.[74]

Using this line of reasoning, I operationalize ideology as the degree of party identification with nationalization. The more intimately a party is identified with nationalization, the more difficult it will be to privatize, and the more limited the scope of privatization will be. It is precisely the close identification with state ownership that colors a party's conceptualization of the role of the state. The legitimation that this identification affords to SOEs limits the range of a party's alternative conceptualizations of the appropriate role of government. Consequently, parties intimately involved in nationalizing enterprises are not likely to support privatization. In the event they do, the scope of the proposed program will be limited.

When times are good, politicians cherish the identification of a successful economic strategy with a particular party. They strengthen and promote this identification as much as possible to enhance their electoral success, particularly with highly visible policies, such as nationalization, that run through to the very core of party ideology and have been espoused with considerable fervor. In periods of economic crisis, however, disassociating the party from the policy becomes problematic. This is particularly true when SOEs are commonly viewed as failures. A possible reversal in policy requires action on two fronts. On the one hand, politicians not only have to dispel the public's perception of their lack of responsibility for failures, but they must also demonstrate the ability to reverse course. It is much more difficult not to receive at least part of the blame when the same party has been intimately involved in advocating and implementing ambitious nationalization programs.

The second element having an effect on privatization is political strategy, the ability of party leaders to overcome opposition from within and the degree to which opposing parties can propose credible alternatives. Leaders must be able to convince their own party members of the "rightness" of their decision. Because nationalization goes to the core of a party's view of the state, a move in the opposite direction is likely to draw criticism from within. Although this type of criticism can be coated in ideological terms, it may also manifest itself in the form of political struggles for power. First, party leaders must go against years of tradition and party doctrines as to the appropriate economic role of the state. Achieving this goal is not impossible, as Chirac proves, but doing so involves considerable risk. Certainly, it limits the range of sectors in which privatization can occur. Under these conditions, SOEs that provide some sort of public service, such as utilities or infrastructural industries, are not good candidates for privatization. In contrast, SOEs that operate in competitive markets—that is, sectors that are subjected to either domestic or international competition—are more likely to be privatized. It is much easier to justify the sale of SOEs in commercial markets by treating them as nonessential activities to the maintenance of the state.

Second, criticism, or at least pressure, may be forthcoming from affected groups. It is reasonable to expect political parties that have been intimately involved in nationalizing and operating SOEs to have a political stake in maintaining these corporations. If nothing else, the managers of these enterprises are likely to lobby hard either to block the sale or to dictate the terms of the sale so as to yield the most benefits to the company and to themselves. In addition, parties that are closely affiliated or influenced by unions are more likely to oppose privatization, given traditional union support for state ownership. Conversely, parties that are influenced heavily by employer associations and business interests are more likely to support privatization because many businesses stand to gain by entering a previously untapped market or by buying shares in the newly privatized companies.

## A Policy in Search of a Rationale?

Finally, policy outputs depend heavily upon coupling the streams at critical moments in time labeled *policy windows*. When windows open, viewed here as opened by election outcomes, policy entrepreneurs try to take advantage of the political climate by attaching a problem to their pet solution. In other words, privatization is not likely to develop as a response to a particular problem; as Kingdon argues, "advocacy of solutions often precedes the highlighting of problems to which they become attached."[75]

Although Kingdon does not make the case explicitly, the rationale for such paradoxical behavior rests with the lack of goal clarity. The model assumes a situation of problematic preferences where policymakers often do not know what they want. Indeed, ambiguity is frequently employed as a political tool to build coalitions to either maximize candidate appeal among voters or to forge a legislative consensus.[76] Nevertheless, even though politicians do not know what a country's problems are, they need to appear as if they know how to fix them. As a result, espousing appealing solutions first, however vaguely defined they may be, is politically more beneficial because it gives the impression of a course of action without having to define what is the precise problem to be addressed. For example, advocates of privatization are likely to find it expedient to call for selling SOEs regardless of whether such sales are designed to reduce public expenditures, curb union power, or foster competition, provided proponents are viewed as action-oriented individuals. Besides once the solution is known, the problem becomes easier to define because the parameters of what is politically feasible have already been set. The concreteness of action, therefore, reduces the universe of possible goals and renders their identification a much easier process.

The essence of coupling rests with the logic of timing. Each factor's impact is conditional upon its specific combination with the other streams at a given moment in time. A change of personnel at the pinnacles of political authority, for example, will not necessarily result in the adoption of specific policies. One might well ask why the French privatized in 1986 and not 1966 since the same party governed in both occasions. The answer, according to the multiple streams approach, lies in the context—that is, the values of the other two factors at that time and the institutional arrangements within which coupling is made.

The emphasis on coupling makes the model stand out in two important ways. First, coupling gives the model a dynamic quality that differentiates it from "static" structural approaches. Coupling suggests that the effects of each stream are not additive. Rather, only a combination of all three streams at once can result in the adoption of a specific solution. No one stream determines the process. Moreover, the fact that coupling takes place when policy windows open also frees the multiple streams approach from deterministic effects. Policy windows open for a short period of time, therefore policies need not follow unidirectional trajectories but can change or even reverse course as windows open and close.

Second, the process of coupling enables me to probe the usual problem-solution sequence found in conventional models of policy formation. The multiple streams approach is uniquely qualified to provide theoretical substance to empirical observations concerning the rationale of privatization. Some analysts claim that British privatization is really a policy that does not have a rationale.[77] Others point out that there was no official document in the early stages of Thatcher's privatization articulating a clear rationale.[78] A practitioner intimately involved with the process puts it even more bluntly: "from the inside we [the British government] had no coherent policy . . . it came upon us gradually and by accident and by a leap of faith."[79] Certainly, an approach emphasizing a rational process of policy formation would be unable to convincingly test these claims because it assumes consequential order. In the argument presented here, however, problems are conceptualized as flowing separately and independently of solutions. Because privatization is not a problem-unique solution, it may be attached to different problems at different times. It is therefore entirely conceivable for privatization to be proposed as a solution to a variety of problems. Moreover, the point that solutions frequently look for problems rather than the other way around suggests *ex post* rationalization. Although the model's emphasis on independent streams and timing provides for both problem-solution sequences, following Kingdon's line of thought, I expect privatization to be more likely a policy in search of a rationale.

## Conclusion

So far I have examined several perspectives on privatization. After finding their answers to be incomplete, I presented a more promising framework for thinking about policy formation and constructed an argument regarding privatization. The argument that guides the analysis in the ensuing chapters is that privatization is brought about by coupling three factors in critical moments in time: available alternatives generated in policy communities, high government borrowing needs, and the ideology and strategy of governing parties. In part 2 I examine the argument against the British experience, and in part 3 I do the same with the French.

# Part 2
# Departing for Britain

Laistrygonians and Cyclops
angry Poseidon-you won't find them
unless you bring them along inside your soul.

## CHAPTER 3

# Politics and Problems

Having laid out the argument in theoretical terms, I now turn to an examination of the evidence. Using the multiple streams approach, I seek to illuminate the reasons that brought about privatization first in Britain (part 2) and then in France (part 3). Although the analysis concerning the British case focuses largely on the period since 1974, it is also enriched with references to earlier periods. The debate over state ownership is certainly not new, and in part, the arguments put forth by proponents and opponents of privatization are embedded in past successes or failures of SOEs. Policy choice, in other words, is bounded by inheritance.[1]

To set things up at the outset, during the course of industrialization all capitalist states developed a mixed economy—that is, an economy in which the state has a large capacity to intervene and that sanctions both state and private ownership[2]—with different purposes and limits. Countries that industrialized first have traditionally viewed the sovereign entrepreneur with suspicion. Early success through reliance largely on private initiative precluded an extensive commercial role for the state. Instead, SOEs were expected to operate only in cases of "market failure," when market solutions (private firms) would not produce optimal outcomes. In contrast, in countries that industrialized later, the state took an active interest not only in bolstering the private sector, but also in becoming an entrepreneur in its own right. Britain and France represent opposite poles on this continuum; Britain's "defensive" view of state ownership contrasts sharply against France's "strategic" view. As a result, the privatization debate was cast differently in these two countries.

Table 3.1 provides figures on the British privatization program. Interestingly, SOEs were profitable before they were privatized, shattering the argument by proponents of privatization that the state cannot run commercial activities profitably. This is an important theme to which I will return later in the chapter. Prior to privatizing electricity in December 1990, the British sold 29 major businesses affecting approximately 800,000 jobs.[3] By July 1993, receipts from the sales yielded an estimated amount of £45.9 billion (table 3.1). In the span of twelve years, Conservatives succeeded in privatizing major SOEs in all but two sectors: coal and railroads. Following the

**TABLE 3.1. The British Privatization Program, 1979–93 (£ million)**

| Corporation | Net Proceeds to Government | Profit (Loss) before Sale |
|---|---|---|
| British Petroleum (1979) | 276 | — |
| (1981) | 8 | |
| (1983) | 543 | |
| (1987) | 5,322 | |
| British Aerospace (1981) | 43 | 52.8 |
| (1985) | 347 | |
| Cable and Wireless (1981) | 181 | 64.1 |
| (1983) | 263 | |
| (1985) | 580 | |
| Amersham International (1982) | 60 | 4.8 |
| National Freight Corporation (1982) | 53 | 4.3 |
| Britoil (1982) | 626 | 423.1 |
| (1985) | 426 | |
| Associated British Ports | | |
| (1983) | 46 | 5.5 |
| (1984) | 51 | |
| Enterprise Oil (1984) | 382 | 83.2 |
| Sealink (1984) | 66[a] | 12.8 |
| Jaguar (1984) | 297[a] | 50.0 |
| British Telecom (1984) | 3,681 | 990.0 |
| (1991) | 5,350[b] | |
| (1993) | 5,000[b] | |
| British Shipbuilders Warship Yards (1984–85) | 54[a] | 18.0 |
| British Gas (1986) | 7,731 | 782.0 |
| British Airways (1987) | 850 | 195.0 |
| Royal Ordnance (1987) | 185 | 26.0 |
| Rolls Royce (1987) | 1,028 | 120.0 |
| BAA (1987) | 1,183 | 84.0 |
| Rover (1988) | 150 | 28.0 |
| British Steel (1988) | 2,437 | 207.0 |
| 10 Water Corporations (1989) | 3,480 | 636.0 |
| Electricity Corps. (1990) Distributors | 5,200[b] | — |

**TABLE 3.1—*Continued***

| Corporation | Net Proceeds to Government | Profit (Loss) before Sale |
|---|---|---|
| Electricity Corps. (1990–91) | | |
| Power generators | 5,040[b] | — |

*Source*: *Hansard, House of Commons* Written Answers 27 April 1990, cols. 357-60; Rodney Lord, ed., *Privatisation Yearbook, 1992* (London: Privatisation International, 1992), 6–9; and *New York Times*, 30 June 1993, D2.

[a]Proceeds went to parent SOEs as follows: Sealink to British Rail; Jaguar to British Leyland; Warship Yards to British Shipbuilders.

[b]Figure represents asset value.

Conservative victory in the spring of 1992, Major's government announced plans to sell them, too.[4]

Why did Thatcher's government elect to privatize SOEs in some sectors but not others? Following a political logic, I argue that privatization rose high on the agenda and was finally adopted because of the interplay of three streams or factors in critical moments in time: (1) the policy stream, which included alternatives generated in policy communities; (2) the problem stream, which involved high government borrowing needs; and (3) the broader political stream, which encompassed party politics. The Conservative electoral victory in 1979 and again in 1983, 1987, and 1992 opened four policy windows that provided policy entrepreneurs with opportunities to push for selling state assets. Privatization was adopted in oil and telecommunications because policy entrepreneurs were able to couple privatization to a pressing problem, curbing government spending, and to a receptive political audience. In contrast, partial coupling has not yet led to privatization in railroads, although significant changes are in store for British Rail (BR). Despite ideologically committed Conservatives, the inability to attach privatization to a specific problem explains why it has not yet taken place.

The analysis aims to answer three questions. First, why has privatization gained such prominence on the British government's agenda? Second, what factors account for the adoption of privatization? And third, what reasons explain the percent of ownership ceded? The answers are organized in two chapters. In chapter 3, I examine the political and problem streams. Because they are the same for all three sectors, I discuss them first. In chapter 4, I first analyze developments in the policy stream for each industry separately—oil, telecommunications, and railroads—then look at the process of coupling. The main argument is that the interplay of all three factors at the same time explains the reasons for and limits of privatization in the United Kingdom.

## The Political Stream

Issues become important and particular policies are adopted partly because of a receptive political audience. In this section, I examine whether and how party ideology and strategy affected privatization. The central argument is that parties that are able to dissociate themselves from state ownership are more likely to privatize than are others. The analysis is divided in three parts. First, I trace the evolution of state ownership in Britain and the political association of Conservatives and Labour with state ownership. Then I discuss how Conservatives tried to dissociate themselves from state ownership during the 1970s and 1980s. Finally, I discuss opposition from certain members of the Conservative party and from Labour to illuminate the Conservative strategy that finally tilted the balance in favor of privatization.

Being the first country to industrialize, Britain became a champion of free trade and private enterprise. The spontaneous nature of British industrialization, the private ownership of banks, and a relatively weak Crown whose powers were already severely curtailed by the landed aristocracy contributed to Britain's laissez-faire policies.[5] Because of Britain's head start and the political strength of its financiers and industrialists, state ownership was minimal and concentrated largely on running traditional operations such as ports and the post office. So long as the economy continued to grow, the Crown generally remained committed to these liberal doctrines.

### Early Socialist Calls for Nationalization and the Morrisonian Model

That situation was dramatically altered with the advent of World War I. Under the pressures of war, the state took over many defense- and energy-related industries, showing that despite mishaps, the government could operate commercial enterprises with reasonable success. Convinced that governments could operate industries as efficiently and effectively as could private entrepreneurs, the Trades Union Congress (TUC) increasingly demanded wider measures of nationalization. Influenced by unions, Labour adopted a new constitution in 1918. In it the party committed itself to securing "the common ownership of the means of production."[6]

Interestingly, Conservatives (also known as Tories) were the first to set up SOEs: the British Broadcasting Corporation in 1926, the Central Electricity Board in 1927, the London Passenger Transport Board (LPTB) in 1933, and the British Overseas Airways Corporation (BOAC) in 1939. Limited in size, scope, and political significance, SOEs took an organizational form that would greatly influence the nationalizations carried out by Labour after World War II. Even more interesting is that details of this instrument, the public corporation, were most clearly articulated by Labour's Transport Minister, Herbert Morrison.

Because of its importance for the subsequent privatization debate, it may be fruitful to briefly describe the theory upon which the public corporation rests.[7] Creating an SOE is deemed necessary for social and economic purposes; in the LPTB case, some felt that unified control under state ownership would increase the quality of the provided service, decrease charges, and maintain socially necessary but economically unprofitable routes in the name of the public interest.[8] SOEs using public funds for public purposes should be accountable for the performance of their functions. This accountability, however, should not unduly impinge on the management of the enterprise. In that context, legal, financial, and managerial autonomy are emphasized as an essential requirement. First, to perform their commercial function, SOEs have to acquire their own legal personality separate from government departments. Second, SOEs should not depend on financial support from the state. Morrison clearly, and perhaps prophetically, states the risks involved: "[State financial guarantees] might well have encouraged a spirit of slackness, or even recklessness . . . all might be tempted to say, *"Well, after all, the Treasury is behind us."*[9] Third, managers should be free from tight ministerial and bureaucratic control and should maintain informal consultation with the appropriate minister only in matters of broad policy. Under this scheme, worker control, but not participation, is rejected on the grounds of enterprise autonomy.

Despite the merits and popularity of this type of nationalizing "at arm's length," several questions remained unanswered. Why should public corporations be run more efficiently than private firms? Why would a simple change in ownership necessarily mean that managers would now pursue the general, and not their own, self-interests? Nevertheless, by the end of the 1930s, this organizational form dominated Labour's proposals and became the guiding principle of the Nationalization Acts that followed World War II.

## Postwar Nationalization: To Plan or Not to Plan

The general election of 1945 brought a Labour government to power, headed by Clement Atlee. Although the issue was controversial, nationalization was considered essential toward achieving the ultimate goal of economic planning. "Fundamental nationalisation," Atlee said in 1945, "had got to go ahead because it fell in with planning, the essential planning of the country."[10] Linking state ownership and planning, however, cost Labour dearly because the failure to implement planning also undermined the rationale behind nationalization.

The nationalization program involved the transfer of entire sectors, not just specific enterprises.[11] The first act brought the Bank of England in February 1946. In contrast to France, however, Labour left commercial banks under private ownership. Next came the coal mines, followed by the revival of BOAC, whose activities had ceased because of the war. Interestingly, aircraft construction was left up to private entrepreneurs, such as Rolls Royce, and the state became the industry's most important customer. In January 1947 the British government completed the acquisition of the remaining shares in Cable and Wireless, a company with considerable telecommunication links between Britain and the Commonwealth. The same year also witnessed the passage of the Transport Act, which called for the nationalization of various trucking concerns and the railroads, and the Electricity Act. The Gas Act of 1948 brought into state ownership the entire gas industry, and the Iron and Steel Act of 1949 provided for the transfer of the securities of ninety-six companies operating in that sector.

British nationalization was largely a partisan issue. Heavily influenced by unions, Labour considered nationalization an important step toward achieving the socialist ideal of promoting worker participation and fostering economic efficiency. In contrast, Conservatives remained opposed to the principle of nationalization, expressing reservations in some cases, such as coal, and outright hostility in others, such as iron and steel. When they came to power in 1951, however, they accepted state ownership in some industries.

Originally, nationalization was viewed as a stepping-stone toward economic planning. Controlling "the commanding heights" of the economy was going to be an important tool for stimulating economic growth and maintaining full employment. The public corporation model seemed to fit planning well. On the one hand, it involved political control so that the agreed central plans could be successfully implemented. On the other hand, public corporations were sufficiently independent to be able to respond to market signals and let consumer demand influence future investment. Soon planning gave way to Keynesian ideas of demand management.[12] The decline of planning, however, also undermined the legitimacy of SOEs. Keynesian demand management contained little room for state ownership, for after all, the theory was developed to save capitalism and not to establish socialism. What role should SOEs play now? While Labour wrestled with this issue, Tories increasingly came to question the usefulness of SOEs. Although public corporations were supposed to be autonomous, in practice ministerial and financial control was inevitable. The pursuit of full employment policies also made laying off workers politically risky. As corporate deficits increased, SOEs became more financially dependent on the Treasury. Ministers, however, were unwilling to take responsibility for the performance of SOEs. Whereas this outcome suited Conservatives who were skeptical about the merits of state ownership in the first place, it cost Labour dearly.

In addition, the rejection of economic planning, coupled with the nationalization of entire sectors, imposed a heavy cost on the public sector. Nationalization added the responsibility of running SOEs but deprived them of direction and legitimacy. In the long run, nationalization in Britain came to be viewed as the principal tool for reinvigorating specific industries, but it was never used as part of a broader industrial restructuring plan, as it had been in France and elsewhere in Europe.[13] The net result was eventual disillusionment. This feeling is aptly captured by a trade unionist: "The form of *ownership* for a significant portion of the economy was changed by the 1945–50 Labour Government but not *its* control" (emphasis in the original).[14]

### A Continuously Swinging Pendulum

The 1950s witnessed the beginning of a long debate over state ownership. The outcome of the general election in 1951 brought Winston Churchill back to the prime minister's office and a Conservative majority in the House of Commons. Although Tories voted against nationalization, their attitude changed once they assumed power. Churchill made it very clear from the beginning that some form of state ownership in railroads, coal, gas, electricity, and airlines was acceptable. In other instances, however, Tories were resolutely opposed to state ownership. Two industries were targeted for immediate return to private ownership: transport and steel.

Because their opposition focused on road haulage and the monopolistic structure of the industry, Tories immediately announced their intention to privatize state assets in that industry. The Transport Act of 1953 noted that the guiding principle was that selection of alternative modes of transport should be coordinated by consumer choice, not by government. Consequently, the Road Haulage Executive was abolished and vehicles were sold either back to their original owners or to other interested private parties. By the end of 1955, however, it was clear that not all vehicles owned by the British Transport Corporation (BTC) could be sold. In 1956 the government ended the procedure of disposal, leaving BTC with 10,000 vehicles or approximately 25 percent of the original fleet.[15] They were reorganized into what eventually became the National Freight Corporation. Interestingly, the fact that the government "got stuck" with the remaining vehicles questions the wisdom of nationalizing unusable assets and illustrates vividly the "defensive" view of state ownership. For the most part, British governments set up SOEs in businesses that the private sector found unprofitable.

The privatization of steel was a contentious affair.[16] Just as Labour considered nationalization to be the principal tool for industrial rejuvenation, so did Conservatives see private ownership as the principal means of restoring growth. In the 1953 Iron and Steel Act, provisions were made to sell shares, preferably back to their original owners but also to the general public. In this sense, the early privatization experiment differs from recent practice in that preference was given to former owners. Ownership of the steel concerns passed on to the Iron and Steel Holding and Realization Agency, which was in charge of the sales. In addition, the government retained some regulatory powers through the Iron and Steel Board. It was charged with setting maximum prices and, more interesting, with promoting projects in the name of the national interest that the industry was not prepared to undertake. In other words, the state was willing to bear some the costs without reaping any of the profits.

Because of mounting deficits, discontent with state ownership continued to spread even among trade unions and prominent Labour leaders. Unionists were disappointed with inadequate worker participation in formulating policy and managing SOEs. Public corporations, it was alleged, were used by politicians to further their own political objectives and to strengthen the private sector. "The signs," lamented a unionist, "will continue to confirm the [coal] industry's fundamental status as an overburdened yet pliable handmaiden to private manufacturing industry."[17] So-called "revisionist" Labour leaders similarly complained that ownership of the means of production did not necessarily imply control of the economy.[18] Nevertheless, although in practice both Conservatives and Labour were intimately involved in running SOEs, in rhetoric Labour came to be more closely identified with state ownership, particularly after the renationalization of steel in 1967.[19]

### State Ownership and Heath's Legacy

"We are totally opposed to further nationalisation of British industry . . . [and] we will progressively reduce the involvement of the state in nationalised industries . . . so as to improve their competitiveness."[20] With these promises in their 1970 campaign manifesto, Conservatives under Edward Heath recaptured the majority in the House of Commons. During the annual party conference in October of the same year, John Davies, Secretary for Trade and Industry, made it clear that the Conservative government would not prop up lame ducks. In addition, Davies announced a policy of "hiving off"—that is, the sale of SOE operations that were not in the mainstream of their work.[21] Although the government enjoyed a moderate success with the hiving-off policy, it failed miserably in its intention toward lame ducks.

Conservatives kept their hiving-off promise.[22] Certain assets that belonged to the Transport Holding Corporation, for example, most notably the Thomas Cook & Son travel agency, were sold in 1971. The same year witnessed the disposal of some two hundred establishments in Carlisle and Scotland that had been taken over during World War I as part of an effort to control alcohol consumption in munitions factories. The National Coal Board sold its brickworks, and the British Steel Corporation sold its brick-making holdings and tool and steel wire concerns. Despite these sales, however, the main activities of SOEs were not touched. Moreover, the volume of these sales paled in comparison to the giant rescue operation of Rolls Royce.

Despite resolute opposition to further enlarging the public sector, Conservatives came to the rescue of Rolls Royce. This experience had a dramatic effect on the debate over state ownership because it illustrated the "defensive" view in clear terms; despite rhetoric, governments of both the Right and the Left would come to the rescue of ailing private giants. Why did Heath renege on his campaign promise? Three reasons precipitated the takeover of Rolls Royce: (1) There was a need to maintain a British presence in aerospace for national defense purposes; (2) Its historically high growth in engineering and aerospace technology made the company valuable in terms of national prestige because Rolls Royce was considered to be the British answer to American superiority in the industry; and (3) Bankruptcy would result in enormous job losses that would adversely affect numerous communities. At that time, Rolls Royce was the fourteenth largest employer in the country with 80,000 employees.[23] Conservative backbenchers, however, were unhappy with this decision. Two arguments were put forth to silence their opposition. First, the government said that the measure was temporary. Second, "in the view of the Government," said Lord Carrington, then Secretary of Defense, there was no time to make arrangements with private companies to take over Rolls Royce that "would have both kept confidence and ensured the continuation of . . . important defence projects."[24] That was little consolation to dogmatic opponents of state ownership. The message was that despite rhetoric to the contrary, even Conservatives were willing to bolster ailing private firms provided they were large employers and operated in industries in which the government wished to maintain a presence for national defense or prestige purposes. In time, opposition to state ownership from inside the party grew more vocal. Heath's inability to keep one of the Conservatives' major campaign promises was the cause of major embarrassment and a disappointment. Thatcher's remark from her memoirs aptly captures this sentiment of discontent: "After a reforming start, Ted Heath's government . . . proposed and almost implemented the most radical form of socialism ever contemplated by an elected British Government."[25]

In sum, state ownership was largely a partisan issue in Britain. Initially, Conservatives supported SOEs as long as they served specific purposes in a few industries, but in time Tories became disillusioned with state ownership and sought ways to distance themselves from it. To Labour's dismay, nationalization did not bring about the expected results, although the party remained ideologically committed to state ownership. All in all, partisan politics relegated SOEs to the subordinate role of propping up the private sector rather than becoming entrepreneurs in their own right. It was only a matter of time before privatization would replace disillusionment.

### Conservative Ideas Regarding Privatization

Electoral defeat in 1974 led some Conservatives to question the party's conventional ideas. The old consensus politics—that is, efforts not to deviate from the middle ground—was seen as ineffective.[26] Furthermore, the most politically damaging element of the old consensus was considered the acceptance of the need to maintain a mixed economy with heavy state involvement in the production of goods and services. Indeed, privatization became not only a central pillar of Thatcher's economic policy, but also a personal crusade by the outspoken Prime Minister to reverse "the corrosive and corrupting effects of socialism."[27]

Sir Keith Joseph and other Conservatives blamed the party's electoral failure in 1974 on the so-called "ratchet effect."[28] They argued that consensus politics robbed the party of electoral benefits while pushing it further to the left. When Labour was in power, state intervention would increase. When, on the other hand, Tories returned to office, they had neither the will nor the desire to roll back Labour's incursions. Instead, they opted for consensus politics, which effectively meant that every time Labour reassumed office, the middle ground would move further to the left. What was needed, Sir Keith and others maintained, was a "new right," an ideology that would restore Conservative credibility and help frame the terms of the political debate. As a result, several members sought to chart a new course for the party, and by doing so they helped build the intellectual foundations that made privatization politically feasible by enabling the party to dissociate itself from state ownership and blame Labour for past failures. These members, such as Thatcher and Sir Keith, successfully challenged Heath's leadership and began to slowly replace the old guard with members who were ideologically closer to the new leadership. In time, these ideas became the official party ideology that is now commonly referred to as New Conservatism or Thatcherism.[29]

Echoing arguments that are most eloquently articulated by public choice theorists, the new ideology is generally based on the virtues of the free market and is built on four "pillars."[30] First, government activity is viewed with suspicion. Politicians are thought to be motivated by self-interest; they are thus likely to make policies to either promote themselves or reward narrow special interests. This process distorts the function of the market and in effect strips away benefits stemming from free competition. A fervent advocate of privatization and former president of the influential right-wing Adam Smith Institute explains:

[The public sector] is directed to serving the values and meeting the needs of those who direct it and work within it. Its effective monopoly often denies choice by law; and even where it does not, the fact that people have to pay for the public service through taxation removes in most cases the resources with which they could have paid for an alternative.[31]

Hence, there is a need to protect the economy from vote-seeking politicians by decreasing the level of state activity. The most effective way to do this, so the argument goes, is to privatize.

The second pillar of the new ideology is a deep distrust of SOEs. State enterprises are widely regarded by Conservatives as having failed in their mission to provide goods and services in the quantity and quality originally envisaged by the nationalizers. Rather, these industries have grown "fat" over the years, protected by statutory barriers and financed by a seemingly bottomless public purse. Being immune to the discipline of capital markets and to the fear of liquidation, some state managers have lost sight of the pursuit of commercial objectives. In addition, as captives of the political whims of the government of the day, SOEs are used to further political rather than economic aims. As a result, managers do not have incentives to run operations more efficiently, neither can they be held accountable, because evaluation criteria are always ill-defined. "The bureaucrats," says Thatcher emphatically, "are not good in business. They shouldn't have the running of it."[32] This sentiment is similarly captured in various pamphlets published by the Centre for Policy Studies, which was sponsored by Thatcher and Sir Keith. In a pamphlet titled *Why Britain Needs a Social Market Economy,* the Center deviates from old Tory lines to assert that "there is now abundant evidence that state enterprises in the UK have not served well either their customers, or their employees, or the tax payers. For when the state owns, nobody owns; and when nobody owns, nobody cares."[33]

The third pillar is hostility toward unions, particularly the ones in the public sector. SOEs, Conservatives felt, were run by powerful unions largely for the benefit of workers and were used in some instances to further the political aims of union leaders. As a result, these industries in general had poor industrial relations and an equally poor image among consumers and taxpayers. Managers and the government ultimately had to succumb to excessive union demands, bringing about a further deterioration in company finances. In a Conservative report leaked to the *Economist,* Nicholas Ridley forcefully makes this point: "[W]here industries have the nation by the jugular vein the only feasible option is to pay up."[34] John Moore makes the point even more forcefully:

Public sector trade union experience of previous administrations has given their leaders a taste of political power without responsibility. They are all too ready to seek to involve the Government in the interests of their political objectives if not in the interests of their members. Privatisation decisively breaks this link.[35]

The fourth pillar of new ideology is support for the free market on moral grounds. By relying on consumer preferences, the market is seen as unleashing individual initiative, promoting self-reliance, and encouraging responsibility. Furthermore, economic freedom not only fosters economic growth, but is also intimately tied to political freedom. For many Conservatives, the market is regarded as more democratic than politically designed institutions because it is based on free choice and mutual agreement.[36] Consumers, it is argued, are free to choose which goods or services to purchase and voluntarily seal the transaction with a document of mutual agreement: a contract. The uninhibited function of the free market, according to Sir Keith, was—and continues to be—the driving force behind new Conservative thinking. The benefits of this vision cannot be expressed in mere economic terms. In his words,

> We have a vision . . . which provides a framework which encourages people to do in their own interest that which is in the public interest—a framework with plenty of ladders and a good safety net, a society with widespread ownership and therefore with securely based liberties, a society in which people choose between right and wrong, good and evil.[37]

Privatization is the "glue" that binds the four pillars together. It is justified not only on the basis of political expediency, but on moral grounds as well. Selling SOEs obviously helps reduce public spending, at least in the short run, and rids the government of industries that many Conservatives view as political liabilities. Commenting in 1982, a Conservative minister nicely captures the mood: "Look, we're bloody fed up with them. They make huge losses, they have bolshie unions, they are feather-bedded. It seems almost impossible to do anything with them; therefore, the view has grown, get rid of them."[38] More important, however, privatization could help widen ownership. Norman Tebbit, then Trade and Industry Secretary, maintained on the eve of BT's sale: "Real public ownership is when people regard owning shares in their telephone company as natural an event as paying their telephone bills, and a lot less painful."[39] In fact, widening share ownership was crucial to the new doctrine because, as Thatcher put it, "if you look round the world today, you will see in those societies where property is widely shared, freedom flourishes; and where property is concentrated in the hands of the State, freedom is denied."[40]

Interestingly, Conservative ideology turned the tables on nationalization. Whereas nationalization, it was hoped, would give the community control over certain important industries, privatization now claimed to do the same by reversing the direction of the relationship. Ownership by private individuals, not the community at large, entailed real control. Conservatives undermined state ownership by framing the debate as an "us," the voters, versus "them," the politicians, issue. "The more power you put in the hands of government, the less the power of the people. The more in the hands of bureaucrats, the less in the hands of the electors," said Thatcher emphatically.[41] Viewed from this perspective, the already feeble sovereign entrepreneur became an easy target. Privatization became for Conservatives a policy for "taking capitalism to the people."[42]

## Opposition to Privatization

Not everyone was as receptive to the idea of privatization as Sir Keith and Thatcher were. Many Conservatives had to be won over and large numbers of voters converted. Opposition came primarily from a faction of the Conservative party and from Labour. It was precisely the ability to effectively counter this criticism that helped cultivate a broader and more receptive political audience, thereby increasing the likelihood of privatization. After assuming the party's leadership in 1975, Thatcher wisely kept many members of the old guard in her "shadow" cabinet. The division, however, between the new and the old guards—between the so-called drys and wets—became more apparent. "Drys" under Thatcher's leadership favored monetarism and relied on cutting taxes and public spending to foster economic growth and combat inflation. "Wets" under Heath's leadership advocated reflating the economy to reduce unemployment and saw a more positive role for government. There were many who could not easily fit into either camp, but they leaned more toward one or the other side.

Criticism by the "wets" on the subject of privatization was initially weak because the newly privatized enterprises were already operating in competitive markets. In addition, some SOEs were too small to make headlines, such as Amersham International, or had only recently been nationalized, such as British Aerospace. Thus, criticism was low-key, focusing on the particulars of each sale rather than on the principle of privatization itself. As the program began to include large public utilities, however, criticism became more vocal. Accusations of "selling the family silver" came from various Tory quarters, not least of which included former prime ministers. One such celebrated example was Harold MacMillan's remarks to a moderate Tory group. Speaking at the tenth annual dinner of the Tory Reform Group in 1985, he had some harsh words for Thatcher's privatization program, as reported in the *Times:*

> "First of all, the Georgian silver goes, and then all that nice furniture that used to be in the saloon. Then the Canalettos go." Cable and Wireless, "a tasty morsel," had also been sold. Profitable parts of the railways and the steel industry along with the telephone system had also been sold. "They were like the two Rembrandts still left." He said "now we are promised the further sale of anything else that can be scraped up." And turning to Mr. Walker [then Energy Secretary], he added "you cannot sell the coalmines, I am afraid."[43]

Despite such criticism, however, Thatcherites easily won the argument. Privatization proved to be not only intellectually defensible, but also politically expedient. First, the family silver, it was argued, did not belong to the state, but to the people. By selling these enterprises, Tories returned assets to their "rightful" owners. Second, the government had taken great pains to encourage maximum individual participation in the sales by frequently pricing shares well below the postissue market value.[44] As a result, several offers were oversubscribed. Hence, the number of individual shareholders rose to 22 percent in 1992 from 7 percent of all Britons in 1981.[45] By fostering so-called popular capitalism, the government hoped to create a new Conservative power base and to block any Labour moves for renationalization.

The most interesting feature of privatization, however, proved to be the weakness of Labour's opposition, its inability to offer a viable alternative to privatization, and the lack of credibility of its threat to renationalize. In 1974 Labour returned to power with plans to further extend state ownership. In 1975 it passed enabling legislation to create the British National Oil Corporation and the National Enterprise Board, the latter being a holding company charged with bringing firms under state ownership through voluntary agreements. The government also rescued the "lame duck" British Leyland and nationalized sections of the aerospace and shipbuilding industries. By 1979, convinced of the failure of British capitalism, Labour promised further nationalization and possible extension of industrial democracy to all companies employing more than five hundred workers,[46] but the tide was moving in the opposite direction.

In terms of political strategy, Labour was outmaneuvered by Conservatives. Labour reiterated the threat to renationalize shares in both oil and telecommunications. The same pattern can be discerned in most other sales as well.[47] Initially, Labour and unions threatened to renationalize them without compensation, although the policy was abandoned after the 1982 TUC and Labour Conferences. Were these threats credible? The answer is an unequivocal no because employees and sometimes even unions bought shares in the privatized companies. For example, despite industrial action and Labour threats of renationalization, 96 percent of all eligible employees became shareholders in BT. The figure is even higher in the case of British Gas, in which 99 percent of all eligible employees applied for and were allotted shares.[48] In the case of British Rail's Gleneagle Hotels Group, even the National Union of Railwaymen (NUR) itself bought shares despite initial opposition to the sales.[49] Labour and union threats obviously lacked credibility even among their own membership.

The problem with Labour's opposition was much more than just one of political strategy; it was also an intellectual problem. The party's inability to deal with the new reality stems from two related factors: intraparty strife and intellectual sterility. At a time when Tories were moving further to the right, Labourites were following the polar opposite. Torn by factional disputes, the official Labour party line hardened considerably.[50] As a result, Labour continued to offer state ownership and strict financial controls as antidotes to the Conservative onslaught. In a widely accepted argument by the British left, Stuart Holland postulated a new phase of capitalism.[51] Because of increasing market concentration in the hands of large firms and the multinationalization of production, neoclassical assumptions over competition no longer applied. Such changes in the behavior and structure of capitalist enterprises, he argued, necessitated socialist economic policies, of which state ownership is one necessary variant. Holland's ideas, however, did not appear to be very popular with the voters, who didn't really believe they owned a stake in their water or gas companies, let alone had a say in the quality of service provided. The election of 1983 dealt a devastating blow to Labour. In terms of votes per candidate, it was the worst electoral result since the birth of the party in 1900.[52]

Did Labour's dramatic defeat produce the kind of intellectual ferment needed to counter Tories? No.[53] What it did produce was surprise at the popularity of privatization—judged by the number of share applicants—a reemphasis on social as opposed to public or state ownership, and a major critique of past nationalization policies. In a document titled *Social Ownership*, Labour stated:

> Current disenchantment with social ownership is above all rooted in the failure of past Labour governments to adapt to new demands. . . . Many public-owned companies have been highly successful. On the other

hand, post-war Labour governments—anxious to protect essential industries under threat—have also had to take into social ownership industries in serious difficulties.[54]

Yet the 1987 Labour manifesto reaffirmed the party's strong commitment to state ownership, although it did make vague references to alternative institutional arrangements.[55]

There is evidence to suggest that Labour is in search of new ideas. In a powerful critique, McDonald argues that the party has deviated from the principles of an equal distribution of wealth and a framework of popular control of industry.[56] Nationalizing industries does not necessarily serve these aims. Consequently, she concludes, Labour's past theological affinity to nationalization is clearly a mistake, not least because any program of widespread renationalization would be prohibitively expensive. Instead, promoting industrial democracy, creating employee share ownership schemes, establishing more cooperatives, and strengthening the existing regulatory controls of newly privatized utilities are some innovative alternatives she proposes. The latter idea is particularly important because it deviates from previous policy and acknowledges that utilities can be placed temporarily under private ownership, provided an appropriate regulatory framework is in place.[57]

In sum, neither Labour nor the "wets" have been able to stop privatization. Instead, the Conservative party under Thatcher's leadership not only catapulted privatization to the top of the government agenda, but was also instrumental in formulating the enabling legislation. Freedom from ideological affinity or political association with state ownership gave Conservative "drys" the opportunity to make their case forcefully and persuasively. To return to the hypothesis put forth earlier, parties, the book finds, do matter.

### Public Finances and Privatization

Having analyzed developments in the political stream, I now turn to an analysis of the stream of problems. In an interview, Sir Keith Joseph identified the nationalized industries as a cause of Britain's economic decline.[58] Why? What were the problems posed by SOEs, particularly in the period since 1974? The overarching problem was the government's borrowing needs, which were compounded by a deep recession and poor SOE finances. Heavy borrowing needs not only helped bring attention to the issue of privatization, but also provided the main impetus for adopting the policy. In this section I argue that a high government deficit burden enhances the likelihood of privatization.

Government finances had an important influence on privatization. The central government's deficit burden during Labour's tenure in power in-

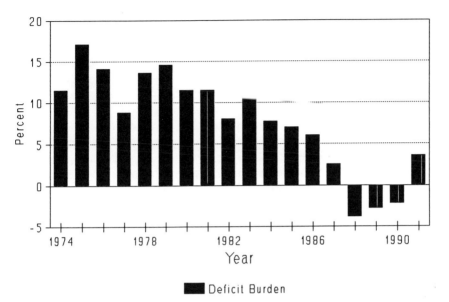

Fig. 3.1. British central government burden, 1974–91, in percentages. Ratio of central government deficit (surplus) over total central government outflows. Negative numbers represent surplus. (From International Monetary Fund, *International Financial Statistics Yearbook, 1990* [Washington, DC: IMF, 1990]; IMF, *International Financial Statistics* [Washington, DC: IMF, December 1992].)

creased dramatically to 17.1 percent in 1975 from 11.5 percent in 1974 (fig. 3.1). It remained high until 1978 when it reached 13.6 percent. During this period, Conservative attacks on the public sector multiplied. SOEs, it was argued, placed too many demands on resources "crowding out" funds destined for the private sector. To reverse the process, the deficit burden had to be eased by containing public expenditures.

During this period, the economy showed signs of a serious crisis. After recording negative economic growth in 1974 and 1975, real growth resumed and by 1979 real gross domestic product (GDP) grew at a modest 2.3 percent.[59] Similarly, inflation remained in double-digit numbers until 1982, except for 1978. Sir Keith and others argued that SOEs contributed to higher public expenditures, which were regarded as the poison rather than the antidote to the recession. They pointed to difficulties in meeting balance-of-payment obligations and the humiliating loan from the IMF in 1976. Hence, influenced by monetarist thinking, the new Conservative leadership concluded that the answer to Britain's economic decline was "too much government." One way to reverse this process was obviously to sell SOEs.

The last straw was dissatisfaction with the financial performance of SOEs. Several, though not all, SOEs were running huge deficits, which further compounded the overall government borrowing needs. Despite an attempt by the Labour government to impose financial discipline on SOEs through "external financing limits," the situation did not improve.[60] The problem was that both SOE managers and politicians were unwilling or unable to adhere to the limits. Thus, managers kept going back to their political bosses with requests for more funds, arguing that if they had more money, they could turn their companies around. Ministers agreed to provide the funds, but they also attached conditions aimed at meeting employment or anti-inflation objectives. The net result was an uneasy financial relationship that under adverse macro-economic conditions grew worse.[61]

By the time Thatcher was elected to office in 1979, Conservatives had come to a consensus that the government's borrowing needs were their most pressing problem. In 1979, the deficit burden had reached 14.6 percent, its second-highest level since 1974. Inevitably the sale of state assets as a possible solution to this problem gained considerable appeal. Since 1980 the burden had been eased, although it continued to remain at high levels until 1985. After reaching 11.5 percent in 1980, it went down to 7 percent in 1985. Privatization was considered a major contributor to this reversal of fortune. In more recent years, the situation has improved dramatically, and in 1989 and 1990, the burden stood at a positive 2.9 percent and 2.4 percent, respectively. This improvement indicates that the central government ran a surplus during these years, which means the "burden" turned into a "blessing." Nevertheless, deficits have returned to Britain. Coincident with the global economic slowdown in 1991, Britain plunged into its deepest recession since the 1930s. Accordingly, the deficit burden in 1991 reversed course and stood at an alarming 3.6 percent.

The aforementioned figures show that high government borrowing needs—that is, the deficit burden—substantially increase the likelihood of privatization. This was indeed the case in the 1970s. The relatively high deficit burden in the 1980s also ensured continued attention to this problem and to the probability that privatization might prove to be a possible remedy. However, as more state assets were sold, the government's borrowing needs decreased. This fact is ironic because it makes the budgetary rationale for privatization less obvious. Because the need to curb public spending was no longer as urgent, privatization planners sought to emphasize alternative justifications. This is not to say that budgetary reasons have eclipsed. Revenues from the sales continue to flow, and as controlling public spending has reemerged as an urgent problem, privatization has once again been put on the forefront. I will elaborate on this important point in the next chapter when I discuss the process of coupling. Suffice it to say at this point that high government borrowing needs had a significant impact on the likelihood of privatization.

## Conclusion

In this chapter, I examined developments in the political and problem streams. I showed how Conservatives were able to dissociate themselves from state ownership and espouse privatization, both as an ideological argument and as a policy. Then I examined how government borrowing needs came to be defined as a pressing problem and how these needs affected the chances of privatization. Having illuminated the workings of the first two streams, I can now proceed to illuminate developments in the policy stream.

CHAPTER 4

# Privatization in Britain

So far I have explored the emergence of a receptive political audience and the rise of a pressing problem. Here I examine the development of alternatives in the policy stream in each of the three industries under investigation—oil, telecommunications, and railroads. Finally, I examine the important process of coupling to show how the interplay of all three streams at the same time helps explain the rise of privatization on the British government's agenda and the policy's eventual adoption.

## Alternatives in Policy Communities

The purpose of this section is to illuminate the dynamics of the policy stream by examining how its two elements—technical feasibility and value acceptability—affect the availability of privatization as a viable alternative. For each of the three industries, I first examine precedent by reviewing earlier successes or failures. Then I assess the politically forged consensus in the various policy communities, and finally, I show how the ability of Conservatives and experts to solve some of the technical problems of a possible sale favorably conditioned the adoption of privatization.

### Privatizing the British National Oil Corporation

For many years, coal was the primary source of energy, but "oil soon seemed part of the Empire itself."[1] The mix of energy sources, however, began to shift in favor of oil after World War II. In 1950, coal accounted for 90 percent of Britain's primary needs.[2] Because of technological changes and falling prices, oil consumption grew at an annual rate of 7.5 percent between 1959 and 1969, and by 1966, Britain had become "a two-fuel economy" with oil covering 40 percent of annual energy consumption.[3] Given the growing importance of oil, there was a clear need to secure adequate supplies.

The discovery of North Sea oil in the 1950s partially alleviated fears of dependence on external sources, but it raised important issues of state control. After negotiating several treaties delimiting the Continental Shelf, the British government began issuing exploration licenses to private companies. The terms of these licenses, however, were very generous because the government hoped for rapid exploration and exploitation. Given "the security of supply" rationale and deteriorating balance of payments, this policy made sense. By 1972, it became evident that oil reserves in the North Sea were enormous. Early estimates projected that by 1985, oil production would range between 2.7 and 3.5 million barrels a day, making Britain self-sufficient within only a decade.[4] Only then did the government realize oil's enormous implications for the British economy.

These new developments caused a fundamental reexamination of U.K. oil policy in favor of more state control. In the aftermath of the oil price hikes of 1973–74, the refusal of oil multinationals to redirect oil supplies from their global stock to Britain, the coal miners' strike (which further exacerbated fears of energy shortages), and public accusations that oil companies were reaping excessive profits,[5] the political tide began to change. Labour pledged in its 1974 manifesto to secure the effective control of oil and gas reserves off the British coast. Out of this vague pledge, the British National Oil Corporation (BNOC) was created in 1976.[6]

*A Corporation Is Born amid Controversy*

BNOC was born amid hostility from oil companies and repeated threats of privatization from Conservative leaders. It is therefore instructive to understand this early beginning to illuminate the process of value acceptability or consensus over privatization forming in the policy stream. On 11 July 1974, the newly elected Labour government produced a White Paper that, among others, announced the establishment of an oil SOE. The proposed enterprise was empowered to build up an expert staff that would enable it to play an active part in the exploitation of oil in the North Sea and to expand its activities downstream—refining and distribution—at a future date. What was the government's reasoning behind the creation of BNOC? Eric Varley, Secretary of State for Energy, stated in December 1974:

> [I]t remains the Government's aim to ensure that oil production from the United Kingdom Continental Shelf builds up as quickly as possible over the next few years to the level set out [before]. This will help our balance of payments, contribute to government revenues, stimulate our industries and make our energy supplies more secure. It will also be an important contribution to the development of the indigenous energy resources of the industrial world.[7]

Retreating from original plans of outright nationalization that were not only expensive but also opposed by several prominent Labour members, the

Labour Party opted for state participation in existing and future licenses. Thus, BNOC was to negotiate with oil companies in the North Sea a 51 percent participation in existing operations. Furthermore, the corporation was to carefully monitor, control, and participate in future licensing agreements. Negotiations were to be voluntary, and persuasion and consent were the order of the day.[8] In cases in which oil companies made the initial investment, they would receive their share of after-tax revenue from the National Oil Account (NOA), which was set up to finance BNOC. In cases in which state participation was gained midway through production and development, however, BNOC would pay its share of future costs, but it would not reimburse the developer for costs already incurred. Initially, BNOC could borrow up to £600 million, which could be increased to £900 million with the consent of the Energy Secretary and the Treasury. The government also anticipated that by the early 1980s, BNOC's annual surplus would reach £2 billion or even £3 billion.[9]

Antipathy toward BNOC was widespread among most major oil companies.[10] A close observer and later architect of Thatcher's privatization policy lucidly captures the industry's sentiment:

> The oil industry at large loathed the whole idea [because it feared BNOC would] act as a "spy" on behalf of the Government. There was a fear that BNOC would use the commercial intelligence it so gained to set up in competition against them in a host of businesses.[11]

Company opposition centered around four concerns. First, multinationals were resentful that the SOE was allowed to take 51 percent of their early finds, although later BNOC was to share 51 percent of both stake *and* risk in all oil fields. Second, they feared for the security of their oil supply. In case of an emergency, company executives argued, the government could divert via BNOC up to 51 percent of the company's oil in the North Sea. This would leave multinationals, such as Exxon or Shell, unable to meet their downstream needs and ultimately put in jeopardy existing commitments to its customers.[12] Third, oil companies resented that BNOC did not have to pay the widely disliked petroleum revenue tax (PRT). This led to accusations that BNOC, in addition to being an SOE, enjoyed unfair commercial advantages. A commentator hit the nail on the head when he observed:

> But the fear among companies now is not that BNOC will fail to pay for itself, but that it may actually live up to its own promises of behaving like a commercial operation. A good entrepreneur takes all the chances he can get. Distrust of BNOC stems from the feeling that it will get too many chances.[13]

By virtue of its financial success, which was made possible by considerable state support, and plans to move downstream, it was obvious that BNOC was becoming a fierce competitor, a development unwelcome among oil industrialists who wished to protect their oligopoly. The fourth and biggest objection centered around the SOE's role as an advisor to the British government. Oil companies loathed the idea that BNOC had access to confidential information concerning exploration costs and potential production capabilities. They could not accept BNOC's dual role as a competitor and an adviser to the government. Lord Kearton, BNOC's first chair, argued this was precisely the reason for creating a state corporation.

> What you want is tax revenue. But if you want that, the essential thing is to have information about such matters as estimated North Sea reserves, since it is such information that determines Britain's oil policy. Our participation agreements will give us access to more information than ever before.[14]

Inevitably, oil companies agreed to BNOC's participation. Being such reluctant partners, however, also made them anxious to get rid of their competitor. Their hostility found fertile ground among Conservative leaders.

Initially, the Conservative party issued warnings against creating an oil SOE.[15] Patrick Jenkin, a Conservative spokesman on Energy, argued against committing huge sums of money in the North Sea. Instead, other measures such as taxation would be more effective. The first call for privatizing BNOC came in early fall 1975. Speaking on the BP exploration rig Sea Quest, Margaret Thatcher, the new leader of the Conservative Party, prophetically pledged that a Tory government would be committed to privatizing North Sea oil, provided it could resell what had already been sold to the government.[16] Replacing Jenkin as Energy spokesman, Tom King announced in 1977 that under Conservative rule, BNOC would lose its privileges and operate as a commercial company. His concern centered on BNOC's dual role as a regulatory agency and a state oil company, the well-known "poacher versus gamekeeper" dilemma. How could a company lay down the rules of the game and simultaneously be a participant in it? As oil company, it would have an incentive to bend the rules, but as regulatory agency, it would need to enforce them. This dual role gave BNOC an unfair advantage, a point frequently echoed by oil multinationals operating in the North Sea. As a result, private companies would be unwilling to drill in the region and therefore production would decrease, bringing eventual loss of revenue for the government and jeopardizing the supply of oil to the UK market. To transform it to a commercial company, King argued, would require forcing the corporation to pay PRT and terminating access to the NOA. It is clear from King's argument that Conservatives did not view the sovereign as a legitimate entrepreneur in its own right. David Howell, who later was to play a key role in the privatization debate as secretary for energy, carried the argument a step further. He not only opposed using BNOC as a government "spy," but also urged not to use oil revenues to fund nationalized industries. He thought these revenues should be used to either reduce taxation or stimulate private business investment.[17]

*A Period of Dramatic Change*

The period up to 1979 led to substantial changes in Britain's oil policy, which eventually made the option of privatization technically more feasible and acceptable to many specialists in the oil community. Three factors help explain the change. First, oil revenues were lower than expected. Although offshore production by BNOC and multinational oil companies rose to 770,000 barrels per day in 1977, revenues from PRT remained unexpectedly low. The taxation system contained several loopholes, allowing oil companies to deduct large capital expenditures before paying taxes. Consequently, in 1977, the government received only $456 million in taxes and royalties compared to $2.02 billion projected two years earlier.[18] Second, the sale of 17.3 percent of the government's stake in British Petroleum (BP) in June 1977 provided an example of raising revenue without increasing taxes.[19] The fact that Labour was able to raise £564 million, a figure which represented 11.1 percent of the overall central government deficit for that year, certainly provided food for thought for the Conservative leadership. Third, the loan from the IMF that was negotiated in 1976 provided an additional impetus to find new sources of revenue and curb public spending. Not only did the loan reveal the extent of the government's problem, but it also hurt British pride. It was embarrassing for the second-largest (at the time) contributor to the IMF to have to request funds from the lender of last resort. For Britons, this was a position reserved for Third World countries.

These combined factors led to increased pressure to modify BNOC's status. In October 1978, Labour committed under union pressure to further extend state ownership. "In time the oil companies," said Anthony Benn, Secretary of State for Energy, "will have to be moved from being concessionaires to being contractors, so that ownership of the resources is in the hands of the nations themselves."[20] Any plans to nationalize were unrealistic, given the huge amounts of possible compensation, funds that the British government simply did not have.

This extreme position by Labour left Conservatives with plenty of room to maneuver. Addressing the Young Conservatives' National Advisory Committee in 1978, King called for an inquiry into the activities of BNOC.

Characterizing the SOE as a failure, he claimed that BNOC stood to lose £15 billion because of "bad faith, broken promises and political arm-twisting."[21] In the same speech he stated that further nationalization, referring to Benn's pledge, caused uncertainty and delayed the development of marginal oil fields. Finally, he voiced his party's concern with the security of vast amounts of commercial intelligence amassed by BNOC. This was the same objection raised by oil companies a few years ago. The two sides, oil companies and the Tories, had come to a broad consensus concerning BNOC; its powers had to be curtailed. On the other hand, Labour and the unions had pushed themselves out of the picture. Although ideologically appealing, nationalization was not financially feasible.

## A Policy Window Opens

Although privatization was an option being considered, it was not high on the government agenda. The Conservative manifesto of 1979 made only a vague promise to review the activities of BNOC as soon as the party assumed office. Following electoral victory, however, in the spring of 1979 a policy window opened. After some structural changes in BNOC, the idea of a possible sale gradually gained currency among oil experts as it became easier to implement.

The new government took office amid alarm over the supply of oil. Following events in Iran in the winter of 1978–79, oil prices began to rise. By June 1979, the price of oil rose to $20 a barrel, an $8 increase in a period of just eighteen months.[22] Price hikes and fears of shortages of supply put privatization on the back burner because it was precisely security of supply that made BNOC essential: it was not an opportune time to sell oil assets. Instead, Conservatives fulfilled their campaign promise. David Howell, the Energy Secretary, ordered a complete review of all the activities of BNOC. Before the recommendations of the report were made public, however, Howell had already stripped BNOC of its right to be exempt from PRT. The report of the civil servants sided with BNOC's management: the SOE should stay in business, but some of its powers were nonessential. Howell immediately seized the opportunity to take away additional privileges, paving the way for an eventual sale. Access to the NOA would be ceased, exploration activities reduced, preferential treatment in licensing rounds ended, the right to sit on operating committees concerning fields where BNOC did not have a direct interest revoked, and its advisory role to the government terminated.

Still, Howell wanted to go further. He continued to press for an injection of private capital. Two options were circulated at the time. In the first, BNOC could be split into separate trading and exploration companies. While the state would retain the trading company, it would offer shares of the exploration arm to private investors. The second option included a sale of part of or all state oil assets, giving preference of purchase to U.K. companies, particularly BP. The plan immediately encountered fierce opposition from the company's former and current managers. Lord Balogh, a prominent Labour leader and former BNOC deputy chair, said that the government behaved like traitors. BNOC's chair, Lord Kearton, concurred. Because the SOE was financially successful and was able to secure oil supplies to Britain throughout the crisis of 1979, it should not be broken up; rather, it should remain a state company.[23] By mid-August, the government's intentions became clearer. As part of the government's plan to reduce the PSBR, the Treasury demanded a £400-million contribution from BNOC.[24] In addition, preparations for a sale of 5.3 percent of the government's stake in BP established a precedent and provided additional impetus to sell BNOC.

It was difficult, however, to build consensus around the same option. BNOC managers countered government demands with their own proposal. Instead of restructuring the SOE and selling its assets, they favored the idea of issuing bonds tied to BNOC's financial performance and the price of oil. Being a highly profitable producer of a commodity whose price was skyrocketing at the time, BNOC could conceivably satisfy Treasury demands and still preserve its structural integrity.[25]

In the course of evaluating the technical feasibility of these proposals, civil servants found privatization highly unappealing. BNOC had no capital structure, a limited business base, and a complicated taxation system. Asset valuation, a necessary prerequisite for any equity sale, would present formidable problems. In addition, the creation of a new company, which was at the heart of the privatization option, could create a legal nightmare as it involved separate negotiations with each company in 21 partnerships and 150 offshore blocks through participation in licenses.[26] Instead, uncertainty in the oil market, Labour's threat of an all-out battle in the event "the seed corn of the future" was sold, BNOC's stiff opposition, and the sheer complexity of a sale carried the day. In September 1979, the government announced it was shelving plans to sell BNOC and proceeded to reduce its borrowing through advance sales of oil.[27] A battle was won, but the war was far from over.

*Britoil Saves the Treasury*

Although privatization was removed from the public agenda, it continued to be debated in government circles. Howell was determined to have it his way. The key was to break the corporation in two. Once this technical obstacle was overcome, private investors could be lured more easily to buy into the more profitable operations. In a strange way, BNOC's own success proved to be its biggest handicap because success made it a more likely candidate for sale. The SOE was able in just four years to build from scratch assets valued at

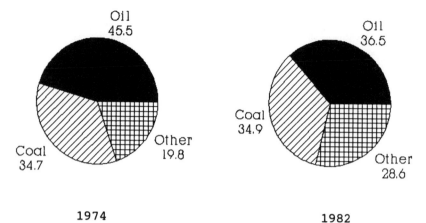

Fig. 4.1.   Inland energy consumption in Britain, 1974 and 1982, in percentages. (From Central Statistical Office, *Annual Abstract of Statistics* [London:
HMSO, 1985].)

£2.5 billion in 1980.[28] Equity share in North Sea oil production grew to
85,000 barrels per day (b/d) in 1980 and was expected to rise from 100,000
b/d in 1981 to 150,000 b/d in the mid-1980s.[29] More important, by the end
of 1981, BNOC estimated that it would have repaid the £451 million taken
from the National Oil Account and $400 million of the $825 million loan
raised by a consortium of U.K. and U.S. banks in 1977.[30] Strong demand
growth also increased BNOC's appeal to private investors. Although its share
of overall U.K. consumption fell from 45.5 percent in 1974 to 36.5 percent
in 1982, oil continued to be the largest single source of energy (fig. 4.1). As
a board officer pointed out in 1980, BNOC's share of recoverable offshore
oil reserves stood at 800 million barrels. Furthermore, the SOE was the most
active developer of oil in the North Sea, being responsible for 23 of the 54
wells drilled in the area in 1979.[31]

BNOC's relative financial health also proved to be its fatal attraction.
As Conservatives were looking for ways to reduce public spending, they
increasingly turned to SOEs for the answer. SOEs had to either reduce their
borrowing or face the possibility of a sale. BNOC belonged to the "unfortu-
nate" category of profitable companies. Since 1979, BNOC was posting a
profit, and by the early 1980s its profits were projected to rise to £700 million
(assuming prevailing market conditions in 1980).[32] By selling it, the government would not only be able to sever its relationship with an SOE, an action
in perfect harmony with prevailing Conservative ideology, but also receive a
handsome profit from the sale. Obviously, BNOC finances shattered the myth
that all British SOEs were unprofitable. Moreover, the corporation's
profitability made it a sure bet to attract investors. By 1980, BNOC was

posting a net profit ratio of 7.5 percent, while in 1981, it rose to 8.1 percent.[33] Indeed, institutional investors showed substantial interest in a possible sale of BNOC holdings as early as 1979.

Before the SOE could be sold, however, there had to be a broad consensus among specialists in the policy community. Although Labour and unions remained resolutely against any privatization scheme, BNOC's opposition suffered a serious setback as new BNOC managers softened and finally reversed their position. Following Lord Kearton's fortuitous retirement in 1979, the new interim chair, Ronald Utiger, appeared more amenable to the idea of attracting private capital. Instead of opposing a sale, as his predecessor had done, the new chair asked the government to introduce private capital in a way that would safeguard the corporation and the national interest. The final tilt in the balance came with the appointment of Philip Shelbourne as chair of BNOC. The appointment followed his giving advice to the Department of Energy on ways of injecting private capital into BNOC, although his recommendations were not made public. BNOC's new leadership, which by now also included a former Shell executive, was clearly friendlier to government objectives. The new appointment caused a serious dispute among senior BNOC executives, resulting in the resignation of a board member, Alastair Morton.[34] By appointing Shelbourne, Howell was able not only to replace a leading opponent to privatization, Kearton, but also to get rid of potential future headaches by Morton, who had already sided with Kearton on the issue. This move helped create a wider consensus on privatization. The stage was thus set for the final battle.

Having gotten many, but by no means all, BNOC senior managers on his side, Howell introduced in the House of Commons the Petroleum and Continental Shelf Bill on 13 February 1981. The bill announced the breakup of the corporation and the subsequent sale of the exploration arm. The trading side would remain under state control to continue trading oil that BNOC handled under participation agreements and to preserve the security of oil supplies under firm state control amid worries over oil shortages. Nevertheless, the bill did not specify in detail the particular mechanism of disposal. Was the government going to issue shares or sell off assets? Howell and Shelbourne were keen advocates of share sales. However, others in the Cabinet, Parliament, and BNOC argued against a sale because such action could weaken BNOC's bargaining power vis-à-vis oil multinationals and because it was financially unwise to sell off one of the government's biggest revenue earners.[35] The complexity of the privatization option, Labour's successful stalling tactics, and the legislative timetable finally forced Howell in late March to drop the bill for that session of Parliament. The government had simply run out of time.

The summer of 1981 proved fateful for BNOC. The question was how to infuse private capital into the corporation.[36] Two options had reached the top of the agenda. As two legal advisers to Britoil recall, consideration was first given to recapitalization. This scheme preserved the company's structure and included the issue of bonds tied to BNOC's oil production and price levels. Apart from technical problems, the most serious objection was political: the bond would not affect the Public Sector Borrowing Requirement (PSBR). Because reducing government deficits was a political priority, an option that would not affect, let alone reduce, the PSBR was bound to fall on deaf ears. The government consequently decided to abandon this option and pursued the other alternative, privatization.

Although there were still many technical details to work out, privatization provided several economic and political benefits. First, a sale of equity of the newly created exploration arm of BNOC would not only take the SOE off the government books, but it would also bring in substantial revenue to the Treasury. Initially revenue was estimated to range between £1.2 and £2 billion, but the actual figure was much less, £626 million, because of adverse conditions in the world oil market at the time of Britoil's sale. Second, privatization would force political interference in day-to-day operations to cease. Howell, however, overlooked the fact that it was the same government that did not give its approval for additional capital investment to develop the Clyde oil field two years earlier because of fears of raising the PSBR.[37] Were the Conservatives, a cynic might ask, trying to save the corporation from themselves? Third, hiving off a part of but not the entire BNOC would allay fears raised by Tories in Parliament over the security of oil supplies. By keeping the trading arm firmly under state control, the government could ensure the continued supply of the UK market. Fourth, a sale would substantially weaken BNOC's powers, thereby fulfilling a Tory campaign promise and satisfying disgruntled oil companies. Finally, the government would not sell the entire corporation, but only 51 percent of it. This action was thought to be ideal because the state both transferred ownership to private investors and retained control as the largest shareholder.

As drafts of the Petroleum and Continental Shelf Bill circulated in government circles, opposition to the sale grew stronger. In October 1981, Labour pledged to renationalize any BNOC assets that were sold. Merlin Rees, opposition Energy spokesman, called the proposed sale a "parliamentary, financial and national disgrace" and vowed to fight it line by line.[38] Later in the year, two senior BNOC officials resigned over disagreement with government plans. This development was particularly embarrassing to Nigel Lawson, the new Energy Secretary, as he was pushing the Oil and Gas (Enterprise) Bill through Parliament. The opposition, however, could not muster enough support to win. Using their parliamentary majority, the Tories imposed a guillotine motion limiting debate on the Bill—something Labour had done seven years earlier when it was trying to create BNOC—and passed it in late spring 1982.

According to provisions of the Act, Britoil was established in August 1982 and 51 of the company's shares were sold off in November. A second offer to dispose of the remaining shares held by the government was carried out in August 1985. Following that sale, the government retained, in addition to a few shares concerning an employee bonus scheme, only its special-rights-preference share, which it eventually gave up when BP finally took control of Britoil in February 1988. The 1982 Oil and Gas (Enterprise) Act also broke up the British Gas (BG) monopoly and separated the oil interests from the rest of the company. They were eventually sold off in the Enterprise Oil offer in June 1984. The government's stake in BP was further reduced from 51 percent in 1977 to 1.8 percent of the total BP ordinary-share capital in 1988.[39] Having been stripped of most of its assets and many of its privileges, BNOC fell upon hard times. Rapidly falling prices and an oversupply of oil in the mid-1980s dealt the final blow. Alick Buchanan-Smith, Secretary of State for Energy, formally announced on 13 March 1985 the government's intention to abolish BNOC and replace it with the Oil and Pipelines Agency, which was to retain largely regulatory powers. After the passage of enabling legislation, BNOC's assets were transferred over to the new agency, and the SOE was officially dissolved on 27 March 1986.

In conclusion, the privatization of BNOC provides a glimpse at the dynamics of the policy stream in a way that confirms the usefulness of the multiple streams approach. The idea of privatization incubated among circles of the Conservative Party and found fertile ground among major oil companies. With the Tory advent of power in 1979, a policy window opened. As the government sought to redefine its relationship with BNOC, several options competed to receive serious attention. Two elements within the policy stream influenced the availability of privatization. Initially, technical difficulties dampened thoughts of selling BNOC. Distinguishing between trading and production and exploration, however, enhanced the policy's feasibility. The company's healthy profitability and the high demand growth for oil also ensured the adoption of legislation. A relatively broad consensus among members of the policy community further helped privatization. Although unions and Labour denounced privatization, BNOC's competitors, the Conservative government, and senior management—following Lord Kearton's fortuitous retirement—endorsed the sale.

Is this pattern generalizable? Does privatization incubate among certain specialists in policy communities and then squeeze through a policy window onto the government agenda? Are the aforementioned criteria—technical feasibility and value acceptability—significant in enhancing an option's chances for adoption in other sectors as well? The analysis will address these questions by next examining privatization in telecommunications.

### Privatizing British Telecom

Like oil, privatization in telecommunications follows a similar pattern of policy formation. The issue of privatizing British Telecom (BT), however, is more complex, entailing questions of liberalization and regulation in addition to that of ownership. In this section I first examine early developments that led to state ownership and subsequent organizational changes that established precedents making an eventual sale more technically feasible. Then I proceed to describe the creation of BT and the liberalization of telecommunications. Finally, I specify the relevant options that received governmental attention and illuminate the factors that enhanced the consensus over privatization.

*Early State Ownership and Organizational Change*

The early development of British telecommunications was entrusted to private firms.[40] Budgetary considerations, however, and the desire to protect revenues from telegraph services quickly made state ownership an attractive option. Initially, competition among many small service providers in local communities did not pose a threat to revenues of the Post Office's monopoly on electric telegraphs, but after the merger of several firms into the United Telephone Company in 1879, the threat became apparent. Fearing loss of revenues, the Post Office (PO) launched a successful campaign to nationalize telephony in Britain. After a select committee report, the takeover date was set for 31 December 1911. Protecting revenues from telegraph services, better amortizing capital costs, and coordinating the development of telegraph and telephony provided the impetus for creating the new government agency. Even if telephones proved to be successful, the PO reasoned, the state and not private firms could reap the profits.

Although several proposals calling for the reorganization of the PO were put forth in the interwar years, they went for the most part unheeded. They did reveal, however, a certain element of disunity among actors in the telecommunications community that played a pivotal role in the eventual privatization of British Telecom. Pressure from business users prompted an inquiry by a select committee in 1920. It concluded that PO practices hindered rather than promoted telephony, particularly in rural areas. Moreover, the choking effects of budgetary controls by the Treasury impeded long range planning and development.[41] PO management adamantly opposed any separation of postal from telecommunications services, fearing shrinkage in personnel and funding allocations. Postal unions concurred with management, but unions representing telecommunications engineers supported separation, resenting that profits were consistently diverted to cash-poor postal services. Even though several members of Parliament known as Memorialists and the Bridgeman inquiry in the early 1930s recommended reducing Treasury control over capital expenditures and running the telecommunications authority—or telco for short—more like a business, the government remained unconvinced. Ridden by enormous public debt, neither the Treasury nor the PO wanted to give up the telco's profits.

Following World War II, the tide slowly began to change direction. The Post Office Act of 1961 instructed the postmaster general to run the telco more efficiently as a semi-autonomous business although shortages of funds for capital expenditures became more acute. Criticism was also leveled against the PO's management for its negative attitude toward telecommunications and poor planning capabilities. Momentum for structural change began to build, and the Post Office Act of 1969 finally transformed the PO from a government agency to an SOE. Although this change confirmed the commercial nature of telecommunications, it came as a mixed blessing, because while output more than doubled from 1963 to 1973, finances turned sour.[42]

*The Creation of British Telecom*

In the 1970s public confidence in the quality of both postal and telecommunications services rapidly fell while dissatisfaction with high prices began to rise. Faced with such pressure, politicians scrambled to find ways to modernize the system and cut costs.

Although privatization of postal deliveries received brief attention at the time, no consideration was given to selling off telecommunications. Instead, considerable attention was paid to restructuring the PO into two separate entities: post and telecommunications. These early arguments are important because of their precedent-setting nature. Splitting the PO led to the creation of BT and facilitated the liberalization of telecommunications; both developments paved the way for eventual privatization. Telecom managers, the Post Office Engineering Union (POEU), and several consumer groups argued for the breakup. The PO's director general at the time repeatedly emphasized the "natural" distinction between the two services by contrasting the capital intensiveness of telecommunications with the labor intensiveness of postal delivery and by emphasizing the different rates of growth of the two services.[43] Lending additional weight to pro-separation arguments were the findings of the influential Carter Report.[44] The POEU, representing mainly telecommunications workers, also favored the split because it provided an opportunity for future pay raises.[45] In contrast, the Union of Post Office Workers (UPOW),

which organized mainly PO staff but also represented telephonists and tele-
graphists, opposed the split, counterarguing it was unnecessary and expensive
because it would result in duplication of central services.[46] The Labour government, however, did not act immediately. Although it agreed in principle
with many of the report's recommendations, it eschewed the issue and instead
proceeded to experiment with industrial democracy.[47]

The election of 1979 brought a new government to power. A policy
window opened and new issues squeezed onto the government agenda. Sir
Keith Joseph, the head at the Department of Industry (DOI), terminated the
experiment with industrial democracy and pushed the restructuring option to
the top of the agenda. Concurrently, privatization proposals began to circulate.
Sir Keith told Tom Jackson, general secretary of UPOW and chair of the
Trades Union Congress (TUC), that he was considering splitting the PO and
"giving over part of telecommunications to private industry."[48] Both major
unions, UPOW and POEU, opposed the move. It was not clear, however,
what exactly Sir Keith's plans were. Did the invitation to private industry
envisage an outright sale or a bond issue, or did it simply aim at curbing the
state's monopoly while keeping the proposed telecommunications authority
under state ownership?

By the autumn of 1979, Conservative plans became clearer. Although
aiming at creating a new authority and liberalizing telecommunications, the
plan also included the possibility of participation by private capital. First and
foremost, the Cabinet agreed to the separation of PO and the creation of BT.
This is a crucial development because it helped rid BT of the financial drain
coming from postal services, making it more attractive to potential private
investors. It also made asset far easier to value, which increased the technical
feasibility of a potential sale. Second, the government clearly was determined
to end the monopoly in sales of terminal equipment. These two goals were
not new; they were recommendations put forth by the Carter Report in 1977.
The Conservatives, however, appeared to have a third goal as well. It was
reported that the new telecommunications authority was "likely to join the
list of state corporations" in which the general public, along with employees,
would be offered shares.[49] The privatization of BT was obviously an option,
but as subsequent practice shows, it was not high on the government agenda.
Instead, Conservatives elected to pursue the first two goals.

In 1981, the government introduced the Telecommunications Act. In
addition to authorizing the sale of Cable and Wireless, a state telecommunications company with experience in the Commonwealth, it separated telecommunications from postal services, but BT was to remain under state control
as a public corporation, and the act liberalized the supply of certain types of
terminal equipment. A few months later, Conservatives took liberalization
one step further. Early in 1980, Sir Keith asked then state-owned Cable and

Wireless to take leadership in developing an alternative network. Accordingly, the company succeeded in forming a venture named Mercury with Barclays Bank and British Petroleum, which initially owned 20 and 40 percent of Mercury, respectively, but their shares eventually were bought off by Cable and Wireless. In October 1981 a license was granted to Mercury to set up a rival network that would link up twenty-six major British cities with optical fiber cables and provide trunk and international services to business customers.[50] These early developments strengthened the argument for BT's privatization by making it more technically feasible and politically acceptable. BT was a commercial entity in its own right, and it would be easier to propose its sale now that parts of its business were subject to competitive pressures.

## To Sell or Not to Sell

Although the Conservative government liberalized parts of telecommunications equipment and services, it did not pay serious attention to privatization. In fact, privatization of telecommunications was not mentioned in the 1979 Conservative manifesto; neither was the policy community seriously debating proposals to sell off BT. Instead, the debate centered around restructuring PO. As I argued earlier, the creation of BT as an SOE and the partial liberalization of telecommunications acted as precedent setters, paving the way for the ensuing process of privatization. Where did the option originate? How did it gain prominence on the government agenda, and why did it take the form that it did?

Having addressed liberalization to the limited extent that they did, Conservatives moved to tackle the next important question. How was BT going to finance its massive capital investment program? There was a fairly wide consensus that telecommunications services in Britain were inferior to those of other major industrialized countries.[51] Table 4.1 confirms the conclusions of the Carter Report and other studies on the subject.[52] Despite progress in the 1970s, Britain was falling behind its continental neighbors France and West Germany. Investment in U.K. telecommunications relative to GDP fell from 10.7 percent in 1974 to 6.5 percent in 1982 while that of some other countries increased. In addition, U.K. telecommunications remained highly labor-intensive relative to France and West Germany.

Modernization, however, meant massive capital injections. As long as BT remained an SOE, funds would have to come from the Exchequer, something that a government committed to reducing public spending was reluctant to do. It was precisely the unwillingness of Conservatives to fund BT's modernization program that created friction between the corporation and the government and made privatization more appealing. In the crucial months prior to and following the creation of BT in 1981, senior management found itself at odds with the government. Throughout this period, Sir George Jefferson, BT's chair, emphasized the need for increased investment and expressed his frustration with the financial limits imposed by the Treasury. In his words,

> We recognize the need to control public expenditure but unless we can find ways of matching finance to the real need, the ability of commerce and industry in the United Kingdom to be competitive will be seriously impaired by lack of a good telecom network.[53]

How could BT acquire additional financing? Leaving the option of issuing bonds aside for the moment, the company could either generate the funds internally or borrow from the Treasury. With a self-financing ratio of approximately 90 percent, which is very high by normal commercial standards, BT would have to raise user charges to avoid external borrowing. Yet higher prices for telecommunications services were unpopular and might not raise adequate funds. Thus, the other available option was the one most frequently used by SOEs: the public purse. The Treasury, however, imposed strict limits on the amount of funds BT could borrow. Following marathon negotiations, the Treasury finally agreed to increase the corporation's external financing limit (EFL) for 1981–82 to £380 million from a proposed £180 million. Nevertheless, the amount still fell short of BT's request for £500 million, leaving a gap of £120 million. Moreover, a pledge to invest £2 billion annually (at 1980–81 prices) until 1985 to modernize the country's telecommunications system further widened the gap.[54]

Which members of the policy community supported privatization? Similarly to the case of oil, the answer is to be found in government circles—more specifically the Treasury and to a lesser extent DOI. Unlike the case of oil, however, privatization was not widely debated in the policy community prior

TABLE 4.1.   A Comparison of Telecommunications Systems in Three Countries

| | Britain | | France | | West Germany | |
|---|---|---|---|---|---|---|
| | 1974 | 1982 | 1974 | 1982 | 1974 | 1982 |
| Density of Penetration[a] | 34.1 | 50.7 | 23.6 | 54.1 | 30.2 | 51.0 |
| Telecommunications Investment as Percentage of GDP | 10.7 | 6.5 | 5.2 | 7.0 | 7.6 | 7.4 |
| Employees per 10,000 Main Lines | 201.6 | 128.8 | 142.5[b] | 84.0 | 156.2 | 89.7 |

Source: International Telecommunications Union, Yearbook of Common Carrier Statistics (Geneva: ITU, 1984).

[a]Telephone sets per 1,000 inhabitants
[b]Figure is for 1977.

to the government's announcement to sell BT. Furthermore, neither private industry nor unions were consulted, and even BT itself was caught by surprise. Despite government rhetoric to the contrary, it appears that neither privatization nor the subsequent regulatory regime received careful consideration prior to drafting the telecommunications bill.

As in the case of oil, two options were serious contenders to solve the problem of financing: recapitalization and privatization. Initially BT's management and the Department of Industry favored recapitalization. BT's chairman proposed three ways of raising funds outside treasury constraints.[55] BT could issue (1) subscriber bonds, (2) bonds yielding a fixed rate of return, or (3) bonds tied to BT's sales and performance. While DOI favored the third proposal, the Treasury remained against recapitalization in principle and was more favorably disposed toward privatization.[56]

The technical difficulties associated with the bond issue were quite serious. The principal problem was the rate of return that could be used to attract investors. It seemed that City investors would require a return 3 or 4 percent higher than that of government stocks and an implicit guarantee that the government would not try to restrict BT's profits. The issue of BT's performance, however, was a double-edged sword. On the one hand, the bond's success depended on BT's profits. On the other hand, eliminating controls on tariffs would leave BT operating as a monopolist, without incentives for increased efficiency. For the Treasury the questions were whether BT should borrow in the capital market at rates higher than those it could get from the treasury and how the loans would affect the PSBR. It made more sense for BT to borrow from the Treasury because that option was cheaper. This argument diminished the appeal of the bond but fostered political unease because it meant that the Treasury had to raise the corporation's EFL and thereby increase the overall deficit at a time when it was seeking ways to reduce it.

On the other hand, an outright sale of equity also presented formidable technical difficulties. Was the government going to break it up into regional authorities or was BT going to be sold as a single entity? A breakup would be expensive and time-consuming and would yield a lower sale price. Selling BT as a single entity, however, would raise serious regulatory concerns. In addition, should the government sell the entire enterprise, or should it retain a certain percentage of ownership to mollify critics? This is obviously a formidable array of questions that made privatization a difficult option to implement.

Nevertheless, privatization was the solution that finally bubbled to the top of the government's agenda. Why? Two factors weighed heavily to its favor. First, the technical feasibility of an outright sale was substantially enhanced by BT's internal reorganization and the experience accumulated from the successful sale of other enterprises at the time. Ironically, reorganization began when BT was still under state ownership and contained two components. The first, BT's cultural transformation—that is, the change in the "dominant behavioral norms, value systems and the spirit of the organization"[57]—was made possible by recruiting senior managers committed to changing the SOE to a more commercially viable corporation. Two appointments were especially important, that of Sir George Jefferson and that of Deryk Vander Weyer, who in 1983 became deputy chair.[58] Both managers had built distinguished careers in the private sector and were committed to making BT both more sensitive to customer needs and more profit oriented.[59] An important complement to cultural change was BT's structural transformation. Its purpose was to enable the SOE to adapt to a rapidly changing environment, particularly since liberalization brought limited competition in equipment manufacturing. Beginning in 1982, decision making was decentralized and individual profit centers were introduced.

Apart from BT's organizational change, privatization gained credibility as a viable option through the success of other sales. In fact, as I argued previously, privatization was not an idea "indigenous" to telecommunications. Rather, it was put on the broader government agenda in 1979 as a general way of dealing with the problems of SOEs. The valuable experience that the government acquired through other sales, particularly the sale of local council houses, made the possibility of BT's sale more feasible because it revealed that privatization could attract considerable voter support and be carried out in a relatively short period of time without significant political opposition—BT's privatization was the first to encounter strong opposition—and with substantial financial rewards for the Treasury.[60] Indeed, by February 1982, the British government had obtained £568 million[61] as net proceeds from sales of SOEs, with the sale of Britoil scheduled for later that year. This point illustrates the process of spillover discussed in chapter 2. Once a precedent is established in one policy area, it becomes relatively easier for similar change to be advocated in other areas as well.

Technical feasibility was enhanced by BT's salability. Despite the need for modernization, the corporation remained a highly profitable enterprise. Partly because of its monopolistic position, BT's net profit ratio stood at 14.4 percent in 1984 after a peak of 16.2 percent in 1982 and a strong 16.1 percent in 1983.[62] In fact, when BT was created in 1981, the SOE posted a profit ratio of 12.5 percent. Officials in the Department of Trade and Industry (DTI) were certain, and were later proven right, that they would have little trouble finding buyers.

Apart from financial health, BT had excellent demand prospects (table 4.2). The diversity and speed of technological advances created a soaring demand for telecommunications services in Britain and elsewhere.[63] The size of the telephone system measured by the number of telephone sets connected to the public network, grew from 13.2 million sets in 1974 to 19.9 million sets in 1980. As an SOE, BT also witnessed an increase in size from 20.2 million sets in 1981 to an impressive 22.8 million sets at the time of its sale in 1984. This constitutes an increase of a little over 72 percent in a ten-year period. Total national traffic also increased from 19.1 billion sets in 1974 to 27.8 billion sets in 1981 to 29.5 billion sets in 1984. Perhaps more impressive has been the growth of the data transmission system. It grew from 69,000 terminals in 1980 to 98,600 terminals in 1983, an increase of 43 percent in three years! With such high demand prospects and proper marketing, BT could easily be transformed from a boring utility to an exciting growth company whose stock would yield a high rate of return. Just as in the case of oil, such was subsequently the case. Interestingly enough, however, substantial growth had already been achieved under state ownership. This point supports the claim made earlier concerning the defensive role of the state in Britain. In cases where private interests stood to gain, the sovereign entrepreneur was vulnerable to a sale.

Although technical feasibility was important, it was by no means enough. Value acceptability among members of the telecommunications community was equally significant. Some authors argue there was no consensus in the policy community as to the desirability of privatization.[64] Judging from the level of opposition to the Telecommunications Act, one could find merit to the argument. Dissent, however, was more apparent than real. Many groups that opposed the act expressed concern with specific regulatory provisions and not with the notion of privatization itself. Their concern was partly placated by inserting amendments based on the assumption of a *private* BT. The main sources of opposition were unions and Labour.

As already mentioned, the idea of selling BT was pushed vigorously by the Treasury. Fighting between the Treasury and DOI over the best way of

TABLE 4.2.  Patterns of Demand for British Telecommunications Services, 1974–84

|  | 1974 | 1980 | 1981 | 1982 | 1983 | 1984 |
|---|---|---|---|---|---|---|
| Size of the System[a] | 13.2 | 19.9 | 20.2 | 20.8 | 21.4 | 22.8 |
| National Traffic[b] | 19.1 | 26.6 | 27.8 | 28.6 | 29.1 | 29.5 |
| Size of Data System[c] | — | 69.0 | 81.5 | 93.3 | 98.6 | — |
| Size of Postal Services[d] | 11.2 | 10.4 | 10.2 | 10.2 | 10.4 | 10.8 |

*Source*: International Telecommunications Union *Yearbook of Common Carrier Statistics* (Geneva: ITU, 1984; 1990); Central Statistical Office, *Annual Abstract of Statistics* (London: HMSO, 1985).

[a]Million telephone sets.

[b]Billion calls.

[c]Thousand terminal equipment connected to public telephone and telex networks.

[d]Billion letters, printed papers, newspapers, and parcels.

allowing BT to raise capital continued for a whole year. Initially, DOI appeared to be winning the argument, but the announcement of the bond issue was postponed several times.[65] Finally, the Treasury had the last word, aided by a consensus in government to reduce public spending and by BT's better-than-expected 1981 financial returns. The stage was set, and the decision was finally announced.

On 19 July 1982, Patrick Jenkin, the new Secretary of State for Industry, announced to the House of Commons the government's intentions to sell 51 percent of BT.[66] He further noted the need to establish a new regulatory body, the Office of Telecommunications (Oftel), to regulate telecommunications and control BT's possible monopolistic behavior. What were the government's goals behind privatization? In his address to an OECD conference, J. Butcher, Under Secretary of State for the Department of Industry, states that

> our intention is to convert British Telecom from a "PTT" in the traditional mould into a dynamic private company; fully responsive to market demands, free from Government restraints and able to raise investment capital on a commercial basis and on a scale which will allow it to make full use of the coming opportunities.[67]

The publication of the government's intentions highlights three points. First, despite a promise to give up commercial control, the government intended to continue exercising control through ownership. But if the state was to remain the single largest shareholder, how could this solution address previous concern? How could the new hybrid realistically raise funds in capital markets without implicit government approval? Wouldn't investors look for some sort of government guarantee?[68] Moreover, the government announced for the first time its intention to shift from ownership to regulation, a less visible, indirect form of control. Some of Oftel's powers that were later added to the 1984 Telecommunications Act included advising the Department of Industry; issuing and revising the licenses of BT and its competitors to promote more effective competition; exercising control over tariffs;[69] and promoting the interests of consumers, users, and equipment manufacturers. Evidently, the government intended to retain considerable indirect control over the company despite the sale of BT.

Second, there was a marked shift in emphasis away from competition. John Moore, then Financial Secretary to the British Treasury, clearly articulated this shift: "We will encourage competition *where appropriate but where it does not make business or economic sense we will not hesitate to extend the benefits of privatisation to natural monopolies*" (emphasis added).[70] While the debate in the telecommunications community focused on the far-reaching implications of recent liberalization measures, the government formally introduced privatization without seriously curbing BT's monopoly powers prior to the sale. This raised questions about the ability of equipment manufacturers to compete with BT in a limited range of products and cast doubt over the commercial viability and competitive "threat" posed by the nascent Mercury project. Instead, the government explained its decision as motivated by the desire to free BT from financial constraints and government interference. Although it reaffirmed its commitment to competition and efficiency, the government placed primary importance on financial considerations.[71] This is a key point because up until that time, the theoretical case for privatization was made largely on the grounds of increasing competition and improving efficiency.[72] In practice financial considerations were of paramount importance in previous cases as well, such as Britoil.

Third, it was the first time that the government openly attributed to BT a "national flag" carrier status. Not breaking BT up, it was argued, would enable the company to maintain economies of scale and to compete in foreign markets while retaining a strong home base. Characteristic of this view is Sir George's allusion to BT as the "battleship of the British fleet."[73]

Value acceptability—the degree of consensus—in the telecommunications community had to be politically forged. Although the unions immediately condemned the privatization proposal, BT's management and the City maintained guarded optimism. BT had already won the battle against a separation along regional lines, a breakup that the unions also opposed. Although Margaret Thatcher herself and Alan Walters, economic advisor to the Prime Minister, favored the division, BT argued against it for four reasons: (1) There would be a problem finding buyers for BT's unprofitable parts; (2) There was a risk of substituting a national monopoly with regional monopolies; (3) It would further infuriate the unions; and (4) It would diminish BT's ability to compete on a world scale.[74] Nevertheless, the company was somewhat surprised that privatization came so soon. BT was busy reacting to new demands posed by liberalization and was skeptical about having to respond to further exigencies created by privatization. The City also advised against haste, pointing out that the sale of 51 percent of a company whose assets were valued at £8 billion at the time would make it the biggest sale to that date. The market certainly ran the risk of financial indigestion.

The government, however, was determined to press ahead and forge a consensus. In November 1982, Jenkin introduced a hastily drafted Telecommunications Bill. The unions were the first to lead the attack. To better coordinate their efforts, they decided to form the British Telecommunications Union Committee (BTUC). The decision to launch a public campaign was itself significant because it signaled a change from the low-key approach the union had adopted with the privatization of Britoil.[75] They opposed the bill, arguing that (1) privatization would end BT's obligation to provide a public service to the community as a whole; (2) privatization might result in loss of jobs; (3) a private BT would have an incentive to reduce or eliminate unprofitable rural services; and (4) new procurement policies would have harmful effects on British equipment manufacturers.[76] Until that time, approximately 95 percent of BT's equipment was purchased from domestic suppliers. Because the new legislation enabled BT to shop worldwide for its equipment, workers in domestic companies—75 percent of whose output went to BT—faced possible massive layoffs. In addition to mobilizing member support, the union campaign also included letter writing to both Conservative and Labour politicians,[77] direct lobbying of MPs in Parliament, and coordination of efforts with other opposition groups.

Two important points need to be made concerning union strategy. First, the labor movement contained several seeds of disunity, some of which were planted earlier. The importance of the precedent established by the 1981 Telecommunications Act was not simply that it enabled the government to take liberalization a step further, as the White Paper claimed, but that it also helped split the unions. Although all BT unions opposed privatization, some in the supply industry favored the sale of BT.[78] Thus, privatization found unions with bridges to cross and bruised egos to mend *before* any real opposition could be effectively mounted. It is clear that the timing of the announcement was partly motivated by the government's keen awareness of the opposition's weakness.

Second, privatization signaled the breakdown of the previous consensual policy style and the unions' increasing marginalization, at least temporarily, from an insider to an outsider group. Indeed, consultation with unions concerning privatization amounted to a few meetings with the minister. Relations with the government further deteriorated, and by early 1982 the minister instructed civil servants to cease discussing the subject with unions.[79] In a little over two years, unions found themselves not only off the center of decision making—note the Labour experiment with industrial democracy in the 1970s and its subsequent termination by Thatcher—but also fighting for political survival. It was feared that privatization would seriously diminish union strength. These fears were subsequently realized.

Equipment manufacturers also opposed the Telecommunications Bill, arguing that it was designed to squeeze them out of the market. Liberalizing BT's procurement policy, they claimed, would potentially harm the industry; whereas BT remained de facto the main purchaser of their output, British companies stood to lose the right of being BT's main suppliers. Thus, they proposed restricting BT's market share of terminal apparatus to 25 percent.[80] The majority of their proposals were rejected, although the government later agreed to allow subscribers to provide their own first telephone. Interestingly, some of these concerns were also voiced for different reasons by unions. The difference was that although equipment manufacturers did not oppose privatization in principle, they feared the predatory behavior of a private BT. They were not alone.

A coalition of diverse groups criticized the bill as well. The Post Office Users National Council (POUNC), whose functions would be taken over by Oftel, complained that Oftel's director could not adequately safeguard consumer interests and look after BT's welfare. Other organizations such as the National Farmers' Union, local councils, and Rural Voice—which was part of the National Council for Voluntary Organizations—expressed concern over the potential loss of rural services. Although general Conservative thinking argued against viewing telephone services as a social obligation,[81] some Conservative MPs disagreed.[82]

Finally, opposition parties openly questioned the wisdom of the bill. Stan Orme, Labour's "shadow" industry minister, reaffirmed Labour's preference that BT stay under state ownership and argued that liberalization would result in massive layoffs and a flood of foreign imports.[83] Ian Wrigglesworth, representative for the Social Democratic Party, also lamented the haste of the bill and its lack of serious attention to the implications of a private monopolist in telecommunications.[84] Nevertheless, the government did not have the time to put the bill to a vote because of the general election in June 1983.

The Telecommunications Bill's long career in the Commons should be credited to Labour's delaying tactics, a notable example of which was John Golding's eleven-hour filibuster.[85] The delay strengthened rather than hurt the bill, however. First, it enabled Conservatives to make it an issue in their 1983 manifesto and claim a mandate upon return to power. Second, the actual sale was not really delayed because the government had always said that it planned on selling BT after the general election. Third, the delay forestalled the installation of the regulatory regime, thus giving BT the opportunity to raise prices.[86] Finally, union tactics delayed the entry of Mercury, thereby increasing BT's value as a source of information for the government.[87]

On 29 June 1983, a new bill was introduced by yet another Secretary, Cecil Parkinson, at what is now the Department of Trade and Industry. The new bill contained several modifications, most notably the guarantee of BT's right to supply the prime instrument and the company's commitment to maintaining rural services. These provisions were included largely because of pressure by interest groups showing that the government was trying to obtain a certain degree of consensus among members of the telecommunications community. Whereas many groups opposed the bill, their concerns did not focus on privatization. Rather, the government was able to isolate the main source of opposition, the unions, by accepting several amendments that did not affect the substance of the bill and at the same time placated a substantial number of concerned groups.

Despite a long public debate, arguments against the privatization of BT remained isolated and often took the form of dogmatic battles in the House of Commons. The government finally overcame two sources of opposition, industrial action by the unions and Lord Weinstock's public protest, and cemented the consensus over privatization. The POEU had inherited from the Post Office a tradition of frequent consultation with management over policy matters and a reputation for getting its way. By 1982, however, it became apparent that the old consensus was coming to an end.[88] Sir George Jefferson constantly reiterated his claim that liberalization necessitated a change in BT's management-labor relations because the consultation practices of the past, he argued, were inappropriate in the light of new realities.[89] In August 1983, the POEU took action. Engineers refused instructions from BT to connect Mercury to the main network, claiming it would threaten their job security. Mercury took the union to court, charging the POEU with causing a breach of contract between BT and Mercury.[90] In the meantime, industrial action spread to BT's services in London. Several, but not all, engineers staged a strike in Central London, disrupting mainly international telephone lines. Before the two sides were able to inflict serious damage upon each other, however, the High Court reversed the decision of a lower court; the POEU was found to be in breach of contract.[91] Engineers remained divided over responding to Mercury's challenge and in a rare acceptance of defeat, they agreed not to pursue the case. Finally, depleting funds, the fear of being sued for damages, and disagreement among its membership forced the POEU to scale down its campaign against BT. The unions had challenged plans for BT's privatization and lost.

The second major development of this period was Lord Weinstock's protest. It is important to discuss it in some detail not only because he headed GEC, a telecommunications equipment manufacturer, but also because his criticism, unlike that of so many others, focused on fundamental assumptions of privatization. First, he questioned the notion that a transfer of ownership would by itself generate efficiency. He concluded that "by itself public ownership does not . . . emerge as an obstacle to efficiency . . . it is all a matter of management."[92] Good managers, he argued, could be found in both public and private sectors. Second, he doubted whether the bill went far enough to create true competition. Since BT would remain the main operator of the telecommunications network and the main supplier of terminals, there was little Oftel could do to control an "all-powerful patron." Given that the new regime would remove BT from parliamentary scrutiny, there was risk of inadequate control.

Weinstock's points are very important. During the bill's second reading in the House of Lords, Lord Cockfield, Chancellor of the Duchy of Lancaster, argued that BT's privatization was mainly a response to considerations of competition and efficiency.[93] If, on the one hand, better management was the key to efficiency, as Weinstock pointed out, and given that the government was satisfied with Sir George's tenure, why the rush to privatize BT? If, on the other hand, the key was to be found in competition, the bill left much to be desired. With this in mind, Weinstock was justified in asking; "[I]s it wise to hand out monopolistic licenses and concessions without a properly considered and coherent national programme of communications?"[94] Oftel, whose powers were not clearly specified in the bill, was considered too weak to control a private BT. Besides, only 55 percent of the company's revenue was really subject to price regulation at the time of BT's privatization.[95] In addition, prior to its sale BT retained a formidable market share. At the time of its sale, BT was a virtual monopolist in four out of six major products.[96] To be sure, Weinstock's protest may not have been entirely altruistic. Being the managing director of GEC, he had a direct stake in the outcome. For this reason, Whitehall viewed his remarks with skepticism and irritation, particularly since domestic equipment manufacturers were slow to respond to new export opportunities, contrary to government hopes.[97] Nevertheless, politics prevailed and Weinstock's criticism went unanswered.

The process of forging a consensus was nearly complete. One final actor's agreement remained. Despite initial hesitation, BT managers argued in favor of privatization. Although they did not place the issue on the government agenda, they were certainly influential in shaping the final outcome. BT conducted a careful campaign which included numerous briefings of politicians.[98] When the bill was being debated in 1982, BT's corporate affairs department organized briefings of politicians to educate them of its position or reassure them of the continuation of certain services. Throughout the winter of 1982–83, BT maintained a presence in the House of Commons, attended all 35 sittings of the standing committee, and was even able to put up its own amendments. Following the June 1983 election, 150 new MPs were elected to office. BT immediately went to work organizing group briefings in Parliament and in Gresham Street, BT's headquarters. It continued to maintain a representative in the Commons who dutifully distributed parliamentary briefs written by BT. The strategy finally paid off. BT avoided divestiture of its constituent parts and convinced the government of "light rein" regulation.[99]

In sum, privatization in telecommunications followed a similar pattern to that of oil. The main difference was that the idea did not bubble up from within the narrow policy community. Rather, it was placed on the broader government agenda and spilled over to telecommunications through the Treasury. PO's SOE status as early as 1969, the separation of telecommunications, and the liberalization measures taken in the 1981 Act established precedents, which then enhanced the chances of privatization.

In addition to the spillover, the availability of the privatization option in telecommunications depended on two factors: technical feasibility and value acceptability. Despite valuation problems, the SOE's reorganization and the substantial experience the government acquired through previous sales greatly enhanced privatization's credibility as a viable alternative. BT's high profits and strong demand growth dramatically enhanced the policy's chances to not only receive serious consideration, but also to be adopted. Value acceptability among members of the policy community also improved the odds that the policy would receive serious consideration. It is worth noting that many members of the community opposing the Telecommunications Bill did not really object to privatization in principle. Rather, their opposition focused on obtaining certain guarantees, such as the continuation of rural services or reciprocal access to foreign markets, on the assumption of a *private* BT. In the crucial early stages of agenda setting, only the Treasury and later the DOI pushed for selling BT. Sensing the direction of the prevailing winds, management quickly joined the effort to ensure that the law protected BT's interests. Not unlike the case of oil, unions were against the sale, but two things were different this time. First, unions organized a highly visible public campaign and engaged in industrial action against BT. Second, there were signs of disunity among postal unions, telecommunications unions, and unions in the supply industry. Equipment manufacturers were not against privatization per se, but rather sought to dismantle BT's monopoly. The impact of intellectuals on the privatization debate appears limited save for the two government-commissioned reports written by academic economists. Moreover, several diverse groups coalesced at different times in the House of Commons and especially the House of Lords to propose amendments to the bill.

The case study of telecommunications highlights three important points. First, the state continues to retain considerable control over a private BT. The government remained until recently the single largest shareholder, albeit in a minority position. In December 1991, the government sold an additional tranche of shares, bringing its stock to 25.8 percent, down from 47.7 percent. The actual percentage fell even lower, to 22 percent after bonus shares are taken into consideration.[100] The remaining shares were disposed in July 1993. Furthermore, the 1984 sale removed BT from parliamentary scrutiny under direct government regulation through Oftel. Second, the case highlights the importance of privatization as a means of restructuring power relations among members of the policy community. Just as in the case of oil, unions were left outside the policy process. Unlike oil, however, the telecommunications community was restructured to give more power to BT's management and to include new members, namely, Oftel and Mercury.[101] Third, the debate on privatization shows that telecommunications in Britain is losing its social service status in favor of a more commercial view.[102] For instance, the debate whether to continue unprofitable rural services, maintain services for people with special needs, and subsidize services in favor of domestic residential users, as well as the preference for minimal regulation, illustrate Conservative determination to bypass issues of social inequality and public accountability[103] in favor of promoting private enterprise and the profit motive. As I will show in part 3, however, other European countries are less willing to pay this price for "liberating" telecommunications.

### Railroads: Still under State Ownership?

The case of railroads presents a different picture. Like oil and unlike telecommunications, the idea of privatizing British Rail (BR) was debated long before the Conservative advent of power in 1979. Similarly, both oil and railroads are subject to intense competition from other sectors, although rail has been in a long-term decline. Unlike oil, however, railroads share many common points with telecommunications in that they both constitute a service. Thus, the issue of privatizing railroads involves, among others, such complex questions as dividing national operations into regional authorities, hiving off assets, regulating BR, and continuing to service unprofitable routes. The most important difference from the previous two cases, however, is that BR has not yet been sold, although dramatic changes are currently taking place. In this section I trace the privatization debate in railroads and identify the major sources of support and opposition in an effort to illuminate the factors that enhance or impede the availability of privatization as a viable policy alternative.

*Early Debates over Privatization*

The idea of privatizing British railroads is very old indeed. Ever since Labour nationalized BR in 1947, the SOE faced chronic budget deficits and declining demand for services. Despite various efforts to resuscitate BR—for example, the Modernization Plan introduced in 1955 and Dr. Richard Beeching's streamlining attempts in the 1960s—the SOE increasingly relied on state subsidies.[104] Although some Conservatives had initially supported nationalizing the railroads,[105] the party as a whole grew increasingly irritated with BR's poor finances and strong unions. By the early 1970s, BR became in Tory eyes the symbol of state ownership's failure, a "lame duck, part of the soft morass of subsidized incompetence."[106] It is therefore not surprising that members of the railroads community, particularly those with Tory ties, have spent countless hours searching for ways to cut subsidies and improve BR's financial health and quality of service.

The Labour government's commitment in 1974 to continue financing

BR's deficit in the form of public service obligation (PSO) payments led to an unflagging debate. Opponents voiced two major concerns. One strand of opposition called for increased efficiency, with the ideal goal of an eventually self-financing railroad.[107] BR, it was argued, was not doing all it could to bring costs down. Because these advocates found no compelling evidence of social and environmental benefits from rail transport, they concluded that increased financial support was not the answer to BR's problems. Rather, tight financial control, a structural change to divisions with separate management and accounts, and a hiving-off strategy would dramatically improve corporate finances. Some of the candidates suitable for sale included freight traffic, parcel service, and entire electric railway systems in Glasgow, Merseyside, and Tyneside. Opposition to additional rail subsidies also came from the "rail conversion" lobby. Rather than focus primarily on BR's finances, this lobby took a broader view of rail transport, arguing that many rail routes should be paved and converted to roads.[108] Proponents viewed rail as a declining industry with little chance of ever attracting enough passengers to turn BR around. This change was not only inevitable, but also part of a wider structural transformation of the British economy. As Sir Alfred Sherman, then director of the Tory-sponsored Centre for Policy Studies, argued that rail had to give way to automobiles and other more sophisticated modes of transport just as railroads had displaced stagecoaches two centuries earlier. Thus, the privatization debate during the 1970s took the form of either hiving off or closing down rail routes to expand the road network.

*Conservatives and Privatization in the Early 1980s*

The advent of Conservatives to power in 1979 provided a window of opportunity for the rail conversion lobby. It was thought that a Conservative Secretary of State for Transport would not have the same political or emotional attachment to BR or the unions and would thus be more amenable to radical change. The lobby also had some powerful allies in the new government. Sir Alfred became a speechwriter for the Prime Minister while Ian Gow, Conservative MP for Eastbourne, was appointed as Thatcher's parliamentary secretary. Gow gained a reputation as one of the fiercest advocates of privatization during the tenure of the preceding Labour government. Alan Walters, economic advisor to the Prime Minister, was also known to be critical of BR's proposed massive capital investment program and sympathetic to transferring certain rail lines to private operators. In addition, the fact that Sir Peter Parker, chair of the British Railways Board, was a former Labour candidate for Parliament caused many Conservatives to view BR with even greater suspicion. It seemed that privatization was an idea whose time had at long last come.

For its part, BR had a hard case to argue. Because of antiquated equipment and fast-rising deficits, it had only three options available: (1) close down routes and streamline operations to improve the balance sheet; (2) embark on a massive investment program to both attract more passengers and increase productivity; or (3) sell assets. Sir Peter chose to pursue the second option, but he encountered opposition, mainly from the Treasury.[109]

Faced with government reluctance that sometimes edged on hostility, BR turned to the other two options to supplement funds for its investment objectives. Because closing down routes was highly unpopular, not only with the unions, but also with politicians, privatization seemed like a good alternative. Sir Peter first entertained the idea of injecting private capital into BR subsidiaries in 1977.[110] According to *Railtalk,* the Board's publishing handout, the objective was to expand the business outside public-sector financial constraints without giving up majority shareholding or managerial control.[111] As pressure on BR's EFLs mounted, the idea gained wider appeal. This time, however, the Conservative government added a new twist. Attracting private capital, DOT argued, would not be possible without taking control of the subsidiaries away from BR. Sir Peter's plan had backfired. Although he initially proposed the plan as an additional way of funding subsidiaries, the government presented it as the only way to do so. Selling profitable subsidiaries would sink BR deeper into the red, however, making privatization a self-fulfilling prophecy. The greater the number of profitable SOEs that were privatized, the more inept the sovereign entrepreneur appeared to be and hence the greater the need for further privatization.

Initially, Norman Fowler, then Secretary of State for Transport, denied reports that proceeds from the sales would be diverted to the Treasury.[112] There was a catch, however; although proceeds would stay with BR, it later became evident that the amount would be deducted from its EFL, thus offsetting any monetary benefits from the sales. On 12 December 1980, Fowler introduced a Transport Bill authorizing the sale of such BR subsidiaries as Sealink, Hovercraft, British Transport Hotels, and the nonoperational property of BR. Resistance from the Board was mixed because injecting private capital was, after all, its own idea. The National Union of Railwaymen (NUR) openly opposed the sale but was not able to stop the bill in Parliament. By July, the bill became the 1981 Transport Act.

The sale of BR's ancillary services was made possible by a number of factors. First, it was technically feasible because the assets were small and services operated separately from the main rail network. Because they operated in already competitive markets, proper valuation was not difficult to obtain. Moreover, the subsidiaries were generally in good financial health.[113] Second, there was a fairly broad consensus among members of the policy community that owners would operate the services equally well or even better than BR. The consensus was facilitated by the fact that the services were peripheral to core operations and their sale would therefore not affect the main rail network. Just as in the case of oil and telecommunications, the driving force behind privatization was the Treasury and its doctrinaire desire to curb public expenditures. It was BR's frustration with inadequate funding that originally led to the idea of seeking private funding for BR subsidiaries.

In sum, the hiving-off strategy was fueled largely by the government's ideology and desire to cut public spending.[114] Although some subsidiaries were sold off, BR's main business was not affected. Despite a long-standing debate, injecting private capital or introducing private ownership in railroads remained an elusive goal.

*To Privatize or Not to Privatize*

Several factors enhanced the availability of privatization in the policy stream. Following the appointment of a new chair, Sir Robert Reid, in 1983, BR embarked on a major restructuring program to improve its image and finances. Included among the government's objectives were the following: to run railroads efficiently providing good value for money; to reduce the PSO grant by 25 percent over three years; to operate parcels and freight more like commercial (profit-making) activities; and to encourage private investment in railroads. The relentless pursuit to trim down costs brought a sharp improvement in BR's balance sheet. Government support was reduced, and the corporation's deficit fell. Whereas government support—that is, grants as a percentage of rail revenues—increased from 29 percent in 1979 to 53 percent in 1982, by 1988–89 it fell to 25 percent. Similarly, BR's deficit in 1988–89 was cut in half from £1 billion in 1982.[115]

BR's restructuring had a profound impact on the debate over privatization. On the one hand, it enhanced the appeal of privatization, just as in the case of telecommunications. Being on the road to financial solvency certainly increased BR's chances of attracting private investors. On the other hand, there was a clear shift in emphasis away from BR's public service mission outlined in 1974. Although the government reaffirmed its commitment not to close down major routes, largely because it would be politically very costly, it became obvious that its primary interest was improving BR's balance sheet and reducing the level of funds disbursed by the Treasury. In a manner similar to telecommunications, railroads was stripped of its status as a social service in favor of a more commercially oriented activity. In stark contrast to practice in other European countries, profits became the bottom line.

Following Thatcher's reelection in 1987, Conservatives grew increasingly confident that privatization was a viable alternative. By 1988, the Downing Street Policy Unit was seriously considering two options: liberalization and privatization. Liberalization involved operating BR's existing five sectors as autonomous entities with possible private participation. This option also envisaged the creation of an independent regulatory commission and the lease of track time to private companies. Privatization included several competing variants: (1) selling BR as a single unit; (2) splitting BR into a number of regional, privately owned companies loosely based on pre–World War II divisions; and (3) separating infrastructure from operations and selling both. Conservatives were largely in favor of privatization. Pressing for it were several Tory MPs. For instance, former minister Gow argued that the public was in favor of privatization. In contrast to earlier years when people thought BR would "remain for all time in public ownership," he claimed that "the climate of opinion and the experience of recent years has [sic] transformed that belief."[116] But he offered no proof to substantiate his claim, and judging from the experience of prior sales, public opinion was not likely to favor a sale.[117] James Paice endorsed the sale as the only way for BR to gain access to adequate funds. This argument, however, implicitly acknowledged the choking effects of Treasury control, putting the blame for BR's inadequate funding squarely on government shoulders. For its part, DOT maintained a cautious optimism. As David Mitchell, then Minister of State for Transport, emphasized in the House of Commons, privatization was only one of the options considered.

Technical feasibility enhanced the appeal of some options and dimmed that of others. Liberalization was relatively easy to implement. BR could be separated along existing divisions, requiring few changes during the transition period. Moreover, creating Ofrail, the proposed regulatory body, would not be a major problem because there were several British regulatory models to follow. Privatization, on the other hand, was more complicated. Selling BR as a single unit was feasible provided it was preceded by appropriate valuation. In 1989, DOT appointed Samuel Monagu, a merchant bank, to put a value on BR's assets. The figure, cited in a leaked DOT memorandum, ranged between £10 billion and £15 billion, although sale proceeds were expected to be considerably less given BR's precarious financial situation.[118]

Breaking up BR was even more difficult. Because of daunting valuation problems, divisions along lines other than those currently existing would be extremely difficult. A sale of existing sectors, however, was likely to attract limited interest because several sectors were still in the red. By 1988, the Provincial sector covered only a third of its costs, while InterCity and Network SouthEast covered 87 percent and 83 percent of their costs, respectively. Even if the latter two sectors were sold, rural rail service would still suffer because, according to academics as well as government officials, it was (and continues to be) simply unprofitable.[119] The Provincial network under private ownership would require either substantial route closures or considerable subsidies. Whereas Conservatives lacked the political determination to confront a powerful rural lobby and rail enthusiasts, Treasury officials remained displeased at the prospect of having to maintain an annual subsidy of £500 million.[120]

Value acceptability also loomed important in the privatization debate. Several members of the policy community favor privatization, although there appears to be little agreement over how to do it. DOT initially seemed more sympathetic toward the idea of setting up regional companies offering a full range of services, similar to the situation in the interwar period.[121] Several factors, however, militated against it. First, the proposed companies would not benefit from economies of scale. Because BR currently holds 7 percent of the U.K. passenger market and approximately 9 percent of freight transport, a separation along regional lines would create several companies with high fixed costs and a market share of perhaps 1 percent. In addition, fragmentation would not necessarily increase competition, while it could potentially lead to difficulties with international freight transport through the English Channel because of differences in loading gauges with other European rail systems. Finally, aside from being slow and unreliable, privately owned railroads in the interwar period rarely made enough profits to pay a dividend. Returning to the "good old days" of the Western Railway and the London and North Eastern Railway is just too problematic in the 1990s.

An amendment to this solution was put forth by another study published under the auspices of the influential Centre for Policy Studies.[122] Instead of separating rail along regional lines, the study proposed a hybrid scheme under which the InterCity and Freight networks could be sold as separate companies running over other companies' tracks. The remaining parts of BR could then be integrated on a regional basis, selling each company with its own tracks and trains. Although this scheme overcomes the problems posed by its predecessor, it still does not address the issues of complex timetables and subsidization. Subsidizing Network SouthEast is a particularly sensitive issue, not only because it covers the London commuter system, but also because the current general economic downturn forced the government to abandon its plans to stop subsidizing it.[123]

In the spring of 1989, DOT's preferences began to shift toward the idea of creating a national track authority and several independently operated companies. This option, originally proposed in a report by the Adam Smith Institute,[124] rested upon the claim that ownership could be divided between tracks and trains. A private company could thus be created vested with ownership of infrastructure—track and signals. It would in turn lease track time to private companies running competing national services, much the same way airlines do. The advantage of this option, according to then Transport Secretary Paul Channon, "is the potential for introducing competition into the provision of train services."[125] Competition would theoretically increase efficiency and bring rail services closer to customer needs. In addition, pricing would be subject to strict regulatory control by an independent body.

There are two problems with this option. First, it is not clear whether privately owned companies would be willing to run services on a national level. Quite the contrary, profit-minded managers would be motivated to concentrate on profitable routes and surrender the rest to other modes of transportation. Thus, competition on a national level would be marginal. Second, this option does not address the problem of cross-subsidization. At the heart of this debate lies the distinction between social and commercial objectives. Some argue it is possible, at least in theory, to differentiate between the two.[126] By eliminating the distorting effects of subsidies, it is argued, operators will be better equipped to satisfy social needs and meet their financial targets. It may well be, for example, that increasing the frequency of trips offered is more cost-effective than setting artificially low prices. Others disagree.[127] It is not possible, they claim, to disentangle the social and commercial railways, for two reasons. First, overlapping services necessitate that rail journeys be treated as a large set of interconnected trains rather than as discrete shuttle services. Second, passenger resistance to changing trains en route means that revenues may have to be distributed among several competing services. Thus, withdrawing a service may either reduce revenue in other services if they are complementary or increase it if they are substitutes. Breaking up BR would thus produce dubious benefits and certainly create problems.

For its part, BR counterproposed the company's sale as a single unit. Although Sir Robert Reid initially did not want to be involved in the privatization debate, the chair later broke his silence to warn against the dangers of breaking up BR.[128] In an interview on the BBC program "Panorama," he stated his case in unmistakable terms: "I see a broken-up railway [with] lots of little companies which are not properly co-ordinated as a great disadvantage to my customers because there will be constant friction."[129] The economic attractiveness of BR plc, as this option became known, lay in the acceptance of BR's cost structure, the high proportion of fixed costs, and the advantages of uniform operating systems. The option was also politically attractive because it had the *tacit* support of consumer groups and unions. On numerous occasions the Central Transport Consultative Committee, the railway watchdog, warned that breaking up the rail network would be disastrous to consumers.[130] Similarly, unions appeared willing to settle for the plc alternative although they remain opposed to privatization in principle.[131] Finally, the option also appealed to the Treasury because it maximizes proceeds from the sale; sale proceeds are inversely related to competition. The lower the competitive pressures on the newly privatized industries, the higher the share price is likely to be.[132]

Recognizing the complexity of the issue, the government decided not to make a decision until after the general election in 1992. At the same time, successive Transport Secretaries made abundantly clear the Tories' ideological commitment to selling BR. The issue was not whether to privatize BR but how. The question then arises: Is privatization really necessary? The only likely benefit of a sale is a cultural transformation to a more commercially oriented organization. Yet, the experience of British Telecom and dramatic improvements registered in British Airways and British Steel illustrate that such a transformation is possible even under state ownership. SOEs can be run profitably—or at least losses can be minimized—without privatization. Selling BR, on the other hand, presents a serious drawback in that such an act may reduce accountability. The problem rests not so much on the fact that scrutiny shifts from Parliament to a potentially shortstaffed and underfunded regulatory body. Rather, it is possible that managers pressured to meet financial targets may compromise, or be perceived as compromising, the safety of the traveling public. While the danger certainly exists with a publicly owned BR, as the Purley and Clapham crashes tragically demonstrate, the chances of compromise are greater with more cost-minded private managers. In other words, if the government cannot enforce strict safety regulations in a corporation that it owns, it is much less likely to do so in a company that it doesn't.

The announcement of the government's privatization plan in July 1992 and the ensuing controversy are illustrative of the complexity of BR's sell-off. At the outset, it should be noted that the term *privatization* is somewhat of a misnomer; it differs from previous experience in Britain because there will be no share-selling to individuals, a major ideological justification for every previous privatization. Even Prime Minister John Major describes the scheme as "semi-privatization," while John MacGregor, the Transport minister, occasionally refers to it as "commercialization."[133] In reality, the plan, which will take roughly ten years to implement in full, involves a radical restructuring of BR operations, the sale of some services, and contracting out most of the rest. In this sense, the Railways Act of 1993 has more in common with privatization in the United States than with previous British sales.

In the White Paper,[134] Major's government unveiled a proposal to split BR into two units: (1) Railtrack, which will own, maintain, and operate the infrastructure and passenger services that will be gradually franchised to private operators; and (2) freight and parcel services, which are to be sold off, although it is not exactly clear whether they will attract private interest because they are both operating at a loss.[135] The aims, according to the Paper, are to improve quality of service, maintain safety and essential passenger services, offer opportunities for employees, safeguard the benefit of a national timetable and through ticketing, and continue developing the environmental benefits of rail. However, leaving aside the quality of service objective for the moment, it is unlikely that the new system can meet these objectives any better than the old system has. Developing environmental benefits and maintaining safety, essential services, or a through-ticketing system could be accomplished just as well or even better by a company with overall responsibility for the entire network than by numerous companies with limited responsibility over segments of the network.

Although this scheme avoids many pitfalls of previous proposals by incorporating elements from several of them, it still leaves important questions unanswered.[136] The plan does not address the problem of "cherry picking." Because private operators are likely to bid for services with profit potential, BR will be stuck in the short run with the least profitable routes that will further increase its losses. This may weaken the company's long-term earning potential and lead to an increase rather than a decrease in subsidies.[137] Besides, because Railtrack is not allowed to bid for franchises and thus will be deprived of major revenue sources, it still will need huge sums for modernization. In addition, because franchisees will now bear the full commercial risk, they will undoubtedly be tempted to cut costs, which translates into possible staff reductions and probable retaliatory action by employees. If, on the other hand, franchisees are subsidized to ensure a continuation of services, will this reduce incentives for increases in efficiency and quality of service?[138] Moreover, being responsible for infrastructure does not assure BR that new funds will be injected for much-needed modernization, although the Transport minister has recently made such promises, and it still leaves the company vulnerable to constraints imposed by the Treasury. The biggest challenge, however, according to Sir Bob Reid, the new BR chief who by coincidence has the same name as his predecessor, will be charges for access to the lines.[139] How are prices going to be set, and will the proposed regulatory body have enough funds, staff, and information to determine "fair" pricing levels and resolve discrepancies? It is not at all clear whether Ofrail will be able to adequately allay these fears.

Interestingly, the unveiled plan was met with more dissent than agreement. Tories in the Transport Committee of the House of Commons criticized the plan as unworkable. Robert Adley, the chair, dismissed it as "a masterpiece of academic theory."[140] Speaking to Labour, Brian Wilson accused the Transport minister of acquiring more power through the proposed sell-off while Nick Harvey, a Liberal Democrat, called it a "complete dog's breakfast." User groups and the unions expressed similar sentiments. BR managers appeared divided. Although Sir Bob gave the plan a qualified approval, several managers, such as Chris Green, director of InterCity, disapproved of plans to franchise some routes. Perhaps the concerns of opponents can best be summarized by George Walden's, Tory for Buckingham, complaint: "[A]nyone can run a line. What we need is someone to run a railway."[141]

Nevertheless, much of the opposition has been silenced by backtracking on some points and subsequent clarification. This result reveals that consensus in the policy stream is politically forged. For example, although it was hoped that subsidies would gradually be eliminated, at the request of several opponents of the plan, it does not appear this will be possible. In addition, the issue of competition was clarified. Although originally it was taken to mean competition of providers on the same routes, it later became apparent that was just wishful thinking.[142] There will be competition in bidding for franchises but exclusivity in running the service so as to increase the earning potential of private operators. Perhaps this might induce gains in efficiency, because the award will presumably be made to the lowest bidder, but it will not necessarily result in improving quality of service in the short run because the award will create a local monopoly for a period of time. Moreover, the high initial investment to purchase rolling stock, equipment, and such will probably deter many potential competitors in many "unprofitable" routes.

The availability of privatization as a viable alternative is also influenced by technical feasibility. Is BR really salable; would a sale appeal to private investors? The case of railroads reveals a reluctance to privatize unprofitable SOEs. In 1978 BR showed a small profit—defined as percent group profit or loss on ordinary activities before exceptional items over total revenues—of 0.3 percent.[143] By 1980, the situation was reversed and BR was losing 2.1 percent. During this time, calls for privatization increased, but BR was not sold. In 1983 a policy window opened with Thatcher's reelection. Several subsidiaries were sold, but BR as a whole was not profitable enough to attract substantial private interest. During the rest of the decade, BR had some good years, but in the 1990s, profitability took a nosedive: in the fiscal year 1991–92, it stood at a negative 4.5 percent. Partly because of the recession, BR registered pretax losses of a colossal £144.7 million in 1991–92 (the figure includes exceptional items such as proceeds from asset sales), compared to losses of £10.9 million the previous fiscal year. This has decidedly dimmed hopes of attracting private interest, particularly from small investors. Not surprisingly, there will be no sale of shares to the general public.

Another indicator influencing salability is low demand for rail services. The figures are indeed disappointing. Demand for goods transported by rail in the United Kingdom fell steadily, from 21.6 billion ton kilometers (tkm) in 1974 to 19.9 billion tkm in 1979 to 17.9 billion tkm in 1989.[144] Although demand for passenger transport fares somewhat better, the figures are not promising. Passenger transport by rail fell from 36.1 billion passenger kilometers (pkm) in 1974 to a low of 32.9 billion pkm in 1976 and rose to an estimated 40 billion pkm in 1989, a meager 8 percent increase over fifteen years. Similarly, the number of passenger journeys has risen only slightly; from 732.8 million in 1974 to 743.5 million in 1989.

Perhaps more revealing are figures showing competition from available substitutes, especially road transportation. While rail captured 15.3 percent of the market in 1974, its market share continued to fall to 10.6 percent in 1979 and 8 percent in 1989. On the other hand, the share of goods transported by road fell slightly from 63.5 percent in 1974 to 61.8 percent in 1989. The difference was picked up by air transport. The situation is similar concerning passenger transport. Figure 4.2 records trends in passenger traffic by rail and by road during the period 1975 to 1989. I chose 1979 as the base year to illustrate the differences before and after Conservatives came to power. Passenger transport by rail remained relatively steady for a period of ten years before it began to rise in 1985. Passenger traffic by road, however, increased at a rate faster than that of total passenger traffic, indicating that roads are the preferred long-term mode of transportation. This fact presented serious problems to privatization planners. It helps explain the hesitation to sell BR despite political willingness and the final decision to contract services out rather than to sell the company. Simply put, private investors would not have bought BR "as is."

In sum, the availability of privatization as a viable alternative was influenced by two factors: technical feasibility and value acceptability. Lessons from previous asset sales enhanced the technical feasibility of carrying out a potential sale of BR. However, the SOE's fragile financial health and long-term decline in demand finally dashed hopes of a possible sale. There was also a fairly wide consensus concerning the idea of a sale, with sharp disagreement as to the precise details, even after the government's announcement. Some managers and consumers were in favor of privatizing BR as a single entity. Unions might have supported this option, although they remained opposed to privatization in principle. Nevertheless, just as in the case of British Telecom, the government was able to forge a consensus by accepting amendments and by making concessions to various groups. In contrast to oil and telecommunications, think tanks have played a major role in the debate over privatizing railroads.

Three conclusions emerge from the preceding discussion. First, like the case in telecommunications, privatization is not likely to place BR outside state control. Quite the contrary, the current plan envisages considerable regulatory control in the form of price ceilings, subsidies, and safety regulations. Although the government promises to give up some commercial control of the industry, it is equally unclear whether politicians can be removed from the driver's seat in the area of investment. The biggest problem facing BR is access to large sums of capital. In Sir Bob Reid's words, "to refurbish the

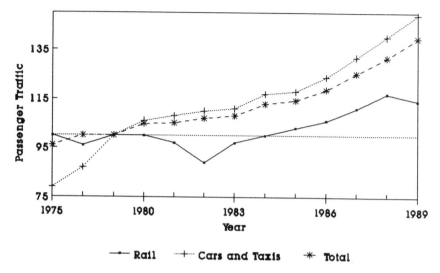

Fig. 4.2.    Passenger traffic trends in Britain, 1975–89. Figures for 1989 are provisional. Total figures include rail, cars and taxis, motorcycles, pedal cycles, and air. (From Central Statistical Office, *Annual Abstract of Statistics* [London: HMSO, 1985; 1991].)

existing railway and to develop new railway [*sic*], we need to spend at a consistent level of more than £1 billion for the next 10 years."[145] This complicates privatization plans because it does not absolve the state of its responsibility to finance investments. Equally revealing is the point that private investors interested in short-term profits may be unwilling to finance rail projects that take five or ten years to yield returns.[146] Second, the Channel Tunnel exposes British Rail to more direct international competition, posing both risks and opportunities. Unlike telecommunications, BR is not the flagship of the British transport fleet. Furthermore, because of Treasury unwillingness, BR's investment has fallen behind that of railroads in other European countries. As a result, only 24.8 percent of the total U.K. rail network had been electrified by 1987, as opposed to 33.8 percent in France, 41.9 percent in West Germany, and 57 percent in Italy.[147] Third, just like telecommunications, railroads under Conservative rule appear to be losing their social service mission. For the most part, BR is viewed as an investment that must yield an economic return. Hence, talk of providing a public service is increasingly being replaced by the language of efficiency. In Sir Robert Reid's words: "We understand that our long term future depends on our efficiency and our attractiveness to our customers. The static language of the PSO in

1974 . . . cannot be the guiding light for UK railways in the year 2000."[148]
As I will later show, other European countries, most notably France, view
their railroads from a totally different perspective.

## Coupling

The analysis so far has focused on each stream or factor separately. In this
section I complete the argument by examining how the streams were joined
together in critical moments in time. By doing so, I will highlight the institutional features of the British system that constrain or enhance the likelihood
that certain issues will rise to the top of the government agenda and that
particular policies will be adopted.

Why did Tories privatize BNOC? Some argue it was the result of the
contradictions of state ownership. Public choice theorists, for instance, maintain that the nature of the governmental process distorts the market and creates
inefficiencies that weaken the case for state ownership.[149] Moreover, political
meddling in management's affairs made the task of management much more
difficult. State participation or ownership in the oil industry was contentious,
and only by turning BNOC over to the private sector could "people within
and without the industry . . . relax about its intentions."[150] Others dismiss privatization as a policy based on ideological grounds. The tide, one analyst
claims, still runs in the opposite direction, toward more state intervention.[151]
The findings in this study show that both views point to inappropriate conclusions. In contrast to the bleak image that many British SOEs projected at the
time, BNOC was a profitable, well-managed enterprise that served governmental objectives well. Privatization, therefore, was not a solution to economic problems, such as inefficiency, but rather, a politically forged decision
to forego ownership in favor of other forms of state control. Tory ideology
was doubtlessly important, but privatization was much more than just a passing fad.

The idea of privatizing BNOC incubated in Conservative circles. Large
oil multinationals also showed hostility to the newly created SOE. Privatization at the time, however, was politically infeasible because it was not an item
on the Labour government's agenda. Labour was interested in strengthening
rather than weakening BNOC's role. Furthermore, the state encouraged the
company to seek funding from private investors to ease pressure on government expenditures and enhance its legitimacy as a viable commercial under-
taking. Indeed, BNOC's $825 million loan from twelve British and American
banks in 1977 signaled an important deviation from conventional borrowing
arrangements pursued by British SOEs.[152] BNOC was able to obtain the loan
through forward sales of oil without a government guarantee, illustrating the
point that SOEs could indeed raise funds in capital markets as companies in

their own right. This point stands in direct contrast to claims by Conservatives that loan arrangements with SOEs were inconceivable without explicit government support.

The general election of 1979 opened a policy window. The advent of the Conservative Party to power provided a political audience that was more receptive to the transfer of state ownership to private hands. Although the 1979 Tory manifesto promised to review BNOC's privileges, observers at the time did not think that Conservatives would actually sell the corporation.[153] Such views, however, underestimate the importance of coupling. Party politics is important but not the only variable that has an effect on policy-making. It should be emphasized that Conservatives, in contrast to Labour, *perceived* the government's borrowing needs as being unacceptably high. Thus, public expenditures—and by extension, state ownership—were defined by Tories as a problem worthy of serious attention. This definition increased the appeal of privatization over recapitalization because the former provided a permanent solution. That was the final piece to the puzzle. The political stream was ripe, and the way the problem was defined made it easier to attach to it a particular solution, privatization. When opportunity came, the three streams were coupled and privatization was finally enacted.

The case of telecommunications presents a similar pattern of coupling, with minor deviations. In contrast to oil, privatizing telecommunications was not widely discussed prior to 1979. Rather, the issue was first placed on the broader political agenda and then spilled over to telecommunications. The spillover process was further facilitated by a precedent established with the creation of BT and the partial liberalization of the U.K. telecommunications market in 1981. These developments enhanced the chances of privatization because association with liberalization made it possible to legitimize privatization.[154] The sale of BT was initially made possible by a favorable political climate. Conservatives were ideologically receptive to the idea of privatizing BT. They were also keenly aware of divisions among unions and the weakness of the Labour Party. Because of BT's size and utility status, Tories knew they were going to meet vocal opposition. Thus, the timing of the announcement of the government's intentions was a carefully calculated political decision designed to catch opposition at its weakest.

Still, it was much more than that. The Treasury and later the Department of Industry and Trade were able to attach privatization to a persistent problem. The government's borrowing needs remained prohibitively high while BT embarked on an ambitious investment program. Privatization's appeal rested on its ability to resolve the government's dilemma quite nicely. It gave the company access to capital and provided a handsome return to the Treasury. In addition, it got BT off the government's books, thereby directly reducing short-term demands on public funds.

The case of telecommunications highlights the importance and tempo-rary nature of policy windows. The first policy window opened in 1979. The sale of BT was not high on the government's agenda because Tories were trying to address other more pressing concerns in the industry. Despite pro-gress, legislation enabling BT's privatization was not passed in time to be implemented during Thatcher's first term in power. This interruption provided Conservatives and Labour with the opportunity to include the issue in their 1983 manifestoes. The second window opened with the general election in 1983. It brought Conservatives back to power with an enhanced majority in the House of Commons and a campaign promise to sell BT. Judging from claims made in its manifesto and on the eve of BT's sale, it is obvious that had Labour won the election, BT would not have been sold off.

The case of railroads is an example of partial coupling. Because it has not yet been possible to join all three streams, BR will not be sold to individ-ual shareholders. In 1979 a policy window opened. The general election brought to power a party receptive to the idea of privatizing BR. At the time, the corporation was unprofitable and overstaffed, and complaints about the quality of service were rampant. In addition, the government's borrowing needs were deemed as unacceptably high. The availability of privatization was also enhanced by placing advocates, like Alfred Sherman, in influential positions. Judging from the bleak picture of the public sector painted by Conservative rhetoric, it seems as if BR were the ideal candidate. Yet it was not privatized. Why? Because the policy could not be attached to a problem. The sale of BR would have had a minor effect on the government's borrowing needs at the time because even if the SOE were able to attract buyers, it would still require substantial injections of public funds to maintain operations and modernize the network. Instead, the government opted for the sale of periph-eral and largely profitable operations that yielded modest benefits to the Treasury by enabling the latter to reduce the company's external financing limits. The general election of 1983 also opened a policy window that did not result in the privatization of BR for largely the same reasons.

In contrast, the policy window that opened up in 1987 presented a real opportunity. The government's overall privatization program was in full swing. Conservatives had not only overcome internal criticism, but had also defeated Labour for the third consecutive time. In addition, the success of the sales of major SOEs, such as BT and British Gas, strengthened the argument for privatizing more SOEs. Despite this euphoria, however, BR still was not privatized. Why? The answer lies in coupling.

Although politicians remained receptive to the idea, there were changes in the problem stream. Partly because of sale proceeds, government finances improved dramatically after 1985. Borrowing needs were consequently per-ceived to no longer be a threatening problem. This fact marked a shift in the official rationale for privatization.[155] In other words, the policy remained the same while the problem to which it was attached changed. Increasingly calls for widening share ownership became more vocal. Thus, privatization began to be seen mainly as a vehicle for increasing the number of individual shareholders in Britain, and improving public finances was demoted to a welcome side effect. This turn of events was compatible with Conservative ideology that envisioned an "enterprise culture" and encouraged the widest possible spread of ownership. But what impact did this shift have on rail?

The crashes of Purley and Clapham catapulted the issue of privatization to the top of the government's agenda. Unfortunately for the government, however, publicity was entirely negative. Safety was given low priority, said John Prescott, Labour's transport spokesman.[156] Investment in modernizing the rail network was perceived to be inadequate. The opposition immediately accused Thatcher of compromising much-needed investment in favor of short-term efficiency gains. The net result was an additional £100 million a year for safety improvements. These additional expenses put a damper on BR's finances that were in need of £829 million from the government to balance the books for 1991–92. Consequently, hopes for privatizing BR in the near future appeared dim. A leaked memorandum written by Edward Osmotherly, deputy Transport Secretary, seemed to dismiss the possibility of selling BR before the end of the century.[157]

At the same time, Cecil Parkinson, then Transport Secretary, reaffirmed at the 1990 party conference the Tories' intention to privatize BR. The question, he said, was not whether but how.[158] This is an example of a policy in search of a rationale. To employ the terms used in this book, the political stream is receptive to the solution, but the problem is missing. Because government finances had improved, maximizing proceeds, although important, was not at the time the overriding concern. Selling BR as a single unit therefore was not likely despite political support. Privatizing several of BR's individual businesses appeared likely because separate but profitable companies could attract more interest by small investors, thus widening share ownership. As I argued earlier in this chapter, the various privatization options addressed different problems. The political stream was ripe and the solution had already been adopted. What remained to be done was to identify the problem.

The general election in 1992 provided yet another window of opportunity. True to their promises, Conservatives have recently announced privatization plans, although full implementation of the plans is years away. Interestingly, there is no talk of widening share ownership or of easing the public-sector deficit burden. This suggests yet another search for appropriate problems. Similarly to BT and based on statements made before and during the 1992 campaign, had Labour won, BR's sale would not have been announced. This would have caused a radical change in the political stream, which would have precluded a coupling of all three streams.

Coupling is a very important process. In two cases, oil and telecommunications, the three streams were joined at critical moments in time and privatization was the end result. In the case of railroads, partial coupling for a long time prevented a final decision. Moreover, the case of railroads clearly illustrates that privatization in the United Kingdom is a policy in search of a rationale.

## Conclusion

I have argued that British privatization was the result of the interplay of three factors: perceived high borrowing needs, party politics, and the availability of viable policy alternatives. Privatization in oil and telecommunications followed this pattern. There was a difference, however. Privatization of BT was not an option widely discussed in the policy community prior to the advent of Conservatives to power in 1979. Rather, it spilled over to the telecommunications agenda partly because a precedent was established through the creation of BT and partly because of accumulated experience from other sales.

The case of railroads further reinforces the argument by showing how the partial interaction of these factors did not result in the privatization of BR. Despite a receptive political audience since 1979, the announcement of firm Conservative plans has come only recently. Two reasons explain the delay. First, the company's fragile profitability and declining demand for rail services coupled with the deep recession currently plaguing Britain indicate a likely lack of interest among small, private investors. Second, Conservatives are constrained by the inability to attach privatization to a problem. Cecil Parkinson, Transport Secretary, made it abundantly clear in the 1990 Conservative Party conference that he intended to privatize BR; the issue was not whether but how. Privatization, however, is only the means to an end. It seemed that Conservatives had already decided on the means and were in search of the end. The case of BR clearly illustrates the point; privatization is a policy in search of a problem.

The multiple streams model has proven useful in illuminating the process of policy formation and explaining privatization in the United Kingdom. Changes in the political stream opened policy windows that enabled policy entrepreneurs to push for privatization. The sale of state assets was then attached as a solution to the problem of high government borrowing needs and found support among members of a party committed to reducing public spending. Extending the approach to cover the entire policy-formation process beyond its original application to agenda setting, I have argued that the likelihood that privatization will be adopted increases when all three streams are coupled. This was indeed the case in oil and telecommunications.

The process of coupling also took the form postulated by the approach. Privatization in the United Kingdom is a solution in search of a problem. This finding lends theoretical substance to empirical observations that the policy is in search of a rationale in Britain.[159] On a more theoretical level, this point runs counter to perspectives on policy formation that assume a problem-solution sequence and further reinforces the view that policy formation at the national level is quite complex and often nonrational. Agendas are not set and decisions are not adopted in a strictly rational manner. The logic of consequential action, in other words, does not explain policy formation well. Instead, the garbage can logic and the structural modifications contained in the multiple streams approach provide a better explanation.

The British case also highlights the political elements of privatization. First, the policy of privatization is an attempt to redefine policy communities by excluding some groups, such as unions, and including others, such as domestic and multinational companies. This transformation process is highly political and depends largely on the governing party's ideology and political strategy as well as on the ability of each community member to influence the final outcome. Second, political influence in the newly privatized companies is likely to continue, albeit in different form. The new approach contains two elements. First, initially the government appeared to favor hybrids as opposed to purely private companies. In both Britoil and BT, the state continued to be the majority shareholder after their sale, albeit in a minority position. Although hybrids have by now been sold, such hybrid arrangements include considerable scope for continuing government influence and have the added benefit of taking the companies off the government's books. Second, Britain appears to be moving closer to the U.S. experience by adopting a framework of regulated, privately owned companies. Government control by regulating BT, British Gas, water, or electricity illustrates the desire to shed the political liability of being perceived by the public as responsible for the performance and accountability of various industries, without necessarily giving up total control. The content of this form of control also differs from the old one; economic criteria are now considered more important. The cases of BT and BR aptly illustrate a willingness to strip industries of their social mission in favor of more commercial tasks. What emerges, therefore, is the realization that the new institutional arrangements do not preclude state intervention. They simply substitute a direct instrument of control, ownership, for an indirect one, regulation.

How generalizable is the British experience? Can the perspective adopted in this study explain privatization in other countries as well? Have these countries followed Britain's approach, or have they moved in different directions? Why? I will now address these issues by analyzing the privatization experience in France.

# Part 3
# On the Way to France

Always keep Ithaki on your mind.
That is your final destination.

CHAPTER 5

# The French Privatization Experience

In contrast to the British, the French pattern of policy-making since World War II has generally involved heavy state intervention and a fairly widespread acceptance of state ownership. This trend continued under President François Mitterrand and most clearly manifested itself in the extensive nationalization program of 1982.[1] Four years later, however, the tide reversed course. The newly elected government under Jacques Chirac's premiership embarked on an ambitious privatization program aiming to reverse Mitterrand's nationalizations and to privatize SOEs brought under state ownership by previous right-wing governments. In 1988, privatization was abruptly brought to an end following Chirac's unsuccessful bid for the French presidency. More recently, however, the issue has resurfaced, first in timid and revised form under Socialist tutelage and later as part of a new privatization program announced by Prime Minister Edouard Balladur in 1993.

SOEs to be sold in the 1986 program included 65 corporations—9 industrial groups, 38 banks, 13 insurance companies, 4 finance companies, and a communications agency—and a television station.[2] In practice, privatization concerned 1,454 companies (including subsidiaries), or 57 percent of SOEs in which the state had majority shareholding.[3] Table 5.1 includes date information and proceed figures on major sales carried out by Chirac's coalition government. Of the 65 candidates, 29 SOEs were privatized, affecting roughly 500,000 employees.[4] In 1993, Balladur announced a sweeping privatization program that included 12 big SOEs that were on Chirac's list in 1986 but were not sold, plus 9 companies not previously offered for sale.[5]

Why did privatization rise to the top of the government's agenda? Why did Chirac privatize SOEs in certain industries but not in others? Why was the program interrupted and why was it later revived by Balladur? The overall argument is that high government borrowing needs, the availability of privatization as a viable policy alternative, and party strategy and ideology help explain the shift away from state ownership. Policy windows in the French case were particularly important because they provided an opportunity for policymakers not only to commence selling SOEs, but also to later cease and recommence privatizing. The analysis is divided into two chapters. In this chapter I examine developments in the broader political stream, then turn to the problem stream and the effect of public finances on privatization. In chapter 6 I examine the availability of privatization in three policy communities—oil, telecommunications, and railroads—in which I specify the conditions that influence its likelihood. Finally, I discuss the important process of coupling and show how the interplay of the aforementioned streams or factors in critical moments in time helps explain the reasons and limits of privatization in France.

## Parties Matter

In this section I examine developments in the political stream and argue that the governing party's (in this case coalition) ideology and strategy have a profound impact on privatization. To do this, I divide the analysis into four parts. First, I explore partisan affiliation with state ownership. Second, I show that, in contrast to Britain, parties of the Right and the Left have for the most part nurtured and expanded the size and scope of the French public sector. Third, I identify the core ideas of the Gaullist party, Rassemblement Pour la République (RPR), concerning state ownership in the 1980s and 1990s. Fourth, I highlight the importance of party politics by showing how the advent of a new party to power can prompt the interruption and revival of privatization.

TABLE 5.1.  Major French Privatizations, 1986–88 and 1993 (in FFr billion)

| Corporation | Proceeds |
| --- | --- |
| Elf Aquitaine (1986) | 3.2 |
| Saint Gobain (1986) | 8.2 |
| Paribas (1987) | 13.6 |
| SOGENAL (1987) | 0.7 |
| BTP (1987) | 0.4 |
| BIMP (1987) | 0.5 |
| Crédit Commercial (1987) | 4.3 |
| CGE (1987) | 8.6 |
| CGCT (1987) | 1.6 |
| Agence Havas (1987) | 2.6 |
| Société Générale (1987) | 17.7 |
| Suez (1987) | 15.5 |
| (TF-1) (1987) | 4.3 |
| Matra (1988) | 1.0 |
| (BNP) (1993) | 27.9 |
| (Rhône-Poulenc) (1993)[a] | 4.3 |

Source: Rebecca Candoy-Sekse, *Techniques of Privatization of State-Owned Enterprises,* World Bank Technical Paper no. 90, vol. 3. (Washington, DC: World Bank, 1988); *New York Times,* 5 October 1993, D5; and *New York Times,* 16 November 1993, D18.
[a]Figure includes November sales only.

Active state involvement has a long tradition in France, and its modern beginnings can be traced to the policies of Jean-Baptiste Colbert, the principal advisor to King Louis XIV. As a mercantilist, Colbert believed that national power depended critically on economic success. Fearful that the unaided behavior of private entrepreneurs would not be conducive to sustained growth, he implemented a program of national development that relied heavily on state involvement, which in rare instances took the form of state ownership, such as the Gobelin and Beauvais tapestries and the Sevrès porcelain.[6] In the interwar years, the desire to extend France's industrial base in branches where private entrepreneurs would not venture on their own led to the creation of mixed enterprises (*sociétés d'économie mixte*). Following electoral victory in 1936, a coalition of left-wing parties, the Popular Front, implemented a limited nationalization program, but in contrast to Britain, the corporate structure that emerged was mixed enterprise. It included the reorganization of the Bank of France—an institution which in contrast to the Bank of England had never really had a purely private character—the takeover of railroads, the nationalization of parts of the armaments industry, and the creation of SOEs charged with developing the nation's energy resources.

The Postliberation Nationalizations

Until World War II, state ownership was limited to a few SOEs and several mixed enterprises. The war, however, brought significant political changes that made state ownership on a large scale more palatable. Unlike in Britain, nationalization was endorsed by parties of the entire political spectrum, including the most influential figure of postwar France, General Charles de Gaulle. The program was not the product of narrow partisan preferences, but rather the "work of the Nation," as some called it,[7] "the holy alliance of the Resistance against private monopolies."[8] The scope of the French nationalization program differed from the British in two respects. First, state ownership in France engulfed more sectors than in Britain. Second, the French did not nationalize entire sectors, in some cases most notably banks and insurance, leaving room for coexistence and competition between state and private firms.

The main program was written up by the National Council of the Resistance in 1944 and was endorsed by all parties.[9] Continuing past practice, de Gaulle's postliberation government espoused the idea that the state should organize and direct the economy to stimulate growth and reduce social tensions. Although the general envisioned considerable freedom for private entrepreneurs, he categorically insisted that the state possess "the levers of command" and "prevent groupings of private interests from running counter to the general interest."[10] The first major nationalization act was passed in December 1944, bringing the coal industry into the public sector. A few months later, the state nationalized all major undertakings in the production and distribution of gas and electricity. In December 1945, the remaining shares of the Bank of France passed into the hands of the state. At the same time, the financial system was reorganized, and four of the largest deposit banks and a large portion of the insurance industry were brought under state ownership.[11] Finally, the state took possession of several individual enterprises such as Renault, Air France, chemical and aerospace factories, and others.[12] In general, it was argued that state ownership was one of the keys to France's economic reconstruction. Despite lofty rhetoric, the program was limited. The influence of de Gaulle and the Catholics compromised the scope of nationalization advocated by the Left, while the departure of the Communists from the government in April 1947 greatly diminished the impetus to expand it. In sharp contrast to Britain, parties of the Center and the Right made it abundantly clear that despite their skepticism, they had no intention of returning the industries to private hands.[13]

## Planning and National Champions

Perhaps the greatest difference between Britain and France was the mission each country attached to SOEs. In France SOEs were viewed as strategic instruments of implementing a national plan. Because there was widespread agreement on the necessity to restructure the economy by government design,[14] SOEs became one of the levers at the disposal of French planners to accomplish this goal. Shonfield aptly summarizes this view:

> Postwar French planning can be regarded as a device that mobilized a number of instruments of public enterprise and pressure, which had been lying around for some time, and pointed them all in the same direction. . . . Enterprises owned by the state, either wholly or in part, fulfill the role of pace setters of the system. The state needs them in the same way that any manager needs an independent yardstick in order to decide the limits of the possible. . . . [State ownership] allows the state's representatives to claim a place on the side of management in the dialogue between planners and producers, and to do so as of right. The state as entrepreneur is taken very seriously.[15]

This situation sharply contrasts with the British experience, where there was no bipartisan agreement on the necessity, let alone the usefulness, of a plan. In the absence of an overall framework, British SOEs lost direction and arguably legitimacy.

The planning effort had two effects on French SOEs. First, it permitted close collaboration between the state and public and private managers so that ideas could be exchanged and concerns raised. This situation helped the state act more "businesslike" in the sense that it kept touch with the private business community. The system was not without problems. Even to its admirers, it was "an elitist conspiracy" and "a rather clandestine affair."[16] This characterization seems justified because planning relied on contacts between a small number of senior civil servants and big business. The creation of this tightly knit elite whose members graduated from the same schools has been well documented and criticized.[17] Moreover, the suffocating effects of the so-called "state bourgeoisie" were prominent themes in the subsequent privatization debate.[18]

The second effect of the planning effort on SOEs was that organized labor was essentially left out of the process. Whether unions were voluntarily underrepresented[19] or de facto excluded, the fact remains that labor did not actively participate in shaping policy.[20] Hence, by not actively participating in decision making, unions could not be blamed for any failures. Being absolved of such criticism partially explains why several decades later Edouard Balladur, the French minister in charge of privatization in 1986, did not exhibit the same high-profile, antiunion enthusiasm that many of his counterparts shared across the Channel. It also stands in sharp contrast to the British experience, where Tories accused public-sector unions of practically running SOEs.

Unlike in Britain, in the ensuing decades, state control in France was enhanced despite opportunities to reverse course. For one thing, state ownership was sanctified in the 1946 Constitution. Its preamble made explicit that sectors that constituted monopolies of fact or provided a public service should be collectively owned.[21] The collapse of the Fourth Republic in 1958 could have ended such legitimacy. Nevertheless, de Gaulle, the founder of the Fifth Republic, did not reverse the nationalizations. Continuing the tradition of using the state to foster national development, he pursued a policy of nurturing national champions. State agencies would target one or two firms within a sector and nurture them by providing low-cost finance, tax breaks, and the like. The purpose was to create companies that would dominate the domestic market and provide France's answer to international competition from American and Japanese multinationals. Many national champions were privately owned, but some were SOEs.

This new form of industrial policy had two effects on French SOEs: product diversification and multinationalization.[22] First, SOEs were encouraged to diversify to the full range of products in their respective industries. Among the major beneficiaries of this period were SOEs that were created or expanded in aerospace (Aérospatiale), nuclear energy (Cogema), information processing (Compagnie Internationale pour l'Informatique, or CII), and oil (Enterprise de Recherches et d'Activités Pétroliéres, or ERAP). Second, SOEs were encouraged to set up ventures abroad. In this respect, French SOEs stand in sharp contrast to their British counterparts. Analysis of the latter's objectives suggests that parliamentary acts had made it practically impossible for them to go multinational. For instance, when British Leyland and British Aerospace were brought into the public sector in the 1970s, the overwhelming majority of their foreign subsidiaries were sold.[23]

The pressure to increase the competitiveness of French industry ultimately placed severe strains on cozy state-SOE relations. Because SOEs were allowed to set up ventures abroad and were increasingly relied upon to stimulate economic growth, state managers became more open about asserting their autonomy.[24] The cooperative framework of the early postwar years was deemed inadequate for dealing with the complexities of an increasingly open economy. Managers openly challenged the wisdom of de Gaulle's *dirigisme*—the formulation of objectives and heavy-handed direction by civil servants—and resented being told what to do. They also resented pursuing strategies that seemed on occasion to serve political rather than commercial objectives.[25]

*Giscard's Tenure and the Socialist Response*

The 1970s witnessed two energy crises and even stiffer competition from abroad. SOE finances deteriorated, and from 1972 to 1976 the rate of self-financing for the entire range of SOEs dropped from 52 percent to 34 percent, while borrowing rose to 52 percent from 38 percent.[26] In principle, Valéry Giscard d'Estaing, the French President at the time, opposed extending state ownership and was lukewarm to the idea of subsidizing SOEs or nationalizing ailing industries. In practice, however, the French propped up lame ducks much in the way the British did. In September 1978, the government of Raymond Barre, the Prime Minister, announced a gigantic rescue operation of the steel duopoly that amounted to nationalization in all but name. The state assumed majority control of Usinor and Sacilor by converting part of their debt to the state—approximately FFr 9 billion—and to other public institutions into debentures.[27]

The Socialists responded swiftly. The deep economic troubles that beset the French economy needed to be met with radical reforms. Nationalization of a number of enterprises in diverse sectors featured prominently as part of an overall reflationary program. First, completing the takeover of the entire banking industry was deemed essential. Since "the aim was to channel vast sums of money directly from the state to industry," nationalizing banks made sense.[28] Second, nationalization was to be selective. To this end, the overall strategy contained defensive and offensive elements.[29] In the face of stiff global competition, declining important industries, such as steel, needed assistance. The aim was to take them over, reorganize them, and return them to profitability. In addition, the state was to seize control of firms in high-growth sectors, such as electronics and communications, with the explicit aim of reviving their commercial vitality. In both cases, managerial autonomy was perceived to be an important ingredient for success. The issue was put to a vote in 1981. Partly because of disunity in the Right and partly because of bad economic conditions, Mitterrand won. During his campaign, he promised to implement his ambitious nationalization program. Once in power, Mitterrand kept his promise.

In contrast to Britain, the concept of a sovereign entrepreneur in the postwar period was endorsed in France to varying degrees by parties of both the Right and the Left. In fact, Mitterrand's nationalizations in 1982 can be viewed as a continuation of a *dirigiste* tradition that bears the stamp of approval of the founder of the Fifth Republic, General de Gaulle himself.[30] Moreover, the policies of economic planning and national champions legitimized the strategic role of French SOEs as indispensable tools for fostering growth. Similarly to Britain, political control and budgetary constraints became issues of intense debate in France, but unlike the British, the French answer stressed managerial autonomy, product diversification, and multinationalization. Consequently, the privatization debate was later framed differently in France than in Britain.

## Core Ideas of the Gaullist Party

Electoral defeat in 1981 and the advent to power of a Socialist president for the first time in the history of the Fifth Republic prompted a reexamination of RPR's conventional ideology. The Socialist nationalizations provided a convenient focus. It was time to move beyond traditional conceptions of French capitalism and construct something new, wrote Balladur, Chirac's minister in charge of privatization and later Prime Minister himself.[31] The Gaullist ideology, treated here as a relatively coherent set of beliefs, relies on the virtue of the free market and is based on three "pillars." The first pillar emphasizes the moral superiority of private enterprise and the free market. Private property is a central element of this new ideology because it fosters self-reliance and responsibility. Closely linked to political freedom, private property enables individuals to enjoy the fruit of their labor and by extension provides incentives for more economic prosperity at the individual and community levels.[32] According to this vision, state ownership is counterproductive because it removes the profit motive, a force that is central to the functioning of a free market, away from the individual and places it in the hands of the state. Doing so subordinates enterprises to arbitrary state powers and imposes the tyranny of planning.[33] Enterprises, Gaullists maintain, become a political football and are used to further objectives that may have nothing to do with, or may indeed be detrimental to, the corporations' welfare.

The second pillar views state ownership as potentially disastrous, not only to enterprises, but also to the state itself. On the one hand, state ownership is seen as a way to strengthen what Balladur terms the "state bourgeoisie." The characteristic mark of French society is "the existence of a synarchy created by the collusion of political power and economic power for the profit of a small group of technocrats."[34] This elite is composed of people who can be found in ministerial offices and SOEs. They are so powerful, it is argued, that they have created a state within a state that is accountable neither to elected officials nor to the laws of the market. Recruitment is tightly controlled and restricted to graduates of the *grandes écoles*. Bureaucrats and managers of SOEs rule according to their own interests; they adjudicate, co-opt, and coerce at will. Their only constraint is that they depend on each other, hence they realize that reciprocity of favors is the only way to assure their survival. Although this sort of policy-making has the advantage of creating a clear and less adversarial conception of the common interest, it also creates rigidity. People may be blocked from entering this tightly knit community, not on the basis of merit, but on the basis of educational background. Hence, it becomes difficult for new ideas to be espoused, particularly if they come from individuals whose experiences and background differ from those of the technocratic elite.

RPR's attack on the state bourgeoisie is curiously interesting because Gaullists helped create and nourish it. British Conservatives, on the one hand, could claim that Labour shared most of the blame for a lethargic public sector because when Thatcher took office in 1979, Labour had been in power for seventeen years since 1945, as many years as Conservatives had governed. Gaullists, on the other hand, could not make the same claim. When Chirac entered Matignon—in the prime minister's office—in 1986, Socialists had been in power for only five of the twenty-seven years since the founding of the Fifth Republic. Socialists simply did not have the time to create a state bourgeoisie; rather, they inherited an administrative machinery with a technocratic mentality.

Some Gaullists also argue that a continuously expanding state runs the risk of collapsing from its own weight. Bringing more enterprises into the public sector, they reason, dismembers the state by placing undue pressure on the public purse. Managerial insistence for more investment financing presents policy-makers with a serious dilemma. If they do not allocate the requested funds, they risk creating perennial losers. Yet, if policymakers decide to give the money, they risk cutting other public projects perhaps equally worthy of funding. The first option is unlikely to be adopted because it casts doubt over the utility of maintaining SOEs. How can SOEs be expected to survive if they cannot be funded? The latter option is more likely, but it is also politically disastrous. Entrenched interests in other areas of the public sector will certainly attempt to block cutbacks. Faced with potentially damaging political discontent, risk-averse politicians will attempt to satisfy everyone by funding as many projects as possible. This situation puts undue pressure on public finances, particularly in times of dwindling revenues and increased hostility toward tax increases among the electorate. Hence, this option creates the problem of perennial underfunding of public undertakings and, if continued unabated, it will ultimately lead to the disintegration of the state.

The third pillar centers on the belief of some Gaullists that the state is a bad entrepreneur. As the former Chief executive officer (CEO) of Elf Aquitaine emphatically claims, "more than others, public enterprises subordinate everything to the act of production, neglecting commerce, profitability, getting themselves into debt without limits."[35] There are three areas in which SOEs are believed to be at a disadvantage: financing, management, and the international market. First, because SOEs are supported by the state, they have the opportunity to borrow funds without being subject to the laws of the market and, more specifically, bankruptcy. The statement of a top-level manager of a French SOE nicely illustrates the essence of the problem: "[I]t doesn't matter that we lose more or less a billion so long as the state is behind us."[36] The very fact that the state is the major source of funds for these corporations, however, means that SOEs are subject to political constraints. Another CEO writing under a pseudonym boldly claims that "it is money that gives the state its sole power."[37] Sound financial management, Gaullists argue, is not usual practice. In Chalandon's words, "financial wisdom is balanced with the rage of investing under the state's whip, for which an investment's merit is measured by volume."[38] Thus, profitability is regularly conditioned, according to Gaullists, by ministerial or administrative directives that are not always clear and often favor political criteria, such as maintaining high employment or supporting projects of high prestige.

This situation leads to the second problematic area; Gaullists argue that SOEs are generally badly managed. This accusation does not mean that SOE managers are incompetent. To the contrary, CEOs are carefully selected from among the best and brightest minds in France. The problem is that many such people are trained in administration, not business. It is therefore the administrative mentality that Gaullists find incompatible with managing business enterprises. "Being a reflection of administration the public enterprise acts slowly and adapts badly and belatedly to change."[39] Finally, environmental change, and more specifically world markets, render SOEs inferior to private enterprises. Because the international environment changes very rapidly, SOEs are perceived as ill-equipped to make certain investment decisions,

mindful that such decisions will be delayed or altered by political delibera-
tion.[40] Alliances with foreign companies, for example, are more difficult for
SOEs to implement because they allow foreign companies indirect access to
public finance. Any time the state subsidizes, say Renault, it also indirectly
subsidizes Volvo, the Swedish automobile manufacturer and until recently
Renault's minority partner.[41]

Privatization holds the three pillars together. It permits the uninhibited
function of the free market by eliminating the distorting effects of state
ownership, hence privatization, argues Balladur, puts the state back to its
proper place and recognizes the irreplaceable role of private enterprise as the
motor of growth.[42] Moreover, it widens share ownership and gives individuals
a stake in their destiny. In a manner similar to Thatcher's Conservatives,
Chirac's Gaullists espoused the notion of popular capitalism as an important
instrument to foster economic efficiency and modernity. Giving employees
and the general public a stake in enterprises, however, aims to do more. It
also gives managers a real sense of autonomy.[43] Furthermore,

> the privatization which we put into effect, characterized by popular own-
> ership and employee ownership, will contribute greatly to limiting the
> role of this state bourgeoisie in the economy and in enterprises, and to
> destroying the traditional circles of its influence and its perennity.[44]

Privatization, then, is for Gaullists a way of reshaping state-society relations
by redistributing power and by altering the pattern by which the state recruits
its members from society.

It is also interesting to note that by selling shares in the Paris Bourse
officials in 1986 hoped to augment the stock market's capitalization by 25 to
30 percent.[45] It was estimated that this action would have given the French
financial market a boost, bringing overall capitalization above that of West
Germany and somewhat closer to that of the big three—the United States,
Japan, and Britain.

When comparing Gaullist ideology with that of British Conservatives,
one is struck by some similarities and many differences. In both cases, the
moral superiority of the free market figures prominently. Moreover, the vision
of creating popular capitalism through privatization seems to have captured
the imagination of the governing leadership on both sides of the English
Channel. Together with an emphasis on efficiency as the most important
objective of business enterprises, these factors explain the rigor with which
both espoused privatization. The similarities, however, end there. There exist
several ideological tentets that help explain differences in the privatization
programs of the two countries.

First, in contrast to British Conservatives, Gaullists limited the scope of privatization by not explicitly attacking unions. Many SOEs that Chirac proposed to privatize had not been in the public sector for very long. In fact, many candidates for privatization, particularly industrial groups such as Compagnie Générale d'Electricité (CGE), Saint-Gobain, or Pechiney, had been nationalized by the Socialists in 1982. Hence, blaming the unions for "holding the nation by the jugular vein," to use Ridley's oft-quoted phrase, was not feasible. Consequently, antiunion rhetoric did not figure prominently in Gaullist ideology concerning privatization.

Second, and more important, Gaullists had a more limited conception of privatization because they had to contend with a strong *dirigiste* tradition approved by General de Gaulle. How could Gaullists reconcile privatization with de Gaulle's idea of a strong interventionist state? Balladur's answer is instructive. According to him, de Gaulle was not an ideologue but a pragmatist. Didn't he declare, asks Balladur, that "in my [de Gaulle's] opinion, in the economy, no more than in policy or in strategy, absolute truth does not exist. But there are circumstances?"[46] After World War II, political and economic imperatives necessitated certain nationalizations. De Gaulle's actions, continues Balladur, were guided by his conviction that at the time this was the best course of action. The nationalizations that accompanied liberation, however, were carried out in 1945–46. De Gaulle could have easily reversed the tide when he helped found the Fifth Republic in 1958; but he didn't. Instead, he legitimized the use of SOEs as "national champions." Why? Balladur again speaks of circumstances:

France in the beginning of the 1960s—with its nationalized enterprises, its price, exchange, and credit controls, its *dirigiste* and corporatist ways becoming almost instinctive—was not ready for a radical change of its economic system. There were other priorities: the necessity to rejuvenate our democracy thanks to solid institutions, the effects of decolonization, the beginning of the construction of the European Community occupied the minds of responsible men. Our economic growth was strong and our country was retaking her place among great industrial nations; we could, one thought, continue down the same path.[47]

Conditions prevailing in the 1980s, however, dramatically constrained the ability of the state to intervene in the economy. French capitalism in the way that it existed prior to 1981, Balladur argues, could no longer serve as a guide to modernity. The new Gaullist vision did not reject the state, but sought to reconcile liberalism with nationalization.[48] Gaullists, in other words, were trying to draw a connection between their traditional belief in the state as guardian of the national interest and liberalism's emphasis on the individual as master of his or her destiny. Whereas British Conservatives viewed government with suspicion, French Gaullists were careful not to attack the state itself. To quote Balladur again:

> This is an important subject, that reflects well our conception of the state. In principle, it is not hostile to the state. To the contrary, it reserves to it a preeminent role: that of guaranteeing to citizens a solid and durable frame that allows them to realize their potential, that of being a strong yet resolute state, respected yet centering around the essential and shedding the accessory.[49]

Hence, the choice of SOEs to be privatized was conditioned partially by ideological predispositions. Balladur made it abundantly clear that his and Chirac's governments would not sell monopolies or SOEs performing a public service.[50]

In addition, two more factors precipitated this decision. First was the existence of possible constitutional constraints. The preamble to the 1946 constitution made it explicit: "Every good, every enterprise, whose exploitation has or acquires the character of a national public service or a de facto monopoly, must become the property of the community (*collectivité*)." This provision was incorporated into the 1958 constitution by means of a preamble. Hence, privatizing SOEs that could potentially fall under this category would face a constitutional challenge, something that might prove politically costly and delay sales. The second factor was the Gaullists' desire to avoid some of the sticky regulatory issues that needed to be resolved prior to any sales. Instead, Gaullists viewed utilities and infrastructural industries as essential services performed by the state and concentrated on privatizing industries in sectors where competition already existed. They also sought to privatize banks and insurance companies. Many of these SOEs were nationalized by the Socialists in 1982, although it must be noted that Chirac's privatization program also included a few SOEs that were nationalized previously, such as Elf, Société Générale, Banque Nationale de Paris (BNP), and a few others. Nevertheless, particularly illuminating is the fact that all but one of the industrial candidates for privatization in 1986 and five of the twelve industrial candidates in 1993 had been brought into the public sector by Mitterrand. Thus, from an ideological perspective, the concept of privatization in France has not touched the heart of the public sector in the way that it has in Britain, although Balladur's program in 1993 has expanded the scope of privatization considerably.

Interestingly and in contrast to initial sales in Britain, the form that was chosen in France called for total divestiture. Speaking before the National Assembly, Balladur made it clear: "I am opposed to the hybrid formulae of mixed companies because in their capital the state remains a minority, theoretically present, but in reality managerially absent and sometimes hostage."[51] One reason for his choice was political. With nationalization, Socialists took up the old Gaullist theme of championing the mixed economy. To clearly differentiate themselves from the Socialists, Chirac and his allies preferred to espouse the "somewhat novel principles of liberalism" which entailed a criticism of state ownership and the mixed economy.[52] The other reason was historical. As Balladur noted, Gaullists wanted to break with the past and chart a new direction for the French economy (at least in theory). Mixed enterprises were a common form of ownership for many French firms, hence the novelty that Chirac could offer to his partisan supporters could only call for total divestiture.

## Support for and Opposition to Privatization from the New Coalition

As mentioned earlier, Chirac headed a coalition government in 1986. Discussing support and opposition from Chirac's partners is important because it strengthens the argument made here that parties matter. Had the Giscardians, for example, been the senior partners in the coalition in 1986, privatization in France, judging from their pronouncements, would have taken a different turn. Even though there was unanimity in the anti-Socialist opposition over the need to privatize, there was no consensus regarding which SOEs to sell. The Gaullists wanted to keep in the public sector all the SOEs that performed a public service or constituted a monopoly. The previous section highlighted the importance of RPR's *dirigiste* tradition as a partial explanation of the Gaullist position. Other politicians, however, had different plans.

The anti-Socialist opposition was divided into two camps: the minimalists and the maximalists. Minimalists, including mostly the RPR, aimed primarily, though not exclusively, at reversing Mitterrand's nationalizations. Included in this camp was a former prime minister, Raymond Barre. He did not "think that the climate of opinion would allow the reversal of the nationalizations of Liberation."[53] For minimalists, the limits of privatization were confined to the competitive sector.

In the other camp were politicians belonging to the group Union pour la Démocratie Française-Réforme (a radical wing of Giscard d'Estaing's party), Parti Républicaine, and others who wanted privatization to go further. They saw a historic opportunity to touch the heart of the public sector in the same way that Thatcher was doing at that time across the Channel. Their purpose was to sell as many SOEs as possible, including some that were nationalized before 1982, such as Renault and Air France.[54]

There were, however, contradictions inherent in both schemes. Although both camps wanted to privatize almost the entire competitive sector, they remained curiously silent about the two steel concerns, Usinor and Sacilor. Why? The immediate answer is profits.[55] Being highly unprofitable meant that these SOEs simply could not attract many private investors; in the event of a sale, share prices would have to be low. Selling them would render the government vulnerable to opposition charges that national wealth—or to use Macmillan's phrase, "the family silver"—would be sold cheaply.[56] Thus, the choice of SOEs to be privatized was driven partially by financial considerations. This confirms the argument that profitability was an important criterion that increased the likelihood of privatization.

The foregoing discussion shows that the anti-Socialist opposition did not agree on the specific limits of the public sector. Some of the differences were hammered out in annual conventions. By 1985, there was ample evidence that the minimalists had won. As Barre put it, "to begin with, we must privatize the banks and enterprises nationalized in 1981–1982."[57] Because they had won the most seats in parliament among coalition partners in 1986, Gaullists were able to impose their will. Consequently, the final list most closely resembled RPR's position. Had the Giscardians been the senior partners of the coalition, the list would have looked different. This point strengthens the argument that the particular complexion of the governing party—be it as majority party or as the senior partner in a coalition—affects the likelihood and limits of privatization.

*Links between the Government and Privatized Companies*

French privatization targeted employees, the general public, and to a lesser extent foreign entrepreneurs as potential buyers in the hope of creating popular capitalism. The government, however, also aimed at another group of investors creating an instrument that later drew a storm of criticism. To avoid instability in the newly privatized concerns, Balladur created an instrument called stable nuclei (*noyaux durs*) in 1986. It was set up for every company except Saint-Gobain and CGE and was composed of institutional investors, each of whom could own no more than 5 percent of the company's shares. Hence, institutional investors were allowed to own between 20 and 30 percent of the shares in newly privatized companies. This instrument was quite controversial and drew considerable criticism from the Socialists. It is worth examining in more detail because it gives us a glimpse of what Gaullists hoped to achieve with privatization.

What is the purpose of stable nuclei? Their creation reflects the weakness of French institutional investors. In contrast to Britain, the preferable method of company financing in France is debt, not equity. The capitalization of the Paris Bourse is low relative to other major industrialized countries, and large institutional investors are fewer in number and far more risk-averse than are their counterparts in Britain. When asked to explain the purpose of stable nuclei, Balladur responded that they were created to avoid spreading all shares among many individual investors, which would presumably leave companies at the mercy of raiders.[58] The stipulation was that participants could not sell their share for a period of two years and that they could not participate in more than two nuclei.[59] Who were participants to these stable nuclei? In the period 1986–88 there were interlocking relations with eight SOEs, thirty-three private firms, and sixteen privatized companies.[60] It is interesting to note the corporate interdependence created by these nuclei and the rather considerable power retained by companies controlled by the state. The sales since 1993 exhibit similar patterns of cross-holdings. Most prominent among investors in stable nuclei are cash-rich banks and insurance companies although industrial giants like Elf and Générale des Eaux are also visible. There are two differences, however, with stable nuclei of the previous period. Most companies buying shares as partners are either private at the time of sale or are soon to be privatized and there are foreign firms included now.[61]

Stable nuclei were the most heavily criticized part of Chirac's privatization. Criticism took two major forms. The first referred to the way these nuclei were formed and the criteria for participation. The criteria were never very clear. According to government sources, they included the investor's stability, the level of private participation before the 1982 nationalizations, and the privatized company's future.[62] It was only natural that such vague guidelines would be criticized. One problem was considerable state control of the management of these SOEs. Balladur replaced many CEOs in SOEs *before* they were to be privatized, with the expectation that these people would oversee the transition of the SOEs to private hands. This effectively meant that the CEOs would remain at the top of these companies, if they so wished, for at least a short time *after* privatization.[63] It also did not escape notice that most CEOs named by Balladur had close ties to the RPR. For example, Jean Dromer, who helped prepare the privatization program, was first at Crédit Industriel et Commercial (CIC) and then at Union des Assurances de Paris (UAP). Jean-Paul Delacour, Balladur's brother-in-law, was promoted to the top of Société Générale. Jacques Friedmann, another architect of privatization and Chirac's close friend, was named CEO of Air France. Jean-Maxime Lévêque, one of the most fervent proponents of privatization and founder of Union Nationale pour l'Initiative et la Responsabilité (UNIR), a think tank with close ties to RPR, headed Crédit Lyonnais; and the list goes on.[64] The other problem concerning the criteria of participation in stable nuclei centered around Balladur's intense personal involvement in the allocation of participants and the fact that so many of them were on the list of SOEs to be privatized. In other words, state control was extended directly by means of SOEs that were not privatized and indirectly by privatized companies whose management had close ties to RPR. The novelty that privatization brought was that these managers could not be sacked with a change in governing parties. In this way, the policy aided in the creation of a "new economic technocracy close to the Gaullist party."[65]

Related to this criticism was also the issue of accountability. Matters of broad policy in SOEs were usually overseen by administrative councils. Preparing for privatization, however, entailed the abrogation of the powers of such councils and the transfer of responsibility directly to the state. In many cases, this effectively strengthened state control because privatization would not have taken place for perhaps a few years. The resulting paradox was a process of "privatization that began with reinforcing state power."[66]

The second major criticism of Chirac's privatization focused on "the intense concentration of interests caused by the highly incestuous nature of the allocation" of stable nuclei.[67] Socialists charged that many companies were permitted to participate in more than two nuclei despite Balladur's assurances to the contrary. Fifteen groups, for example, appeared directly through ownership or indirectly through subsidiaries and management ties in more than two nuclei. UAP, an insurance company, was at the top of the list with seven appearances.[68] All this revealed links around three poles: CGE/Société Générale, Paribas, and Saint-Gobain.[69] Concentration was further reinforced by the ability of nuclei participants to buy back shares from small investors following the stock market crash of October 1987 and the consequent collapse in prices. Concentration by these institutional investors rose in one case, Suez, to almost 50 percent of ownership.[70] As a result, many critics from both the Left and the Right charged that privatization was a program designed to reinforce the state and reward "Edouard's friends."[71] Barre, for example, stated: "[P]rivatization, I have the impression, is a public privatization, that is to say it is done to benefit the state."[72]

For this reason, Mitterrand promised that upon reelection to the presidency in 1988, he would cease the program of privatization. In his letter to the French people, he made it abundantly clear.

> When I announced my candidacy on television, I said that if elected I would stop the [nationalization-privatization] ballet.... The deadline that separates us from the great European market is too close to take the risk of disrupting again the economic landscape.[73]

Mitterrand kept his campaign promise. The consequent dissolution of Chirac's governing coalition and new elections that brought to power a Socialist minority government resulted in the termination of the privatization program.

In 1991, the governing Socialists abandoned their previous "ni ... ni" promise (neither nationalization nor privatization) and expressed an interest in selling shares of SOEs. Subsequent sales included the flotation of a small bank, Crédit Locale de France, in November 1991 and partial emissions of shares in Elf and Total in 1992 and Rhône-Poulenc in 1993, for an estimated total of roughly FFr 15 billion.[74] To some analysts, this reversal of policy might weaken the forcefulness of the argument made here that parties are important determinants of policy. This is not the case, however, because the Socialist plan is qualitatively different from its predecessor. Keenly aware of the need to attract private capital to supplement state support, Mitterrand issued a decree allowing French private and foreign companies to acquire up to 49 percent of SOEs, provided that cash from the sales was used to finance company investments or jobs.[75] This makes the measure qualitatively different from Chirac's privatization because Chirac aimed at relinquishing total state ownership—Elf Aquitaine being the exception in 1986—and because Gaullists used share issues to create "popular capitalism." Ironically, this "new" Socialist scheme is the same one that Michel Rocard, Socialist prime minister in the late 1980s, tried in vein to implement in 1981.[76] Politics, as the old saying goes, rewards those who wait.

The 1991 directive revealed a keen awareness among Socialists of public budget limitations and of the need to attract private investment. The financing instruments used in the early 1980s—such as indexed bonds (*titres participatifs*), nonvoting shares (*certificats d'investissement*), and sales of subsidiaries[77]—reveal a desire to move in that direction, but what is different in this case is the Socialist government's willingness to relinquish ownership rights in parent SOEs. This posture stands in stark contrast to previous policy pursued prior to 1986 and for a short while immediately after 1988. Although the 49 percent limitation was undoubtedly imposed by ideological considerations, the directive reveals the evolution of Socialist thinking vis-à-vis SOEs. It also represents a clever political strategy to define the terms of the privatization debate and to take the "steam" away from Gaullist plans in light of the 1993 legislative elections.

*Revival and Expansion of Privatization*

A landslide victory in March 1993 brought to power the same Center-Right coalition, which promptly revived and expanded its previous privatization program. Just as in 1986, Gaullists took key posts in the new government, with Balladur the Prime Minister this time. In an auspicious convergence of preferences, a member of UDF, Edmond Alphandéry, took the economic ministry responsible for privatization. Just as in the period 1986–88, Gaullists stressed the importance of ideological tenets, such as the promotion of competition and efficiency through SOE sales and the creation of popular capitalism.

In fact, 1.35 million individual shareholders were drawn to the stock market during the 1986–88 wave of privatizations, and 2.5 million first-time shareholders have invested in government-disposed shares since 1993.[78] There are two reasons for this optimism. First, those who invested in Chirac's program saw their portfolios rise in value by 38 percent, partly due to the serious undervaluation of the offered shares. The second reason has to do with revisions in the tax code. Because the tax-exempt ceiling in Sicav money-market funds was reduced in January 1993 to FFr 158,000 from FFr 317,000, Balladur hoped many investors would be attracted to new tax-exempt equity plans.[79] It also did not escape notice that privatization paid off political dividends, too. According to one survey, 70 percent of right-wing voters and 29 percent of left-wing voters favored privatization.[80]

What is similar about the new privatization law, passed on 19 July 1993, and the old one in 1986 is the sale of the entire portion of state holdings in various companies and the return of the stable nuclei. Balladur made it explicit that he viewed these nuclei as necessary because they would enhance the stability of the privatized company, although it was clear that in contrast to 1986, it would be more difficult now to find partners willing to tie up considerable sums for a year or two in times of recession and relative ease of cross-border fund transfers. Moreover and despite his vows, Balladur has engaged in corporate purges, of which Socialists are equally guilty. Several CEOs with Socialist ties, such as Francis Gutmann of Gaz de France, Bernard Pache of Bull, and Loïk Le Floch-Prigent of Elf Aquitaine, have already been relocated or replaced with bosses politically connected to the new government. Similarly to the 1986 privatization program, many of the new CEOs are charged with preparing and presiding over their companies' transition to private ownership. In this way, "Edouard's friends" continue RPR's corporate influence even after privatization.

Two conclusions emerge from this discussion. First, despite criticism, Balladur appears eager to continue the previous practice of state-directed privatization. Second, the replacement of CEOs reveals the continuation of a cycle of politically motivated purges and the creation of economic elites with close partisan ties. Both purges and elites are likely to further sharpen rather than blur political influence on markets. State managers are starting to lose their image of nonpartisan integrity. In addition, selling SOEs enables Balladur to reduce the size of the state bourgeoisie, not by eliminating it, but by transforming it into a partisan bourgeoisie.

There are some differences from the 1986–88 program as well. First, Mitterrand's opposition in 1993 is not as vocal as it was in 1986. His worry this time is with imprudent sales in the aerospace, airline, and oil industries. Such concern can be easily accomodated in two ways: first, the government keeps a "golden share," which allows it to restrict the acquisition of shares in the name of national security; and second, the industry minister can acquire special veto powers over certain managerial decisions that could adversely affect national defense policy. Mitterrand's stance can be explained by his own decision in 1991 to encourage the sale of minority stakes in SOEs. This point reinforces the argument made in this study over the importance of setting a precedent.

Another difference is that despite some internal disagreement, the Union pour la Démocratie Française (UDF) is more eager than it was in 1986 to circumscribe the privatization program along the lines proposed by Gaullists because of the popularity of previous sales and potential regulatory headaches.[81] Giscard d'Estaing, UDF's leader, categorically asserted before the election that France's big utility SOEs in such areas as transport, electricity, and the like would not be sold.[82]

Finally, there is a marked shift in emphasis over the role of foreign investors.[83] Whereas previously foreigners could not acquire more than 20 percent of the shares in a privatized company, no such restrictions now exist. Not only that, but foreign investors have been asked to participate in stable nuclei, such as those of BNP and Elf. Alphandéry attributes this shift to the growing openness of the French economy, but it is more plausible that foreign investors are needed to supplement the shallow French capital market, particularly now that France is in a recession. As one British banker put it bluntly: "[W]ithout foreign investors, the French state will not be able to achieve its objective of raising FFr 50 billion [from privatization receipts]."[84]

In this section I have analyzed the effects of party ideology and strategy on privatization. The identification of the governing party (or coalition) with state ownership as well as its political strategy influence the likelihood and scope of privatization. Chirac's Gaullists confirm this proposition. Moreover, changes in the political stream affect the continuation of certain programs. Mitterrand's reelection to the presidency in 1988 and the consequent cessation of privatization further strengthen the argument. Finally, Balladur's advent to power in 1993 confirms the importance of governing parties. After a landslide victory in legislative elections, he revived the privatization program implemented under Chirac. Precedent was crucial in this revival because Balladur could draw upon previous success to continue and expand the program.

### The Problem Stream: Public-Sector Debt and Privatization

Just as in the British case, high government borrowing needs had a profound impact on privatization in France. They helped bring attention to the issue as well as provided the main impetus for adopting the policy.

The central government's deficit burden rose from 0.18 percent in 1980 to 5.4 percent in 1981 and ballooned to 7.4 percent in 1982 (fig. 5.1). This increase can be partially attributed to the ambitious and controversial nationalization program that Mitterrand implemented in the beginning of his tenure in power. It was also exacerbated by the Left's expansionary policies at a time when France's trading partners were contracting. As the burden increased, however, the anti-Socialist opposition began questioning the wisdom of bringing mostly deficit-ridden companies into the public sector. In fact, Jacques Chirac promised he would privatize the newly acquired companies as early as December 1981.[85]

As time wore on, the government's borrowing needs increased and proponents of privatization became more vocal. By 1983, the central government's deficit burden stood at 7.8 percent. Concurrently, the anti-Socialist coalition reasoned that selling SOEs could partially ameliorate the problem by removing enterprises from government books, reducing state subsidies, and providing handsome returns to the Finance Ministry that could be used to finance the deficit. In the ensuing years, borrowing needs declined to 5.9 percent in 1984 and 6.0 percent in 1985, mainly as a result of austerity measures taken by the Socialist government. In 1986, however, borrowing needs rose to 7.5 percent, creating a situation that Chirac and his coalition perceived to be unacceptable; privatization was the logical outcome.

After a minor improvement during Chirac's tenure in power, the budgetary situation deteriorated. In 1991, the deficit stood at roughly 7.0 percent, while it deteriorated to a stunning 14.2 percent in 1992. Encouraged by the Socialist willingness to partially finance SOEs by selling small portions of the state's equity holdings, Gaullists continued to press for privatization as a way to relieve pressure on government spending. Balladur could point to the beneficial effects that privatization and other measures had on the budget during his tenure as Finance Minister (1986–88). This point further accentuates the importance of precedent. Nevertheless, Socialists and the Center-Right coalition define the problem, in this case the deficit burden, very differently. Unlike the Socialists, Balladur will not reinvest privatization receipts in these companies; rather, he will use them to directly finance the government budget deficit. Neither will he use the money to create jobs except only indirectly. It is expected that a portion of privatization receipts will pay off the debt incurred by issuing job-creating bonds. In short, whereas the Socialists were worried about high public expenditures, the Gaullist-led coalition is concerned with the yawning budget deficit.

It is important to note the differences between British and French public finances. Although levels differed markedly, they were both considered exceptionally high by each country's standards. When Thatcher, for example, took over as Prime Minister in 1979, the British government's burden stood

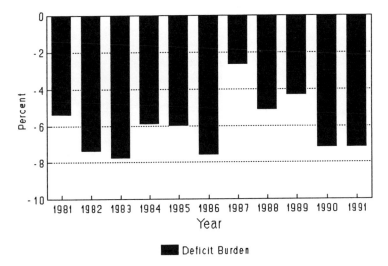

Fig. 5.1. French central government's deficit burden (deficit over outflows), 1981–91, in percentages. (From IMF, *International Financial Statistics Yearbook, 1990* [Washington, DC: IMF, 1990]; IMF, *International Financial Statistics* [Washington, DC: IMF, December 1992].)

at 14.6 percent. This figure compares to an average rate of 12.8 percent for the previous Labour government and a 3.6 percent average burden during Heath's Conservative government in the early 1970s. Hence, based on historical standards, the central government's borrowing needs were judged by Thatcher to be unacceptably high. By comparison, Chirac's advent to power in 1986 found France with a deficit burden of 7.5 percent, which, although not high by British standards, was perceived by Chirac as high because the rate had historically been considerably lower in France. The central government's borrowing needs, for example, stood at an average of 6.5 percent during the preceding Socialist tenure. This figure compares to an average of 2.7 percent during Giscard's Center-Right coalition government. The point that needs to be emphasized is that although problems are sometimes defined by comparing indicators across different countries, as Kingdon suggests, Thatcher and Chirac defined the problem in reference to historical standards of their respective countries.

CHAPTER 6

# The Two Waves of French Privatization

In the previous chapter, I examined developments in the political and problem streams. Here I assess the availability of privatization in the policy stream by reference to two criteria: technical feasibility (the perceived ease of implementation) and value acceptability (the degree of consensus among specialists) in three policy communities: oil, telecommunications, and railroads. Finally, I examine the process of coupling to show how the interplay of all three streams at the same time helps explain the rationale and limits of privatization in France.

## The Policy Stream

In this section I examine developments in each policy community. I highlight the importance of precedent and show how technical feasibility and value acceptability affect the likelihood of privatization.

### Oil: Privatizing Elf Aquitaine

In contrast to Britain, state ownership in the French oil industry was a largely bipartisan issue. Nevertheless, the state has been reducing its ownership in small increments since the mid-1970s. Why? What factors have precipitated the gradual sale of shares? I examine the evolution of privatization proposals in the French oil industry, paying particular attention to the sale of Elf Aquitaine's shares. I first discuss the creation of Elf Aquitaine and subsequent state-SOE relations that helped set important precedents. Then I briefly examine the Chalandon affair because it helped focus attention on privatization. Finally, I show how technical feasibility and value acceptability influenced the likelihood of privatization.

#### Oil and State Ownership

In contrast to Britain, France is not well endowed in energy resources.[1] Consequently, the French state has had to maintain an active involvement in oil by creating numerous SOEs in the beginning and later consolidating them into two national champions. Their mission was to secure adequate oil supplies at "reasonable" prices and to minimize the effects of oil imports on the balance of payments.[2]

The scarcity of oil supplies was painfully felt during World War I. Diplomat Georges Clemenceau's famous phrase aptly captures the strategic importance that the French ascribed to oil at the time: "A drop of oil is worth a drop of blood."[3] Guided by such considerations, the government helped create in 1924 the Compagnie Française des Pétroles (CFP), keeping 35 percent of the shares for itself. World War II witnessed the creation of additional companies. Prospects of oil and gas discoveries in France prompted the creation of Régie Autonome des Pétroles (RAP) in 1939. Two years later, a mixed enterprise, Société Nationale des Pétroles d'Aquitaine (SNPA), was created in charge of prospecting oil in Lacq. True to the spirit of its declaration that the state should possess the "levers of command," the government created another SOE after the war, the Bureau des Recherches de Pétrole (BRP) and charged it with formulating an energy program in the national interest. Although they initially operated as independent companies, RAP, BRP, and state holdings in SNPA were merged by President Charles de Gaulle in 1966 to create the Entreprise de Recherches et d'Activités Pétrolières (ERAP). The new SOE operated under the commercial name Elf. The purpose of the merger, according to ERAP's first annual report, was to create a large enough company whose competitiveness would be preserved by competition with foreign rather than other French oil companies.[4]

From the very beginning, Elf was an instrument of industrial policy groomed to become a national champion.[5] Its mission was to secure adequate oil supplies by exploring "uneconomic" oil in France and the Sahara. Partly because of its SOE status and partly because of the peculiar economic and political circumstances that led to its creation Elf was generously assisted by the state in the form of subsidies that eventually exceeded $1.2 billion.[6] In addition, Elf's creation was strongly endorsed by Pierre Guillaumat, the architect of postwar energy policy and a powerful patron of the corps of mining engineers (Corps des Mines). The fact that he was a committed *dirigiste* and one of de Gaulle's economic advisors also aided the company's close relations to the state. Not surprisingly, top-level managers were heavily recruited from the same corps. In contrast to Britain, this recruitment pattern, which closely followed that of civil servants in charge of oil policy, assured a relatively coherent formulation of policy because participants were trained to think in roughly similar terms. This incestuous relationship, however, accentuated personality conflicts and eventually helped launch the privatization campaign in the 1980s.

Initially, Elf was dependent on state funds. As the SOE grew in size and diversified its operations by vertical integration and multinationalization, it became apparent that state funds were insufficient. Elf possessed oil and gas rights worldwide, but it did not have the capital to implement its ambitious plans. SNPA, on the other hand, had a healthy cash flow from compensation of its state assets. Given the close links between the two firms—Guillaumat was the chief executive of both companies—it was decided that a merger was the best way to solicit funds for Elf. As a result, state ownership was reduced. ERAP, which was 100 percent state owned, merged with privately owned SNPA in 1976 to create Société Nationale Elf Aquitaine (SNEA), whose two-thirds ownership remained with the state. This situation left then President Valéry Giscard d'Estaing's government vulnerable to leftist accusations of creeping privatization.[7] Their criticism was muted, however, because the state retained majority ownership. The merger had two effects: (1) It helped tap into private capital without effectively relinquishing state control; and (2) It established an important precedent upon which Chirac could draw for justification when he proposed the sale of Elf's shares in 1986.

*The Chalandon Affair*

Active state intervention is likely to be resisted by autonomous-minded managers.[8] Such resistance can take many forms, ranging from mild, behind-the-scenes disagreements to open, public confrontations. Conflict, particularly of the latter type, raises the issue of the usefulness and desirability of detailed state direction and creates a fertile environment for possible change. Indeed, the resulting ferment in the oil community following the dismissal of Elf CEO Albin Chalandon's helped focus attention on privatization.

Chalandon's dismissal hit at the heart of the privatization debate. Who has or should have ultimate authority over decisions affecting SOEs, managers or politicians? Following the nationalizations of 1982, then Industry Minister Pierre Dreyfus decided to reorganize the ailing French chemical sector. Under this restructuring program, Elf agreed to purchase the stock of ATO-Cloe, the reorganized chemical operations of Rhône-Poulenc and Pechiney-Ugine-Kuhlmann (PUK).[9] While Elf was to purchase 50 percent of the chemical group's assets, it was agreed that another oil company, CFP (also known as Total), would purchase the remaining half. This division naturally raised the issue of control. When Chalandon complained to Dreyfus about the lack of Elf's control over ATO-Chloe, he was asked to buy back CFP's share with the participation of ERAP. The process of restructuring the newly acquired chemical operations, however, proved to be very difficult. Chalandon refused to compensate CFP, arguing that the funds should be reinvested to financially turn the group around. He also refused to surrender Rousselot to CFP because it was one of the group's few profit centers. CFP immediately demanded arbitration. On 25 May 1983, Laurent Fabius, then Industry Minister, decided that chemicals should stay under Elf's possession. However, Elf was ordered to compensate CFP without ERAP's participation by ceding 3 percent of the Figgs mining company.[10] Chalandon refused to obey a minister who, according to the former Elf chair, "wanted to make public enterprises simple extensions of administration."[11] Two weeks later, Chalandon's contract was not renewed.

The Chalandon affair had significant political repercussions. Although Fabius won the battle, the Socialist government might have actually lost the war. Certainly the affair did more than just damage the Left's credibility of running SOEs in a serious, apolitical manner. It also brought attention to the broader issue of managerial autonomy and was later used by Chalandon to shake the foundations of state enterprise. How could the state commit to managerial autonomy and not intervene in disputes between companies in which it is the principal shareholder? This sort of arbitration inevitably produces political decisions that managers cannot refuse. Although Chalandon's dismissal undoubtedly involved personality and political differences as well—Chalandon had strong ties to the Gaullist party—it demonstrates the curious mix of markets and politics in state enterprise and the ultimate primacy of political directives, whether desirable or undesirable, in the commercial operations of oil SOEs.[12]

*Preparing for a Sale*

It is interesting to note that, as a solution, privatization in the oil sector did not face serious competition from other solutions in the 1980s. In contrast to Britain, the issue in France did not appear to be between issuing bonds or selling shares. In fact, French policymakers finally ended up using both alternatives for reasons that will be explained later. Missing from the French experience with Elf was also the issue of implicit state guarantees regarding SOE access to capital markets. The question in the case of oil was between maintaining the existing ownership arrangements or changing them in favor of private investors.

Selling some of Elf Aquitaine's shares appeared to be a relatively easy policy to implement. Its technical feasibility was enhanced by the fact that shares under the parent company's name Société Nationale Elf Aquitaine (SNEA) were already traded on the stock exchange. Thus, in contrast to the British case of BNOC, asset valuation was a fairly straightforward exercise. The company already issued shares whose value was determined by the stock market. All that needed to be done was to decide what percentage ownership ERAP would relinquish. Elf's profitability enhanced the appeal of a sale. The SOE's profitability ratio remained relatively stable over the period 1981–86. Although profitability dipped to 3.2 percent in 1983 from 4.1 percent in 1981, it regained lost ground and stood at 3.6 percent in 1986. In addition, Elf hoped to attract private investors because of relatively high earnings per share. In relation to Total, which at the time was largely privately owned, Elf fared better. In 1986, Elf earned FFr 43 per share as opposed to Total's loss of FFr 13 per share.[13] More attractive to private investors, however, was demand for oil. A relatively high inelasticity of demand for oil assured French policymakers of private interest in Elf's stock. Figure 6.1 compares oil consumption patterns for 1979 and 1986. In 1979, oil accounted for 59.5 percent of all energy consumption. Although the figure dropped to 43.1 percent by 1986, oil continued to be the largest source of energy in France.

A fair degree of consensus among members of the oil community further enhanced the availability of privatization. Chalandon's departure as Elf's chair created a fertile environment for change. Chalandon himself put the issue on the table almost five months after his dismissal. Speaking at a dinner organized by the French managers' association Comité National de l'Organisation Française, he launched a crusade against state ownership. "The state," he said, "must not substitute itself for entrepreneurs. Its role should be limited to fixing broad guidelines."[14] By virtue of ownership, he continued, the state distorts the laws of the market and ultimately hurts the international competitiveness of French SOEs. This is because politicians want the best of both worlds; companies should maintain high levels of employment and generate profits. This policy, according to Chalandon, can only hurt the companies' long-term commercial viability.[15] Privatization represents a good remedy to the situation. It takes politicians out of the driver's seat and hands control back to managers and the market.

Other former state managers and several intellectuals held similar views. Jean-Maxime Lévêque, former CEO of Société Générale, carried the argument one step further.[16] Apart from finding no economic justification for state ownership of enterprises traded in the stock market, he added that the sale of such stock would generate significant financial benefits for the state. The partial sale of Elf Aquitaine, for example, could bring in approximately FFr 4 billion, funds the state would otherwise lack. On a more theoretical level, others argued for Elf's privatization from an economic perspective. Profitable SOEs operating in competitive markets should be privatized immediately. Because Elf did not produce collective goods, was profitable, and was subjected to international competition, it was a good candidate for sale.[17]

For its part, Elf's new management liked the idea. The oil glut following 1982 and the consequent drop in the price of oil, increasing world competition in refining, and President Mitterrand's strong commitment to developing alternative sources of energy spelled financial trouble for the French oil industry. Particularly hard-hit were the refining operations of many companies operating in the French market. In fact, the number of refineries had been

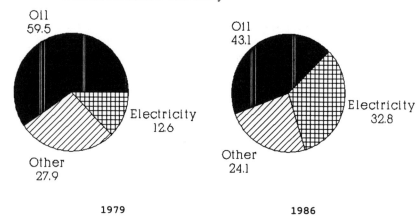

1979                    1986

Fig. 6.1.  French energy consumption by type of energy, 1979 and 1986, in percentages. Electricity figures include electricity generated by hydroelectric and nuclear power. (From INSEE, *Annuaire Statistique de la France* [Paris: INSEE, 1990].)

reduced to 15 in 1985 from 33 in 1973.[18] To make matters worse, experts estimated at the time that profitability in refining would remain low, particularly since oil SOEs from OPEC nations diversified downstream.[19] Faced with such a gloomy forecast, Elf officials were eager to tap into an additional source of funds, but Michel Pecqueur, chair of Elf Aquitaine, was careful not to overemphasize the SOE's enthusiasm. Confronted with the probability of Elf's privatization, he stoically replied:

Denationalisation would not change things much for us. We are already an international company confronted by international competition, and we seek the state's help neither financially nor politically. It would only mean a greater involvement of private shareholders.[20]

Nevertheless, when Chirac's government announced Elf's privatization in September 1986, Pecqueur's enthusiasm over the additional funds became more overt. Elf, he said, was already planning to invest proceeds from the sale on possible acquisitions in oil, chemicals, and biotechnology.[21]

Opposition to Elf's privatization came largely from Socialist quarters and more specifically from Mitterrand himself. In the early months of cohabitation, he hinted that he would not sign any privatization law that included enterprises nationalized before his advent to power in 1981, claiming to be protecting France's national heritage. This threat aimed at blocking the sale of corporations such as Elf, which was set up by de Gaulle himself.

When Chirac's government passed the privatization bill, however, in early July 1986 Mitterrand refused to sign it citing two objections.[22] First, he argued that the law did not provide safeguards for adequate valuation procedures; therefore, there was grave danger that the "family silver" could be sold off at an unfair price, too cheaply.[23] Second, Mitterrand was afraid that control of French companies would be passed on to foreign interests, later clarified to mean non—-European Community (now European Union, or EU) interests.[24] This concern seems particularly applicable to Elf's case because it is a company whose shares are traded not only on the Bourse, but also on the stock exchanges in New York, Brussels, Luxembourg, Frankfurt, Dusseldorf, Basel, Geneva, and Zurich. How could Chirac solve the problem?

In stark contrast to Thatcher's decision to sell the majority of shares in Britoil, Chirac's government decided to sell only 11 percent of shares, maintaining state ownership in Elf at above 50 percent. Privatization would be accomplished by selling stock in the French market and issuing bonds in foreign markets. Why didn't Chirac choose to follow the British example and relinquish majority control? The answer lies in the process of arriving at a consensus in the policy stream. First, it was difficult to privatize enterprises that were brought under state ownership by de Gaulle. Selling Elf was politically risky because it meant not only going against past party policy, but also questioning the wisdom of the premier leader of France, de Gaulle himself. Second, and more likely, the company's strategic role in implementing French energy policy dampened the chances of arriving at a consensus for a total sale. Finally, budgetary considerations made a partial sale particularly appealing. Because the state would not cede majority ownership, it could classify proceeds as additional income in the budget.[25]

Interestingly, the sale in 1986 established a precedent upon which Socialists could draw after their advent to power in 1988. Prime Minister Edith Cresson's government announced in November 1991 that it was going to sell a small part (2.3 percent) of the state's stake in Elf, leaving the state with 51.5 percent ownership.[26] In March 1992, 2.4 million shares were offered internationally and 3.38 million were reserved for French investors, raising FFr 2.08 billion before expenses. In addition to satisfying company capitalization needs, it appeared that Socialists showed signs of greater receptivity toward sales provided that the state retained majority ownership.[27]

Nevertheless, the option of a total sale was kept alive by Gaullists. Concluding a colloquium on privatization in 1988, Edouard Balladur, the minister in charge of privatization, emphatically maintained that apart from retaining a golden share, the state should sell all its shares in Elf.[28] Following the Center-Right's sweeping victory in 1993, Balladur became prime minister and was able to make good on his promise. He included Elf on the list of *privatisables* and prepared it for a sale. To forge a consensus and silence any possible opposition to privatization, Balladur almost immediately replaced Elf's CEO, Loïk Le Floch-Prigent, who was known for his Socialist ties, with Philippe Jaffré, former CEO of Crédit Agricole and a close friend of Balladur. "How can we keep as CEO an architect of nationalization at a time when [Balladur's] . . . government wishes to privatize Elf Aquitaine?" wondered a close aid to Giscard d'Estaing.[29] Privatization was technically feasible. By 1992, Elf had become the largest company in France in terms of total revenues and the largest company traded on the Bourse in terms of capitalization. Keeping it under tight state control made no sense because it was too big— revenues were roughly equivalent to the defense budget—and because it was "more powerful than the majority of ministries," according to a former Elf CEO.[30] In addition, it was a profitable SOE, the net profitability ratio over total revenues was 3.1 percent in 1992 which was 1 percent more than To-tal's,[31] with shares "very undervalued" relative to comparable companies, according to a Merrill Lynch report issued in July 1993.[32]

To maintain a consensus over the sale, the state retains powers of control. Gérard Longuet, Minister of Industry as of this writing, made it clear that the state would retain some control "to reassure those who need it."[33] To alleviate Mitterrand's concerns, Edmond Alphandéry, the minister in charge of privat-ization, also announced in December 1993 that the state would retain through ERAP between 10 and 15 percent of Elf's equity in addition to veto powers granted by a "golden share" (*action spécifique*). It would also name three members to the board of directors, although only one would have voting rights.[34] In contrast to Mitterrand's previous concerns, foreign investors would be invited to buy shares because they already owned 20.8 percent of Elf's stock at the end of 1992.[35] The sale took place on 10 February 1994. Four percent of the 60.3 million shares were reserved for Elf employees while roughly 10 percent went to the nine firms of the stable nucleus, three of which were foreign firms (two Belgian and one Swiss). The total sale brought in roughly FFr 33 billion making it by far the most important and largest privat-ization in France. Shares were predictably oversubscribed partly due to the price of FFr 385, which was slightly higher (2.2 percent) than the price recommended by the advisory Commission on Privatization, but still lower (10.6 percent) than the traded price on 3 February 1994.[36]

In conclusion, the availability of privatization in the case of oil was conditioned by two elements. First, the option was technically feasible. The prospect of selling Elf Aquitaine did not face the serious valuation problems usually encountered in selling SOEs because part of the corporation's stock was already traded on the Bourse. Moreover, Elf was financially healthy and there was strong demand for oil. Second, partial privatization in 1986 enjoyed fairly wide acceptance by members of the oil community, largely because Elf already faced international competition and because the sale would not cede majority control. In 1993, Balladur could draw upon previous sales, including one by Socialists, and press for total divestiture. Nevertheless, the state was still expected to maintain some control even after privatization in early 1994 in the form of equity (10 percent) and a golden share.

## Telecommunications: No Privatization Yet

In contrast to Elf Aquitaine, France Télécom has not yet been privatized. Why? In this section I trace developments in the telecommunications community and assess the availability of privatization relative to other policy alternatives. First, I briefly discuss developments in French telecommunications. Then I look at the difference that Chirac's premiership made in the period 1986–88. Finally, I examine more recent developments in an effort to assess how the two criteria, technical feasibility and value acceptability, influence the availability of privatization in the policy stream.

*State Ownership and Telecommunications: The Early Years*

Similarly to Britain, telephony in France was started by private entrepreneurs, but the government decided in 1889 that a nationalized telecommunications authority was the best way to protect receipts from competing telegraph operations which were also state-owned.[37] Soon, however, the relative backwardness of France's telephones gave rise to calls for reducing state ownership. One critic, Paul Laffont, deputy secretary of the Post and Telegraph Administration, proposed in the 1920s to privatize the telco, arguing that the provision of this commercial service should be left in private hands. Although privatization was rejected by the National Assembly, reorganization, a separate budget, and some planning and funding autonomy were adopted in 1923.[38] Despite these changes, France continued to fall behind other countries. In 1938, it ranked eleventh out of twelve industrialized countries, with just 3.79 telephones per 100 population.[39]

The situation did not improve appreciably until the early 1960s. Although telecommunications services were administratively distinguished from postal services with the creation of Direction Générale de Télécommunications (DGT) in 1941, DGT continued to compete with other government departments, such as defense or education, for scarce funds. It was not until the Fifth Plan (1966–70) that priority for funding was given to telecommunications. Why did the French reverse their policy? Faced with rising unemployment and a widening trade deficit, the government turned to the expansion and modernization of the country's telephone system as a measure of alleviating both. Modernization of telecommunications would also stimulate demand for French-designed equipment and services,[40] attract foreign multinationals wishing to tap into the French or the broader European market, and bring political rewards from voters with improved access to and higher quality of this "public service."

In contrast to Britain, France's telecom operator has until recently remained part of the government's bureaucracy. In 1968, Giscard d'Estaing, then finance minister, proposed separating DGT from the Post Office and granting the former SOE status. Numerous other proposals for organizational reform at the governmental or parliamentary levels were similarly ill-fated.[41] Successive French governments considered these calls too radical, preferring instead tight political control in the name of providing a public service. At a time when Britain granted SOE status to the PO in the name of competitiveness, France was able to achieve success by leaving DGT as part of the bureaucracy. As a result of this precedent, subsequent calls for privatization were interpreted as being too risky.

Because of its legal status, DGT faced special labor-relations and funding problems. Employment was guided by a set of civil service regulations that restricted the organization in terms of hiring and compensation. As elsewhere, top-level managers were and continue to be recruited from special administrative schools, l'Ecole Nationale Superieure des Télécommunications (ENST) and l'Ecole Nationale Polytechnique (l'X). Creative financing, however, has compensated for this and other deficiencies. Unlike its British counterpart, DGT has been allowed since 1970[42] to raise funds outside the limits of public expenditures. Furthermore, setting up joint ventures with private firms provided additional capital from private sources.[43]

*Pressures to Liberalize and Privatize*

Events in the policy stream in France took a different turn from those in Britain, dampening the appeal of privatization as a viable alternative. DGT, which officially changed its name to France Télécom (FT) in 1988, differed markedly from British Telecom (BT) in the early 1980s in two respects: legal status and rate of modernization. First, BT was created as a public corporation in 1981. In contrast, FT acquired similar status only in January 1991. Consequently, there was no precedent set in France in the way that it was in Britain. Second, France was able to modernize its telephone system, keeping DGT as a government department. By 1982, the time when the British government announced its intention to sell BT, France had surpassed the United Kingdom in overall telecommunications development. Using density of penetration as an indicator, we find that in 1974, the United Kingdom had 10.57 more telephone sets per 100 inhabitants.[44] By 1982, the tables were turned. France's density of penetration increased to 54.14 telephone sets per 100 population as opposed to Britain's 50.68 telephone sets per 100 inhabitants. Because of such remarkable achievement, the French were naturally cautious not to embark on radical changes that might jeopardize their success.

To be sure, considerable changes had taken place in French telecommunications. Proposals to transform the organizational structure of the telecommunications sector, however, varied considerably from the British. In contrast to Britain, liberalization and privatization in France were kept as clearly distinguishable alternatives; one could be achieved without the other. In addition, Chirac privatized companies involved in manufacturing telecommunications equipment, an end of the business that was already in private hands in Britain. These variations established a precedent in France that made a big difference in the ensuing debate.

The contradictory nature of DGT's role as administrator and commercial operator aggravated tensions that traditionally existed between postal and telecommunications services and dampened the technical feasibility and appeal of privatization in the French telecommunications community. Similarly to Britain—and just like most other countries in Europe—the telecommunications division was for the most part profitable, and its surplus income was used to finance the postal deficit. Unlike the British case, however, the debate was situated amid the Colbertist tradition of the French PTT.[45] It is much more difficult to reorganize a government agency along commercial lines than it is to restructure an SOE that already operates on commercial logic. Hence, the structural transformation of the Post Office that helped create British Telecom in 1981 was absent from the French case. This absence has important implications for understanding why Gaullists Chirac and Balladur or Socialist Prime Ministers have not yet privatized FT. One of the conditions that facilitated BT's privatization in the early 1980s—its legal status, which made privatization technically more feasible—was marked by its absence in France. Value acceptability also influenced the availability of privatization in France. In contrast to Conservatives in Britain, the Socialist government of Pierre Mauroy was committed to maintaining not only DGT's status, but also many of its monopoly powers as well. Then PTT Minister Louis Mexandeau vowed to restore the element of public service to telecommunications.[46]

Upon his election to the presidency in 1981, Mitterrand implemented his plan to restructure the electronics industry. The industry represented the future, he argued, and France could not afford to be left behind.[47] Accordingly, Mitterrand proceeded to nationalize various companies—many of which manufactured, among others, telecommunications equipment—and organized them into networks of companies with related activities, *filières industrielles,* with the explicit aim of creating "national champions."[48] Indeed, the nationalization of such companies as Compagnie Générale d'Electricité (CGE, now called Alcatel-Alsthom), Bull (the domestic computer manufacturer at the time partly owned by Honeywell), Matra, Thomson, and ITT's former subsidiary Compagnie Générale des Constructions Téléphoniques (CGCT) gave the state direct control over 70 percent of domestic electronics production.[49]

Having acquired control over both telecommunications equipment and network, then Industry Minister Jean-Pierre Chevénement proceeded to restructure the entire sector. First, the Industry Ministry's jurisdictional boundaries were redrawn to cover the entire Post and Telecommunications Ministry so that the latter's resources could be employed to finance the project.[50] Second, several corporations, such as Bull, Thomson, and CGCT, received substantial injections of capital directly from DGT to the tune of FFr 1.7 billion.[51] In addition, DGT under the Socialists also contributed to the general government budget FFr 2 billion in 1983 and FFr 2.1 billion in 1984. In the eyes of many observers inside and outside the agency, DGT had become a "milking cow."[52] Finally, despite DGT's policy to ensure that it had a second French equipment supplier and overriding its objections, Chevénement and later his successor, Fabius, decided that Alcatel, CGE's subsidiary, should absorb all of Thomson's telecom activities, transforming the French telecommunications equipment market into a virtual state monopoly. Confronted with the claim that such a merger would result in lower prices, Jacques Dondoux, DGT's director general at the time, replied with candor: "When there is only one supplier and one customer there is nothing to fix prices. It's a power struggle."[53] Thus, up to 1984, French and British telecommunications policies were moving in diametrically opposite directions; the French emphasized restructuring and concentration while the British practiced liberalization and privatization.

The Socialist honeymoon in power did not last very long. The economic downturn that hit France in 1983 precipitated a partial reversal of course. Public spending was tightened. The decision to use DGT to revitalize the French electronics industry (*filière électronique*) imposed serious financial strains on the state agency and cast doubt over the government's wisdom and ability to single-handedly foster growth and innovation in the entire industry without exposing parts of it to domestic and international competition. This need for capital investment accentuated calls for privatizing electronics firms. Proponents of privatizing DGT, however, were scarce and far less vocal.

Calls for privatization came from groups and individuals. The most vocal call came from UDF-Réforme, a group within the Giscardian party. The proposal, however, remained short on specifics. How could FT be sold? Would any services, say local telephone services, continue to be an FT monopoly? What would the regulatory system look like? Who would be allowed to buy shares? Because of its vagueness, this proposal did not receive wide attention. Another proposal, however, one calling for partial privatization, did stir some controversy. Having been chief of staff (*directeur de cabinet*) of

Giscard d'Estaing's Industry Minister, Michel d'Ornano, and assistant director at Thomson, Jacques Darmon articulated an option that influenced the thinking of Gérard Longuet when the latter became PTT minister in Chirac's and Balladur's government.[54] Darmon took the splitting of postal and telecommunications services one step further. He reaffirmed the view that providing telecommunications services constituted a public service because the preamble to the 1958 constitution stated that monopolies should be in the hands of the state. Because the provision of basic telephone services was a monopoly, he continued, an SOE status seemed appropriate. But he also added: why just transform the legal status of DGT and miss out on the opportunity to introduce private capital? The model of ownership that he proposed for the new company was a mixed enterprise resembling Elf Aquitaine (prior to privatization in 1994), a good producer, rather than Electricité de France, a service provider.[55] In other words, although the new corporation would operate commercially under private law, the state would retain the majority of ownership and therefore maintain effective control.

Creating such a company, Darmon claims, would bring several benefits. First, it would liberate DGT from budgetary constraints imposed by the Treasury, allowing the firm to make investments based largely on commercial criteria. Curiously, the same claim was invoked in BT's case, but in the French case there is a twist. Just as in the case of Elf, there is nothing inherently wrong in the argument that hybrids in which the state is majority owner can raise funds in capital markets in their own right as commercial enterprises. This point weakens the claim, so important in facilitating BT's privatization, that SOEs cannot raise funds without them being construed as implicitly guaranteed by the state and further strengthens the argument made here that British privatization had a strong ideological component. Implicit Treasury guarantees need not hamper SOE efforts to raise funds in capital markets. Second, Darmon points out that his solution would involve a change in human resources. Telecommunications employees would no longer be civil servants (*fonctionnaires*). This is an interesting point not only because it was missing from the British privatization debate, but also because it was vehemently opposed by French unions. Finally, Darmon believes that this particular ownership arrangement would break traditional managerial recruitment patterns. Echoing a similar point also raised by other high-ranking officials,[56] Darmon argues that privatization would result in freely recruiting managers based on individual ability and experience and not according to graduation rank. Given recruitment practices at Elf, however, since that SOE serves as his model, it does not appear as if much will change.[57] Graduates of *l'X* and ENST *are* the labor market for DGT managers.

Although Darmon's views were not shared by many, his position and expertise ensured serious consideration of his proposal. The Socialists were not keen on changing DGT's status, let alone selling parts of it to private investors. Also expressing opposition was DGT itself. In the words of Jacques Dondoux: "If becoming an industrial and commercial enterprise is the only way to adapt, I agree. But, well utilized, the administrative status may be effective."[58] But what about the Gaullists? They had, after all, promised that they would embark on an extensive privatization program upon winning the 1986 election. How did they react?

*Chirac's Tenure: Liberalization without Privatization*

The 1986 elections for the National Assembly opened a policy window. This window presented Chirac with an opportunity to raise new issues and adopt the policies he promised while in opposition. Although privatization was a key issue in Chirac's electoral campaign, selling DGT was not high on his agenda. Instead, the government focused on privatizing telecommunications equipment manufacturers and accelerated the liberalization program that was cautiously started by the Socialists.

Why didn't Chirac sell DGT? His government first had to solve enormous technical problems associated with the agency's status. In contrast to Britain, there was no experience accumulated from other sales. Balladur was preparing to privatize SOEs that were nationalized only recently, many of which were already traded on the stock market. Selling DGT was obviously qualitatively different and infinitely more difficult to implement.

French telecommunications is an interesting case because in contrast to other cases examined in this study, FT has not yet been privatized despite good financial health and a strong demand growth for services. This strengthens the argument made in this book that both technical feasibility and value acceptability are crucial elements of the policy stream. Although profitability has gone down in recent years, FT remains a highly profitable organization. The profitability ratio[59] fell to 2 percent in 1988 from 13.7 percent in 1985 before it stabilized at 5.9 in 1990. Part of the decrease can be attributed to the loss of monopoly in several services. Overall FT's good financial health illustrates the point that the state could attract private investors in the event of a sale. Perhaps more illuminating is demand growth for telecommunications services (table 6.1). The size of the overall telephone system rose from 17.6 million main lines in 1981 to 26.5 million main lines in 1989, an increase of 66.4 percent in nine years. Similarly, total traffic climbed to 98.1 billion pulses in 1988 from 63.0 billion pulses in 1981. Most impressive, however, has been demand growth for data terminal equipment. In two years, it more than doubled, from 5.3 thousand in 1981 to 13.4 thousand in 1983. By 1988 it reached 60.2 thousand terminals, a level eleven times higher than that of 1981. Interestingly, this growth has been achieved while FT remained under state ownership. Although use of alternatives to the telephone, such as postal services, also grew, it is clear that demand for telecommunications services rose enormously during the 1980s.

Privatization of telecommunications was an option that did not enjoy broad support. The question of introducing private ownership into DGT was tied to the issue of changing the agency's status. Although the new government was more receptive to the idea than was its predecessor, the issue was politically risky. This fact helps explain Longuet's lukewarm reception of Darmon's proposal. First, unlike in Britain, Longuet could proudly point to many French technological achievements.[60] Since the late 1970s and under both Giscard and Mitterrand, France had been transformed into a world leader in electronic telephone directory, videotext, picture phones, and data networks. In addition, French industry was highly competitive in public switching technology. France was the only country that could boast having digitized its telephone system virtually "overnight." "In one decade, French telecommunications passed from poverty to abundance, and from a unique product to diversity," remarked Longuet.[61] A great portion of this success could be attributed to a state agency, DGT.[62] "Why change something that works?" wondered another government official.[63]

Support for privatization was not forthcoming from other quarters, either. Management was concerned with possible negative repercussions. Although their desire for autonomy was very real, largely because the agency was being milked for cash, senior managers wanted DGT to stay in the public sector. Concurring with this view were several unions, some of which, such as that of postal workers, did not wish to part with the more profitable telecommunications division. Because of these constraints, Longuet favored the idea of transforming DGT's status into an SOE modeled after SNCF, the French railroads, and placing its activities under the regulatory authority of the Com-

TABLE 6.1. Demand Growth for French Telecommunications and Postal Services, 1981–89

|  | 1981 | 1982 | 1983 | 1984 | 1985 | 1986 | 1987 | 1988 | 1989 |
|---|---|---|---|---|---|---|---|---|---|
| Size of the system[a] | 17.6 | 19.3 | 20.8 | 21.9 | 22.8 | 23.6 | 24.5 | 25.5 | 26.5 |
| Total traffic[b] | 63.0 | 68.1 | 74.5 | 78.9 | 82.9 | 87.0 | 94.6 | 98.1 | — |
| Size of data system[c] | 5.3 | 8.5 | 13.4 | 21.7 | 31.4 | 40.7 | 50.9 | 60.2 | — |
| Size of postal services[d] | 11.6 | 11.9 | 12.1 | 12.5 | 12.9 | 13.9 | 15.3 | 16.5 | 17.8 |

*Source*: INSEE, *Annuaire Statistique de la France* (Paris: INSEE, 1990); ITU, *Yearbook of Public Telecommunication Statistics* (Geneva: ITU, 1990).
[a]Million main lines.
[b]Billion pulses.
[c]Thousand data terminal equipment connected to public telephone and telex networks.
[d]Million letters, parcels, and periodicals.

mission Nationale des Communications et Libertés (CNCL).[64] Although he was able to accomplish the latter, the former remained an elusive goal.

Sales of other companies and the push for liberalization by Chirac deflected attention from privatization. By 1986, it was becoming increasingly obvious that frustration with the inability to integrate the activities of network operator and equipment manufacturers would lead to separate development of the two functions.[65] In practice, this meant the return of various electronics firms to private hands and the opening of the market for value-added telecommunications services. During this period, several companies, such as Matra, CGE, and CGCT, were sold off, and such would have been the fate of Bull and Thomson had the program not been interrupted by the presidential elections of 1988. These sales deflected attention to privatizing the equipment end of the business and took the heat off calls for selling DGT.

Moreover, the process of liberalization accelerated. It must be noted that minor liberalization proposals were put forth by the Socialists, particularly in regard to digital equipment purchases.[66] Despite rhetoric, however, Chirac's government proceeded with caution. In September 1987, Longuet opened up the market for value-added network services (VANS); in December of the same year the cellular phone market followed.[67] Just like their British counterparts, the French did not liberalize the local telephone network. France's liberalization, however, differed from Britain's in one important aspect. Unlike the numerous competitors of BT in VANS, FT lobbied successfully to limit entry to only a few competitors. A good example of such "controlled liberalization" is the carphone market. On the one hand, FT formed an alliance with Matra, then still an SOE, to develop Radiocom 2000. On the other hand, a license was granted to a consortium led by Compagnie Générale des Eaux—the diversified private water company—in conjunction with Alcatel and Nokia of Finland. In contrast to Britain, pain was taken to ensure that French companies led the competing consortium. There was evidently a "French first" attitude toward liberalization, a point that was also corroborated in my interview with a French government official. In addition, because of agency insistence to continue playing a major role in the French market, projected carphone production gave the lion's share to FT. Of the 300,000 subscribers in France, it was projected that 200,000 would be using Radiocom 2000 by 1992.[68]

How did liberalization affect the likelihood of privatization? First, it led to a clear differentiation between the two policies. Unlike Britain, where liberalization was used to extend and legitimize privatization, French policymakers advocated and subsequently implemented one without the other. As long as the two policies remained separate, support for privatizing FT would be low because benefits, such as company growth and innovation, could be accrued with a change in market structure without a necessary change in ownership. Second, emphasis on liberalization focused attention on models from other countries. French officials found the British model counterproductive. More specifically, the PTT minister argued that the British network was kept artificially competitive because of BT's privatization.[69] Oftel deliberately discriminated in favor of Mercury, thereby restraining BT's potential. Hence, following the British model of liberalization with privatization was thought to be unsuitable for France.

Finally, liberalization rekindled the debate over FT's status. How could the government justify an agency that was both a regulator and an operator? Although Longuet in the early days of Chirac's government wanted to change FT's status, Chirac himself was not anxious to do so for fear of an open confrontation with the unions.[70] In January 1988, the PTT minister announced plans to alter FT's status. The plans, however, had to be shelved because of the 1988 presidential election.

*The Socialists Return to Power*

Following Mitterrand's reelection to a second term in office, the Socialists returned to Matignon. Surprisingly, it was a Socialist PTT Minister, Paul Quilès, who finally altered FT's status. Initially, Quilès announced the "rebirth of the concept of public service," a statement that effectively put an end to Chirac's version of liberalization. It seemed that the status of telecommunications would not be altered.[71] Nevertheless, pressure from FT's managers and indirectly from the EU[72] to free the telco from excessive government financial regulations continued to mount. In early summer 1988, Marcel Roulet, FT's director general who returned to his post despite a change in the country's political leadership, emphasized the need to take a more commercial approach to telecommunications. In light of liberalization, it is important, he argued, "to ensure that the management structure of France Telecom [*sic*] evolves before or in connection with any large-scale broadening of competition, enabling it to acquire the same freedom and flexibility as its competitors."[73] It is clear that Roulet associated a more competitive telecommunications environment with a change in FT's status, but he clarified in a later interview that "competition does not necessarily imply privatization. In fact, the choice between public and private is principally political."[74] This attitude stands in stark contrast to the one exhibited by the British, where privatization of BT was the considered to be the "next logical step" to liberalization.

As a result, a consensus began to form, but not in favor of private ownership. The author of an influential report commissioned by the government argued that the postal and telecommunications services should be split into separate bodies, with some financial and managerial autonomy be granted to each entity.[75] Although he did not mention privatization, his recommendations were interpreted by several unions as a prelude to privatization. The communist-led CGT termed it unacceptable, although the more moderate Force Ouvrière (FO) was more receptive to change.[76] Judging from the British case, CGT's fears were not groundless. The split from postal services and the creation of BT established a precedent that facilitated privatization. Not only did this action enhance the technical feasibility of a sale, but it also split the opposition. Nevertheless, support for change was widespread. Despite sharp criticism by Lionel Jospin, then Education Minister, Quilès could count on the support of Michel Rocard, who was Prime Minister at the time.[77] In addition, not only was Marcel Roulet in favor of altering FT's status, but welcoming the accompanying autonomy were also the agency's engineers. "DGT must become a public enterprise," said Michel Huet, president of the Association des Ingenieurs en Télécommunications, so that it can obtain "a large autonomy on its procurement, research, personnel and finance policies."[78]

After marathon negotiations and several amendments in the National Assembly and the Senate, a government-sponsored bill was finally passed on 27 June 1990 authorizing the organizational split between postal and telecommunications services into separate entities. France Télécom became an SOE with special status—that is, without capital. Although the new law envisaged and the Socialist government promised FT considerable institutional flexibility and budgetary autonomy,[79] the Ministry of Finance continued to play a key role. Not only did it influence price levels for services still under monopoly—for example, telephone and telex—but the ministry also claimed that ultimately FT must play a role in the government's industrial policy, just like any other SOE.[80] To this end, the Socialist government has been pressuring FT to inject more funds into Bull, France's ailing computer SOE. In its confrontation with the government, FT resisted such pressure. On the one hand, the Ministry of Finance views this bailout as the corporation's public duty. On the other hand, FT is negotiating to take over Bull's worldwide telecom services in exchange for a check that could total $360 million.[81] Despite the fact that it already owns 17 percent of Bull, FT wants to make it clear that it wishes to no longer be used as "a milking cow."[82] Aided by the European Commission, which is set against member governments subsidizing SOEs, FT appears capable of thwarting the French government's pressure.

In addition to ownership, the state has retained other powers of control. First, until the end of 1993, FT was still obliged to pay the state an annual sum of $2.5 billion to support research and development in other sectors.[83] In addition, regulation of telecommunications services has been strengthened with the adoption of a law on 29 December 1990. FT is no longer regulator and operator because regulation is now firmly under the direct supervision of Direction de la Réglementation Générale (DRG). Furthermore, an administrative council, composed of seven representatives of the state, seven union members, and seven qualified experts, now balances FT's financial decisions—particularly those pertaining to investment and tariffs—with social obligations.[84] In a measure designed to placate unions, FT employees still retain their *fonctionnaire* status, under the new regime.[85]

In contrast to British Conservatives, French Socialists appeared willing to make decisions in concertation with other groups in a way that did not quite fit previous *dirigiste* models of French policy-making. The state adopted a more conciliatory posture toward the unions that resembles, to a limited extent, the industrial democracy experiment at the British Post Office in the late 1970s. To be sure, the French government and FT's management played a key role in shaping legislation. It is also evident, however, that unions played an important consultative role rather than their usual protest style of input.[86] The French model of liberalization without privatization appeared to enjoy considerable support among members of the telecommunications community. But it wouldn't last for long!

*Preparing for a Partial Sale?*

The election of 1993 and the advent of the Center-Right coalition back to power opened yet another policy window. As a result, the new government revived the issue of FT's legal status. Just like in 1986, certain members of the Republican Party, most notably Alain Madelin, raised the issue of privatizing government monopolies such as FT. He argued that economic exigencies favored the dissolution of public monopolies and the transfer of ownership to private investors.[87] In contrast, others in the Center-Right coalition, such as Edmond Alphandéry, the current minister in charge of privatization, wanted to circumscribe the program along the lines proposed by Balladur in 1986. The final compromise resembled Darmon's proposal from the mid-1980s. It was decided that it should be pursued by the Ministry of Industry, which had acquired responsibility for supervising telecommunications. The person heading that ministry was Gérard Longuet, the same minister of telecommunications in 1986. As noted earlier, Longuet was intimately familiar with Darmon's ideas, but he had not pursued the mixed enterprise option in 1986 because he believed that liberalization would be less controversial and easier to implement.

A lot had changed since Longuet's last tenure as minister. The technical feasibility of selling FT shares was enhanced by the change of FT's status in 1991. Accounting procedures were being streamlined to more accurately reflect capital movements (additions and dispositions) and general practices in commercial enterprises. Moreover, FT continued to be highly profitable with strong demand growth potential. Liberalization was well under way despite the fact that 80 percent of FT's operations were still closed to competition. Consequently, Longuet thought the time was ripe to forge a consensus over the partial sale option.

On 19 July 1993, Longuet unveiled the government's wishes to the unions. FT would be transformed to a mixed enterprise, with the state holding onto majority equity.[88] The principal reason given by Longuet was the inability of FT to forge alliances with foreign firms. It was precisely FT's inability to acquire a stake in MCI, the U.S. telecommunications company, that provided the excuse for the proposed change. The change in status would also make it easier for FT to eventually exchange equity holdings with the German telecommunications authority, Deutsche Bundespost Telekom.[89] The announcement came as a bombshell to unions. It effectively meant that employees would lose their civil servant status and the job security that this status implied. It did not escape notice that BT's sale precipitated the departure of 70,000 employees in the period 1988–92, although FT still continues to employ fewer persons than does BT.[90] On 12 October 1993, for the first time in the PTT's history, 75 percent of FT employees staged a strike, which coincided with similar strikes against Air France. Fearing a political crisis similar to that of 1968, Balladur suspended restructuring measures at Air France and Longuet similarly "froze" his proposal for FT. Nevertheless, Longuet changed his tactics but not his mind. At the end of November, he instructed Roulet to bring the unions around and promptly rewarded him by renewing his contract as FT's director for another three years.[91] It seems that state managers and ministers have reached a consensus over the change in FT's status, but the unions have not yet agreed. Details are still sketchy but new government proposals revealed in May 1994 some major innovations. According to government officials, the state would cede 49 percent ownership in FT but it would still safeguard FT employee status as civil servants. In addition, the company would be split in half, unlike BT, with the government hanging onto local and residential services while disposing of the long-distance and international networks along with COGECOM, the holding company of FT's subsidiaries.[92] Whether such changes will take place will depend upon Roulet's skills to forge a consensus with the unions.

To sum up, the availability of privatization in the case of French telecommunications was conditioned by two elements. Unlike oil, FT's status as a government agency impaired the technical feasibility of privatization. The official change to an SOE in 1991, however, and the split from postal services made privatizing FT more likely because they established a precedent. Coupled with high profitability and strong demand growth for telecommunications services, it appears FT could attract private investors in the event of a sale. This does not mean that privatization is imminent. Value acceptability is equally important. The lack of consensus among specialists in the telecommunications community, particularly union opposition, has dampened the likelihood of privatization so far.

The case study of French telecommunications highlights three important points. First, the case points to a gradual, politically forged transformation of the policy community. In contrast to early Socialist efforts to vertically integrate services and equipment, both Socialists and the conservative coalition reversed course and embraced a policy of "controlled liberalization." The entry of companies that were previously denied a chance to compete and the emerging importance of the European Union gradually fragmented the French telecommunications community. The process of fragmentation, however, has followed an interesting path. In Britain, the telecommunications community was opened up by changing the status of unions temporarily to outsider groups. In France, the policy community was enlarged to include outsider groups without changing the status of those already inside it. Employees, for example, have not yet lost their civil servant status and continue to exercise influence through representation in the administrative council and of course strikes.

Second, in a manner similar to Britain, the boundaries between regulators and operators have become clearer and more pronounced. Unlike Britain, however, the operator is state-owned and therefore still under parliamentary scrutiny. Nevertheless, there seems to be an unmistakable trend in both countries toward forms of extraparliamentary control—regulation—and toward granting SOEs more financial and administrative autonomy.

Third, based on the British and French experiences, one can discern a cycle of ownership in telecommunications with a distinct sequence of stages. Each stage establishes a precedent that facilitates the transition to the next stage. In the beginning, the development of telecommunications is in private hands. Then ownership is likely to pass into the hands of governments, which operate telcos as government agencies. Then these agencies are granted SOE status in the hope of invigorating their commercial viability. This change may be either concurrent with a separation from postal services, as in France, or it may precede separation, as in Britain. Then comes a change in state holdings, although the French in contrast to the British will give the state majority ownership in the proposed hybrid. If the British experience is an example of things to come, however, there may be a final stage of gradual divestment that will lead to total private ownership. Although this scenario does not appear likely in France in the near future, the case of Elf Aquitaine, which was Darmon's prototype, increases the possibility that more changes may be in store for France's telecommunications company.

## Railroads: Still under State Ownership

The case of French railroads presents a pattern in the policy stream similar to French telecommunications. Like telecommunications and unlike oil, the French have not privatized Société Nationale des Chemins de fer Français (SNCF). In an interesting divergence from British railroads, privatizing SNCF was discussed neither under Chirac or Balladur nor under Socialist Prime Ministers. In this section I examine developments in the French railroads community, beginning with a brief reference to state-SOE relations prior to 1981. Then I examine in more detail the negative impact that SNCF's internal reorganization in 1982 had on privatization. Finally, I analyze the effects of the two criteria in the policy stream, technical feasibility and value acceptability, on the availability of privatization as a viable policy option.

Similarly to Britain, the French assigned to railroads the goal of helping develop the country. Unlike Britain, however, the French state took an active role early on in maintaining and operating unprofitable routes. In addition, successive governments viewed the railroads as a way to expand their influence in Europe through French civilization.[93] Nationalization in the twentieth century did not come unexpectedly. The inability of private companies to improve financial performance, tighter and deeper treasury control, and the Popular Front's advent to power in 1936 tilted the scale in favor of state ownership. The 1937 law that created SNCF had three goals: (1) unify operations for efficiency purposes; (2) help improve finances; and (3) coordinate the various modes of transport.[94] Interestingly, the newly created corporation was a mixed enterprise in which the state owned 51 percent of the stock with the option to take over the company in 1982. Despite considerable technological innovations in subsequent years, however, stiff competition from roads precipitated a sharp deterioration in company finances. Nevertheless, unlike in Britain, the state's decision in the early 1960s to use rail transport as an instrument for promoting regional growth legitimized the disbursement of generous state subsidies and SNCF's social obligations. Consequently, these precedents strengthened the case for continued state ownership when the issue arose in 1982 and dampened any serious thoughts for privatization when Chirac took over in 1986.

*SNCF Changes Status*

The mandated expiration of SNCF's legal status in 1982 presented policymakers under the tutelage of Charles Fiterman, the Communist Transport Minister at the time, with an opportunity to reexamine state-industry relations and redefine SNCF's mission. Should railroads continue to be subsidized on the rationale they provide a public service, or should they operate on a more commercial basis, emphasizing profitability and a financially determined rate of return? At a time when the British, who were facing a similar dilemma, moved in the latter direction, the French chose the former. This decision had important implications because of the precedent it established. Sanctifying the concept of public service and introducing a more flexible and democratic form of control weakened the case that Chirac could make for privatizing SNCF upon his arrival to power four years later.

Effective January 1983, SNCF's status was changed from a mixed enterprise to an industrial and commercial SOE (*établissement public à caractère industriel et commercial*). The new company was charged with operating and developing the nation's rail network in accordance with principles of public service outlined in the 1982 Transport Act. The act was based on the concept of the "right to transport," which was defined as "the right of every user to travel and the freedom to choose the mode [of transportation]."[95]

Under public service statutes, the new board consists of seven representatives of the state, five competent experts, and six staff representatives, at least one of whom would represent management. Faced with similar problems in railroads as their British counterparts, French policymakers opted for a more democratic form of public service management. Whereas British Conservatives sought to distance the state from BR by emphasizing commercial objectives and hiving off several of BR's subsidiaries, French Socialists moved in the opposite direction. The Socialists' response entailed a firm commitment to public service with generous subsidies[96] under flexible arrangements of state ownership.[97]

The 1982 law also outlined a more realistic assessment of project costs based on two methods that are still in use. Internal SNCF appraisal, on the one hand, is subject to strict commercial criteria, providing the company with the opportunity to view the project from a private firm's perspective. Another analysis, on the other hand, is carried out, taking into account social costs and benefits. For example, although the TGV (*Train à Grande Vitesse*) Bretagne has a 7.4 percent rate of financial return, it scores a 13.6 percent on a social cost-benefit analysis.[98] Use of both methods affords the French state the flexibility to take a broader view of rail policy. Whereas it can keep close track of SNCF's financial situation, the state can also choose to fund projects that will benefit the country as a whole.

SNCF's change in status served as a precedent, dampening the availability of privatization in two ways. First, it made the option less technically feasible by closing the book on the question of ownership. Whereas the expiration of the law in 1982 reopened the debate on the state's equity participation, the Socialist government at the time opted to strengthen it.[99] Second, the change made privatization less likely by granting several groups "insider" status. Although their influence is modest compared to management and the state, new actors, such as workers and subnational governments, have acquired formal powers to participate in making rail policy. In the case of a transfer of ownership, they are likely to offer stiff opposition to defend their status.

SNCF's financial health further dimmed the availability of privatization because even if members of the rail community agreed on selling SNCF, assets would not be salable. After climbing to −19.8 percent in 1983 from −5.7 percent in 1981, SNCF's profitability ratio began a steady decline and stood at −9.3 percent in 1985. In the ensuing years the situation improved dramatically, and in 1989 SNCF was able to record its first profit. The subsequent decrease of profitability, however, to 0.01 percent in 1991 and further deterioration since, coupled with a general stagnation in real total revenues, reveal the fragility of the company's financial health. Overall, the record shows that buying SNCF shares would not be a very profitable investment. This does not mean that French railroads have difficulty obtaining fresh capital. Whereas British policymakers are reluctant to back loans for their SOEs, their French counterparts share no such hesitation. Unlike BR, SNCF can borrow in capital markets on premier ratings—AAA and Aaa from Standard & Poor's and Moody's, respectively—largely because of government support. Although the guarantee was withdrawn in 1990, SNCF was still able to raise 74.3 percent of its financing needs from capital markets in 1991.[100] It is not clear, however, whether SNCF's status as an SOE was not perceived by investors as carrying implicit treasury support.

Demand growth for rail services yields mixed results (table 6.2). Rail passenger traffic, on the one hand, increased from 54,655 million passenger-kilometers (pkm) in 1980 to 59,972 million pkm in 1987, an increase of 9.7 percent in seven years. Freight transport by rail, on the other hand, has fared badly. It has been reduced substantially from 66,370 million ton-kilometers (tkm) in 1980 to 51,330 million tkm in 1987, a dramatic decrease of 22.7 percent! In contrast, roads are facing a growing demand for passengers and freight. Passenger traffic by cars and taxis increased from 452,500 million pkm in 1980 to 536,800 million pkm in 1987, an impressive increase of 18.6 percent. During the same period, freight traffic decreased somewhat, from 103.9 billion tkm in 1980 to 99.9 billion tkm in 1987, a modest reduction of 3.8 percent. It is clear from the table that rail faces stiff competition from road transport, particularly in the area of freight. This point reinforces the argument that potential private investors would be skeptical of buying shares in the nation's railroads.

*Staying on the Same Track*

Value acceptability plays an important role in influencing the availability of a given policy. Unlike other cases examined in this book, there is wide agreement among members of the French rail community to leave ownership arrangements unaltered.

Chirac's victory in 1986 opened a policy window. Privatization, however, was not an available option; in fact, it was not even proposed. Several advocates of privatization specifically excluded railroads from the list of corporations to be sold to private investors. Politicians did not suggest it, academics and researchers did not propose it, and managers did not seem eager to advocate such drastic change. Expressing the Gaullist position, Balladur explained that the principle upon which the French privatization program was based excluded enterprises that performed a public service or corporations charged with running a monopoly.[101] Therefore, privatizing SNCF was not a issue for the Gaullists.

Academics and researchers in think tanks also did not propose selling SNCF. Some, for example, argue that monopolistic corporations must not be sold.[102] There is general political agreement, they maintain, that enterprises in charge of a public-service monopoly should remain with the state. In addition, a possible sale might pose insurmountable political and financial problems. Many such enterprises are heavily subsidized; consequently, a possible sale might be complicated by the heavy debts these SOEs typically incur. Moreover, a transfer to the private sector risks creating stiff opposition by employees. For these reasons, their ownership status should not change.

TABLE 6.2. **Demand Growth of French Freight and Passenger Traffic by Rail and Road, 1980–87**

|  | 1980 | 1984 | 1985 | 1986 | 1987 |
|---|---|---|---|---|---|
| Rail |  |  |  |  |  |
| Passenger[a,b] | 54.7 | 60.4 | 62.1 | 59.9 | 60.0 |
| Freight[c] | 66.4 | 57.5 | 55.8 | 51.7 | 51.3 |
| Road |  |  |  |  |  |
| Passenger[b,d] | 452.5 | 491.7 | 494.4 | 517.3 | 536.8 |
| Freight[e] | 103.9 | 88.4 | 89.1 | 93.0 | 99.9 |

*Source*: European Conference of Ministers of Transport, *Statistical Trends in Transport, 1965–1987* (Paris: ECMT, 1990).
[a]Including road traffic with SNCF fares.
[b]Billion passenger-kilometers.
[c]Billion ton-kilometers.
[d]Figures include only cars and taxis.
[e]Figures include only vehicles less than fifteen years old with three-ton payloads or over.

In an exploratory study to find criteria that justify the existence of SOEs in several sectors, Michel Durupty also adds that social objectives are important.[103] Because SNCF achieves several such objectives as the right to transport and regional economic development, it is best that it remain under state ownership. In contrast, some question the merit of the argument that corporations performing a public service should not be privatized.[104] Why, they ask, should the taxpayer continue to fund SNCF if the service that the company offers could very well be provided by private entrepreneurs? There is, after all, a market with clients who are willing to pay a price for these services. This objection, however, misses the point of providing a public service. Although railroads are to a certain degree a natural monopoly, particularly where infrastructural projects are concerned,[105] SNCF's status is also justified partly on social and political terms. In addition to social objectives, one might include the preference of numerous French governments of both the Left and the Right to promote modes of public transport. Investment nearly doubled (in nominal terms) from 1989 to 1991.[106] Overall, the French spend more on their railroads than do the British. For instance, in 1987 France spent 16.6 percent of total transport investment on railroads, whereas Britain spent only 12.6 percent.[107] Hence, the decision of who will provide a public service is based largely on political factors.

Finally, SNCF's management does not appear interested in privatization. To be sure, some of the issues facing SNCF's management are the same as those facing their British counterparts, such as managerial autonomy, a massive deficit, and safety procedures. Yet French managers view their relations with the French state differently. SNCF tries to adapt the corporation's objectives to those of the French government. Project priorities provide a good example. When SNCF proposed extending the TGV network, the corporation's initial plan accorded priority to TGV Nord because the project would have yielded a higher financial rate of return. The French government, however, wished to extend TGV's Atlantic route because the project had enormous political and social benefits. Developing this route was seen not only as a way to attract votes—after all, 40 percent of the French population lives on the Atlantic coast—but also as an instrument of regional economic policy. Confronted with this dilemma, Jacques Rabouel, SNCF's head of planning and economic studies, responded candidly: "The second TGV line through the north would have provided a better return. But the government said 'you will do the Atlantic before that.' We have our revenue and the state has its own interest, and everybody is happy."[108] This attitude stands in stark contrast with that of BR managers. John Prideaux, director of InterCity, wondered "whether it would be possible to find a shareholder who is quite as unsympathetic to our needs as the Treasury."[109]

Turning corporate finances around is another contentious point. In contrast to the claim that privatization will bring railroads out of the red, an argument frequently made in Britain, French managers have successfully tried to turn SNCF around without the threat of a sale. First, they cut staff levels an average of 5 percent during the past decade, although the rate slowed to 2.1 percent by 1991.[110] It might also be noted that this reduction was achieved despite increases in staff levels in 1982 and 1983, which were the only increases in SNCF's post–World War II history,[111] and despite pressure brought about by a long strike at the end of 1986. Second, investment in technology via developing the TGV network gave a boost to corporate finances. Net profits from TGV service, for example, accounted for 25 percent of total revenue generated from that service in 1985.[112]

Safety requirements have strengthened consensus against privatization. Taking responsibility for a series of accidents that resulted in eighty-four deaths in the summer of 1985, Andrè Chadeau, head of SNCF, resigned. His resignation rekindled the question over railroad safety and further inhibited the availability of privatization. The reason is that cost-minded managers under private ownership presumably have a greater incentive to "cut corners" and are therefore more likely to compromise the safety of the traveling public. Despite improvements in safety procedures, a series of accidents in 1988 prompted the resignation of Philippe Rouvilois, Chadeau's successor. This time SNCF was forced to allocate FFr 4.1 billion over the next five years for improvements in safety particularly in developing systems to control speed and provide better staff training.[113] Not unlike British Rail, it was wisely decided that safety improvements should be undertaken while the corporation remained under state ownership.

In sum, the case of French railroads further illuminates the conditions that impede the availability of privatization. Although the policy's technical feasibility was enhanced by the change in the corporation's status in 1983, profitability and demand dimmed the chances of a possible sale. Value acceptability had a similar effect. Nearly all members of the rail community were in agreement that privatization did not constitute a viable alternative. Instead, they all exhibited a preference for working within the existing ownership framework.

Two conclusions emerge from the preceding discussion. First, similarly to telecommunications, the EU is assuming increasing importance. Although the liberalization measures recently adopted by EU transport ministers do not address the issue of ownership, they seek to break up national rail monopolies. Beginning in 1993, public or private train operators offering international passenger or freight services between EU countries have the right of access to in-between countries' tracks.[114] This means that SNCF will face strong competition from Italian and German railroads. Remaining under state ownership, the corporation seems prepared to face the challenge. Unlike BR, SNCF has invested heavily in high-speed trains, aiming to compete in what is normally considered the airline market. To this end, the corporation recently has received government approval to build a 4,700-kilometer (km) TGV network by the year 2010. Financed largely, though not exclusively, by state and company funds, the project will cost an estimated FFr 180 billion for infrastructure and FFr 29.5 billion for rolling stock, although investment in new TGV lines was expected to fall in real terms in the mid-1990s due to the recession.[115] Not surprisingly, SNCF currently has 15.9 percent of all passenger travel beyond 100 km in France.[116] In so far as the SOE's international aspirations are concerned, Rabouel's response summarizes them well. By the year 2000, "Europe may not be covered by TGV lines but it will be covered by TGV operations, either on new lines or on existing ones."[117] In contrast, BR is currently more concerned with projecting a healthy corporate image in light of the impending sale rather than with expanding internationally. The slow pace of electrification due to fund shortages, delays with the Channel Tunnel, and different gauge standards make an expansion beyond the British Isles highly problematic.

The second conclusion to emerge is that neither the Socialists nor Chirac's or Balladur's coalition governments have challenged the notion of public service in railroads. Unlike the British, French policymakers have sought to promote public transport, which includes rail, backing their support with generous subsidies. French rail managers, in contrast to their British counterparts, have also been able to emphasize commercial objectives while still maintaining a strong commitment to public service. Although there may be conflict among members of the rail community over pricing, investment, or wage issues, there is still substantial agreement on one point: SNCF must remain under state ownership.

### Coupling

So far, I have analyzed the effects of each stream separately. In this section I examine how the streams were joined together in critical moments in time and argue that privatization is more likely when all three streams are coupled. I also compare the French and the British experiences highlighting the effects of historical precedent and of each country's institutional structure on the process of coupling. In contrast to Britain, privatization in France is found not to be in search of a rationale.

The idea of privatization in the oil community incubated among Elf's managers and Chirac's Gaullists in the early 1980s. It must be noted, however, that there was a precedent. In 1977, the Center-Right coalition under Giscard's presidency reduced state holdings to two-thirds majority. Later, Chirac included Elf in the list of SOEs for partial privatization. Diversification plans and long-term oil contracts caused many disputes between Elf managers and their political bosses. Conflict reached a peak with the Chalandon affair. Albin Chalandon, the outspoken Elf CEO in the late 1970s and early 1980s, resigned following a dispute with then Industry Minister Laurent Fabius. At the heart of the dispute rested the Socialist plan to reorganize the chemical sector, which was a major objective of the 1982 nationalizations. Following his resignation, Elf's chair began to publicly question the usefulness of SOEs and openly advocated privatization.

The option was technically feasible because Elf's stocks were already traded on the Paris Bourse. In addition, the SOE was profitable, and given the relative inelasticity of demand for oil, policymakers could be assured of attracting private investors in the event of a sale. Hence, by the mid-1980s, the policy was available in the oil community.

Chirac's advent to Matignon in 1986 opened a policy window. It brought a receptive political audience to power. Moreover, the governing coalition viewed the government's borrowing needs as excessively high and was consequently committed to reducing them. Hence, the three streams could be easily coupled because of Chalandon's ties to the RPR—he was, after all, appointed to a ministerial position in Chirac's government. Indeed, in September 1986, 11 percent of Elf's shares were floated on the Bourse. The Center-Right coalition's victory in 1993 opened yet another window. Balladur seized the opportunity to further reduce the state's equity in Elf. Encouraged by Mitterrand's minor sale of Elf shares in 1992 and the dramatic deterioration of the government's finances that year, Balladur was able to couple the three streams once again in 1993 and included Elf in the privatization program with the aim of almost total divestiture.

The case of telecommunications presents an example of partial coupling. The legislative election of 1986 opened a policy window by bringing a receptive political audience to power. Moreover, the problem stream was equally ripe because the government's borrowing burden was thought to be high. Privatization of France Télécom, however, was not forthcoming. Why? The answer rests with the inability to couple the three streams, because the policy was not available in the telecommunications community. Although the agency was highly profitable, it still remained part of a government ministry. In contrast to Britain, there was no precedent to facilitate privatization, so the debate focused on creating a corporate entity and on splitting postal from telecommunications services. Privatization also did not enjoy wide support among members of the telecommunications community. Thus, there were few individuals or groups willing to invest the time and resources to couple the three streams.

The 1993 legislative elections opened yet another policy window. This time the new industry minister, Gérard Longuet, proposed the partial sale of the state's equity in FT, but he was unable to forge a consensus in the policy stream. Although the problem and politics streams were ripe for a sale, the policy stream was not. Consequently, the streams could not be coupled.

Railroads also present an example of partial coupling. SNCF remains under state ownership, and the process of coupling in this case resembles that of French telecommunications. Despite the windows of opportunity that opened in 1986 and 1993, the three streams were not joined. Once again technical feasibility presented serious difficulties. Unlike FT, however, the problem with SNCF is profitability and weak demand, particularly for freight services. The SOE is generally unprofitable and heavily subsidized, and hardly any individuals or groups in the railroads community proposed privatizing SNCF. The option thus was not available when Chirac or Balladur came to power, and the streams could not be coupled.

Chirac's unsuccessful bid for the presidency also illustrates the temporary nature of policy windows. As Kingdon maintains, windows open for a short period of time. In this case, privatization lasted for only two years (1986–88), although the law envisioned a program spanning a five-year period. Mitterrand's reelection to the French presidency in 1988 and the consequent dissolution of Chirac's governing coalition closed the window. Although the problem and policy streams remained relatively unchanged, politicians were no longer committed to the policy of privatization; hence, there was no opportunity to couple the three streams, and the program was discontinued. The same can be said for the window that opened in 1993. The law envisions a privatization program that will last for at least four more years. Nevertheless, the coming presidential elections in 1995 might bring to power another Socialist president (Mitterrand has said he will not seek reelection). In this case, the streams might not be coupled and Balladur's program will be ceased. The reverse outcome—that is, a victory for a member of the Center-Right coalition currently in power—suggests an opportunity for uninterrupted coupling. In that case, the program is likely to continue.

The multiple streams model has proven useful in explaining the process of privatization in France. The process of coupling, however, was found to work somewhat differently than Kingdon originally suggested, and the comparative nature of the study has helped to identify some of these differences. There are certain institutional features of countries that facilitate coupling. During the first privatization wave in 1986–88, Chirac was able to achieve more than Thatcher had achieved in her first seven years in office. The reason rests with two legal instruments available to French policymakers.[118] First, legislation enabling sales in 1986 and in 1993 took the form of *loi d'habilitation*. This provision permits the government to ask parliament to delegate it authority to rule by regulation (*ordonnance*) for a certain period of time in an issue, in this case privatization, that may cover many industries. In essence, this process limits debate and avoids the emergence of divisions of opinion among the majority in public. In contrast, British Prime Ministers do not have such powers to facilitate coupling of streams in diverse industries under one law. Consequently, the privatization process has been longer and more acrimonious in Britain as each sale has been debated on its own merit. In addition, to further limit debate and hence facilitate the process of forging a consensus in the policy stream and the coupling of streams, French Prime Ministers can declare a bill an issue of confidence (article 49, paragraph 3 of the constitution). The bill will be considered adopted unless the opposition can vote a motion of censure within forty-eight hours, which risks the dissolution of parliament by the president. Both Chirac and Balladur adopted this provision to limit debate and ensure adoption of privatization.[119] In contrast, the absence of such powers in Britain can lead to a more tumultuous coupling process, one that is more prone to amendments and outright opposition among members of the majority party, as the case of railroads amply demonstrates.

The sequence of coupling also seems to be different in the two countries. In contrast to Britain, privatization in France does not appear to be in search of a rationale. Why? Part of the explanation rests with historical precedent. Mitterrand's nationalizations in 1982 conveniently provided Chirac with the rationale that bringing more SOEs into the public sector represented a drain to the public purse. The Socialist nationalizations also gave the opposition an issue that could distinguish their platform in 1986 from the Socialist one. Having been beaten to the punch by Socialists—who since 1983 had partially reversed their expansionary policies in several areas, such as tax reforms, price and credit decontrol, and deregulation of capital markets—Chirac's coalition focused on privatization as a way of offering voters a real alternative.[120] The 1982 nationalizations also enabled the Gaullists to politically distance themselves from state ownership by blaming the Socialists for whatever ills the Socialist policies had created and shifting attention away from the fact that some problems, such as the state bourgeoisie, were actually inherited from the Gaullist past. In contrast, British Conservatives did not have the luxury of such a focus. Consequently, they were forced to search for a rationale.

In addition, the degree of fragmentation affects the sequence of coupling. Unlike Britain, France maintains a centralized decision-making apparatus with a highly disciplined and educationally cohesive state bureaucracy.[121] Policy communities are normally tilted in favor of the state, and interest groups tend to protest past decisions rather than bargain to influence new ones. The relative lack of fragmentation makes the process of policy formation more consequential because fewer actors raise issues and define problems. Indeed, the French privatization experience appears to validate this explanation. In contrast to the British case, French unions were marked by their absence from the privatization debate. In addition, the fact that all the industrial groups for sale were in competitive sectors made it easier to justify a sale. Furthermore, unlike Britain, privatization in France has been entrusted to one cabinet member, the finance minister.[122] The absence of internal dissent between the treasury and sponsoring ministries further facilitated the adoption of a clearly articulated rationale. In addition, the fact that privatization was a major campaign issue in France—much more so in 1986 than in 1993—forced politicians to develop fairly well-articulated objectives concerning their proclaimed intention to take such a bold step. In other words, politicians had to communicate to the public why they wanted to privatize before they could pass enabling legislation. That was not the case in Britain, where it took almost four years to develop a coherent rationale for the policy as a whole.[123] In sum, historical precedent and institutional structure conditioned the process of coupling, making French privatization a policy responding to a well-articulated rationale.

Another explanation of this difference could be constructed if one were to view privatization as part of the process of policy diffusion.[124] Inarguably, the French were intimately familiar with developments across the English Channel,[125] and given that the British happened to privatize first, it may seem as if the French simply later borrowed a rationale that their British counterparts struggled to formulate some years ago. Although this argument is not without merit, upon closer inspection it loses much of its validity. Certainly, memoranda on the British experience circulated widely in the Ministry of Finance, and several British consultants were dispatched to Paris to help lay the groundwork.[126] The evidence, however, suggests that the British were intimately involved in the technical aspects of the implementation phase of the French sales and not in the more political process of formulating a sound basis for privatization. Similarly, success across the Channel partly helped shape political rhetoric, but it did not provide an alternative rationale that the French could not have arrived at independently. The success of the British case simply "greased the wheels" by providing additional impetus for adopting privatization because it revealed the policy's political expediency: selling SOEs on a large scale could be done successfully with major economic and political benefits accruing to the governing party. In contrast, the debate over Mitterrand's wisdom to nationalize several companies in 1981–82 provided the anti-Socialist coalition with the rationale that reversing the tide was preferable, given prevalent economic and budgetary conditions at the time. It is notable that Chirac's promise to privatize came as early as 1981, long before the British were able to formally articulate a coherent rationale for privatization.[127] Consequently, the British experience was used to partly facilitate the adoption and help implement the policy rather than to formulate a rationale for selling SOEs.

## Conclusion

Similarly to Britain, the multiple streams approach is useful in France. The availability of alternatives generated in policy communities influenced the likelihood of privatization. In communities in which privatization was found to be technically feasible and a fairly wide consensus existed, the chances that privatization might be adopted were enhanced dramatically. High government borrowing needs also had an effect on privatization because higher borrowing needs led to increasing calls for privatization. Finally, party politics made a difference. Privatization was brought about by Chirac's anti-Socialist coalition, but following Mitterrand's reelection to a second term in office and the consequent dissolution of Chirac's governing coalition, the program was interrupted. In addition, the *dirigiste* tradition of the Gaullist party and political strategy limited the scope of privatization to reversing primarily, though not exclusively, the Socialist nationalizations of 1982. Following a sweeping electoral victory in 1993, a new Gaullist Prime Minister, Edouard Balladur, revived and expanded the 1986–88 program.

When all three streams were coupled, privatization was the end result. Chirac's election as prime minister in 1986 opened a policy window. Privatization was an available option in the oil community. The policy also found a receptive governing audience and was attached to a problem, the government's borrowing needs, that was perceived to be pressing at the time. Similarly to Britain, privatization was the final outcome in the case of oil, although it was partial in 1986 and almost total in 1994. The cases of telecommunications and railroads, however, followed a different pattern. Although the problem and political streams were ripe in 1986, the policy was not available in either the telecommunications or railroads communities. Hence, in contrast to the British, the French did not privatize the telecommunications operator, although the advent of the Center-Right coalition in 1993 has raised the possibility of a partial sale. Moreover, they kept railroads under state ownership.

The process of coupling, however, was not found to be in the hypothesized direction. In contrast to the British case, privatization in France is not a policy in search of a rationale. Why? I offered two reasons. First, historical precedent, and more specifically the 1982 nationalizations, provided a convenient rationale for the anti-Socialist coalition. Second, the degree of fragmentation affects coupling; less-fragmented policy communities and polities are less likely to produce policies in search of a rationale. The institutional features of the French political system and historical precedent are offered as amendments to Kingdon's framework, showing that privatization, in some instances, is not in search of a rationale.

The French case also highlights the political nature of privatization. Just as in the British case, policy communities are opened up and new actors become involved. Particularly instructive is the process of "controlled liberalization" in telecommunications, by which consortia of French and foreign companies are now allowed to compete with France Télécom for the provision of certain services. Equally important is the role of the European Union. Although not proposing the privatization of SOEs, it has successfully pressured national governments to liberalize certain sectors, such as telecommunications and railroads, and has helped establish precedents that may facilitate possible sales in the future.

In addition, political influence is likely to continue in SOEs and the newly privatized companies. Unlike British ones, French SOEs running monopolies or performing a public service were not sold. Although regulatory commissions were set up in some sectors, such as telecommunications, the operators retained their SOE status. Hence, political control in these corporations remains primarily in the form of ownership. Control in newly privatized SOEs, however, has taken a different path. Despite their composition being altered by the Socialists in the late 1980s, the interlocking corporate relationships created by stable nuclei enable the state to exercise control by proxy ownership. Although the state does not directly own the companies, it maintains an interest through SOEs that are part-owners. Such relationships, particularly between banks and SOEs, were also encouraged by the Socialists in the early 1990s and have been reinvigorated by Balladur since 1993. French privatization suggests that political control in privatized companies is likely to continue, albeit in different form.

# Part 4
# Arrival

Ithaki gave you the nice journey,
without her you would not have made it.
... And if you find her without riches,
she has not deceived you;
having acquired so much wisdom,
by now you must have realized
what Ithaki is all about.

CHAPTER 7

# Conclusion

The aim of this study has been to illuminate the process of policy formation by providing an answer to the puzzling question of why industrialized democracies privatize. Privatization in Britain and France, I have argued, has been brought about by the interplay of three factors or streams in critical moments in time: (1) the availability of alternatives generated in policy communities, (2) budgetary constraints imposed by high government borrowing needs, and (3) the governing party's ideology and strategy. Election outcomes open policy windows and present opportunities for politicians to raise issues and join the three streams. Privatization is more likely to be adopted when all three streams are coupled.

The findings have significant policy implications, but they also go beyond policy concerns and address broader theoretical questions in political economy. In this concluding chapter, I first discuss policy implications for Kingdon's model and the broader multiple streams approach, and then I address theoretical questions concerning the relationship between states and markets and the future of state ownership.

## Amendments to Kingdon's Argument

The findings suggest that Kingdon's model, and in fact the logic of the multiple streams approach, can be fruitfully utilized beyond Kingdon's narrow focus of concern of agenda setting in the United States. The model is a useful analytical tool of the entire process of policy formation (agenda setting and decision making) across several sectors in various countries. Nevertheless, the findings point to several amendments to Kingdon's argument.

In contrast to Kingdon, the present study underscores the primary importance of the governing party (or coalition) in raising issues and shaping public policy. This difference is not at all surprising given the relatively weak role of parties in American politics, but the finding is significant in light of recent controversy in comparative politics over the impact of parties in public policy.[1] Some parties are more receptive to certain ideas than others. The British case aptly illustrates the point. Electoral defeat and the coal miners' strike were the catalysts for a major reappraisal of Conservative ideology in the

175

mid-1970s concerning the economic role of the state. Particularly illuminating of Conservative attitude toward SOEs are John Moore's words: "We were convinced a major cause [of economic decline] was the extent of government control over industry, because we saw then what the collapse of socialism has now made so apparent: state-owned industries will *always* perform poorly."[2] Given such hostility, privatization came as no surprise. While Conservatives were looking for ways to curb the expanding public sector, Labourites, expressing union sentiment, advocated further nationalization. As a result, had Labour won the 1979 election, Britoil would certainly not have been sold. Equally revealing are Labour's pledges to renationalize. It is quite obvious that BT would still be an SOE had Thatcher lost the 1983 or the 1987 elections.

The French case further strengthens the argument. Chirac made privatization one of the most important aspects of his legislative election campaign in 1986. During the campaign, he committed himself to an extensive program of privatization. Socialists, on the other hand, argued against the policy. Given their record until 1986, it is highly unlikely that they would have initiated a program resembling Chirac's privatization. More poignantly, the impact of parties is clearly seen in the outcome of the 1988 presidential election. Mitterrand's return to office for a second term effectively meant the dissolution of Chirac's coalition government. In his campaign, Mitterrand promised to interrupt Chirac's privatization program, and following reelection to the presidency, he kept his promise. In other words, a change in governing parties not only catapulted new issues to the top of the government's agenda, but it also resulted in a change in policy. Balladur's current tenure in office and his privatization program further reinforce the point.

Having said this, I hasten to add that though parties are necessary, they are hardly sufficient determinants of policy choice; where there is a will, there is not necessarily a way. Budgetary considerations impede or facilitate the likelihood that certain policies will be adopted. Indeed, privatization appears to be partially rooted in the widening gap between public expenditures and revenues that was felt in the 1970s and has been exacerbated since then. In times of high economic growth and increasing government revenues, funding SOEs does not appear to be a pressing problem. When government revenues start to dry up, however, or when budget deficits are perceived as unacceptably high, the appeal of privatization increases. Selling SOEs not only takes companies off government books, but it also provides handsome returns for the treasury and gives them access to new sources of funds. It is not surprising, therefore, to find treasury officials in both countries to be some of the most fervent advocates of privatization. In this vein, dichotomies presenting privatization either as ideological or as pragmatic are of limited analytical utility. In so far as the question "Why privatize?" is concerned, the ideology of governing officials does not somehow cloud the real issue; rather, it helps define it, and in this sense it becomes part of the issue. But ideology by itself cannot determine policy choice; some dose of pragmatism, in this case budgetary considerations, is an essential element of the policy-making process. To use the theoretical terms employed in this study, the political stream is important, but the logic of policy choice suggests that solutions be attached to pressing problems. Pragmatism and ideology are therefore not mutually exclusive, but complementary, factors.

Still, policy choice involves more. Competition by alternative options in the policy stream also makes a big difference. Indeed, in line with Kingdon's expectations, in policy communities where privatization is not considered a technically feasible option and where there is no consensus among specialists, privatization is not the final choice. Yet, the findings suggest that the policy stream may operate somewhat differently than Kingdon claims. First, there is not necessarily a long period of "softening up." Ideas do not have to be debated in policy communities for a long time before they receive serious consideration by policy makers. To be sure, the case of privatization in Britain supports Kingdon's claim. Privatizing BR or British Steel are solutions hotly debated in Britain since World War II. The steel denationalization-renationalization cycle in the 1950s and 1960s is a good example of this process. In addition, the spillover of ideas from one sector to the next was also anticipated by Kingdon. The case of BT aptly illustrates the point because privatizing BT was a solution that did not "bubble up" from within the telecommunications community, but instead spilled over from other sectors onto the agenda.

The French case, however, yields mixed results. Privatization was not part of a long-standing debate. As I showed in part 3, until the late 1970s, France had maintained some form of consensus across the political spectrum on the utility and desirability to nurture and strengthen "national champions" in various sectors. With the exception of mass communication and oil, privatization arose as an issue largely in the 1980s. The question previously was whether to expand the public sector, not whether to contract it. Clearly, a country's historical experience with state ownership affects the policy stream and the duration of "softening up." An additional explanation for this cross-national difference is the diverse makeup of policy communities. British policy communities tend to include many actors and provide relatively open access for many groups to influence impending decisions. In contrast, French communities are more tightly knit, unions do not play as big a role, and the state agencies tends to feature more prominently in the process. Given these structural features and *pantouflage,* the French version of the revolving door, it is easier to maintain consensus over the desirability of SOEs, and more difficult for the state to be convinced to give up ownership and relinquish control of its enterprises.

Second in pointing out how policy stream operation differs from King-don's theory, although efficiency and equity are important, the process of arriving at some form of consensus in the policy communities is explicitly political.[3] Governments choose to listen to some groups—for example, equipment manufacturers—but not others—for instance, unions. Moreover, support for particular policies may be politically created by replacing (fortuitously or not) key actors in the policy community, such as SOE managers. The British telecommunications community, for example, was widened to incorporate equipment manufacturers but contracted to exclude unions. The end result was a structural transformation of the community, which in turn altered, at least temporarily, the makeup of consensus. The ability to differentiate between liberalization and privatization, however, led to different results in France. Although in both cases the communities were enhanced to also include regulatory authorities in order to increase corporate accountability, the configuration of the French community did not involve a loss of "insider" status. This finding raises a key point. In contrast to liberalization, privatization involves winners and losers; it is a zero-sum policy. The biggest losers are unions. The French decision to liberalize without a sale—though a partial sale has recently been proposed—shows that the structure of policy communities can be altered with minimal political cost.

Moreover, managerial support for a particular option can also be politically extracted. The case of BNOC is instructive. Consensus was achieved partially by replacing key state managers. Lord Kearton, still BNOC chair when Thatcher came to power in 1979, was adamantly opposed to the idea of privatization. Given the important role that managers play in the process, privatization would have been a difficult task to accomplish without management's support. Consensus was reached after Kearton's retirement with a politically appointed successor who was more receptive to the idea of privatization. A similar phenomenon can be seen in France. When Chirac and Balladur took over Matignon in 1986 and 1993, respectively, they replaced many, though not all, top state managers. As I showed in part 3, the majority of these replacements not only had close ties with the Gaullist party, but many were intimately involved in designing the French privatization program. This fact casts doubt over the claim by some privatization advocates that state managers are eager to break the "shackles" that bind them to the state.[4] To be sure, some managers share this conviction, but others clearly do not. It can safely be concluded, then, that the process of reaching a consensus in both countries was to a large extent politically forged.

Considering each stream separately is important, but it does not provide a complete picture of the whole process. I have argued that the chances that privatization will be adopted are increased when all three streams are coupled or joined at critical moments in time. The process of coupling, however, was found to differ across countries, making privatization in some instances a policy in search of a rationale.

Conventional perspectives of policy formation at the national level view the process as problem-driven—that is, they assume a problem-solution sequence. Both the rational, comprehensive perspective and incrementalism assume that solutions are the result of a careful and relatively clear definition of problems. Policies are designed as responses to specific problems. Whether all possible solutions are considered or only a few that deviate only marginally from previous practice, the problem-solution sequence is inherent.

Kingdon, on the other hand, suggests that the reverse is often true: that policy-making is frequently solution-driven.[5] In contrast to what March and Olsen call the logic of consequential action, policies often are in search of a rationale. When policy windows open, specialists in policy communities try to take advantage of the political climate by attaching a problem to their pet solution. In other words, privatization is not likely to develop as a response to a specific problem. Rather, policy entrepreneurs often develop solutions first and then actively seek out problems that policies might conceivably solve. As March and Olsen put it, "despite the dictum that you cannot find the answer until you have formulated the question well, you often do not know what the public policy question is until you know the answer."[6]

Yet, the logic of timing built into the multiple streams approach does not necessitate that one come before the other. To the contrary, the very conceptualization of independent streams suggests that both sequences could be appropriate at different times. But under what conditions might this be true? The findings here show that historical and institutional features in different countries structure the process of coupling, making one combination more likely than the other. Although privatization in Britain evolved as a policy in search of a rationale, the reverse is true in France. As I explained in chapter 6, Mitterrand's nationalizations in 1982 conveniently provided Chirac with the rationale that bringing more SOEs into the public sector represented a drain of the public purse and therefore selling them was a good idea. Balladur's more recent sales drew inspiration from Chirac's program. In fact, it is no coincidence that Balladur was the minister entrusted with selling SOEs in Chirac's government in 1986. In contrast, British Conservatives lacked such a focus. Consequently, the arrival of a problem prior to formulating a solution depends on historical circumstances. Moreover, the degree of fragmentation affects coupling. A lack of fragmentation, as was witnessed in France, makes the policy-formation process more consequential because fewer actors raise issues and define problems. In short, the findings here refine

180     Markets, States, and Public Policy

the multiple streams argument by illuminating the process of coupling and by specifying the conditions that affect the problem-solution sequence. In addition to historical circumstances, the degree of fragmentation affects coupling; more fragmented policy communities and polities are more likely to produce policies in search of a rationale.

Finally, the model adopted in this study informs and in some instances goes beyond conventional models of comparative politics. Some argue that technology is the determinant variable behind policy choice. Technological imperatives, such scholars maintain, are the major factors explaining changes in industry structure and regulatory environment in such rapidly changing industries as telecommunications.[7] The findings here suggest that such a model of policy formation is clearly inappropriate. Even in sectors with rapid technological change, such as telecommunications, that variable by itself cannot account for the wide variety of policy outputs observed in different countries. Clearly policies are not made in political vacuums; rather, the particular mix of historical circumstances, policy instruments, and institutional arrangements that differ across countries and sectors structure the policy formation process, facilitating the adoption of some options and impeding that of others.[8] Still, the argument made here goes beyond such traditional explanations.

Although the model shares the concerns of explanations that emphasize history and institutions, some of its features help further enrich the understanding of comparative policy-making. To begin with, the conceptualization of different policy and political streams addresses levels-of-analysis concerns. It brings together sectoral events and broader political developments in a coherent and theoretically meaningful way.[9] The model acknowledges the importance of developments in separate policy communities, but it also maintains that their effects should not be separated from their broader political context. This helps eschew the perennial search for the strength of the state by focusing attention on the particular circumstances within which policies are made.[10] Seemingly weak states, for example, such as Britain, may exhibit strong state behavior depending on timing and the country-specific circumstances in each stream—such as the ideological fervor of the governing party, its ability to forge some form of consensus in the policy stream, the problem(s) of the day, and the ability to couple the three streams at opportune times. Thatcher's Conservatives certainly exhibited such ability in regards to privatization, although Major's current government may prove to be less (or more) capable. This point also takes us beyond structurally determined policy styles, be they consultative, consensual, or heroic.[11] Although there are structural features specific to polities and policy communities, policy-making also depends on transient participants, including political appointees such as ministers in the policy and political streams. The fact that Thatcher and other like-minded Conservatives happened to be at the helms of authority during the 1980s, for example, influenced not only the types of policies to be pursued, but also the way policies would be made. It is doubtful that Heath would have pursued privatization with the same rigor. Similarly, Major has shown less enthusiasm for privatization than did his former mentor and predecessor, Margaret Thatcher. Consequently, transient political actors, including those not directly involved in narrow policy communities, can alter in significant ways "customary" patterns of policy-making, at least temporarily. National styles of policy-making, therefore, are more ephemeral and context-specific than previously estimated.

To an extent, the aforementioned argument also addresses Gary Freeman's hypothesis that policies are more likely to converge in the same sector across countries rather than across sectors within the same country. In so far as his hypothesis refers to policy outputs, the study yields mixed results. Limited convergence seems to cut across countries occurring mostly in sectors where competition is the norm, such as oil. In sectors where companies are charged with public service obligations, however, there is considerable variation. As I will discuss at length, policies in industries such as telecommunications and railroads are more influenced by national rather than sectoral conceptions of public service. However, the validity of this conclusion is somewhat limited in light of the single-issue focus of this study and the fact that it refers only to those sectors that are economic in character and not those that include a heavy social component, such as health or education.

Finally, the incorporation of the policy stream and its explicit attention to the evolution of solutions over time and across policy communities provide comparativists with an analytical tool to examine the effects that past policies have on current debates in different national settings. This gives the model a certain sensitivity to differences and similarities in historical trajectories across sectors and countries in an analytically useful way. Furthermore, the notion of coupling gives the model a dynamic quality that differentiates it from the determinism associated with conventional structural explanations or structurally determined policy styles. Coupling suggests that the effects of each stream are not additive; rather, the specific coupling of all three streams at the same time makes the adoption of one policy more likely than another. Moreover, policies can change considerably and even be reversed as a result of different combinations of problems, solutions, and politics. The fact that coupling takes place when policy windows open reduces the risk of determinism without compromising the robust political logic that permeates policy choice. This is not to suggest that policy formation is haphazard, but rather that serendipity and politics are integral elements of the same process.

## States, Markets, and the Future of State Ownership

In this study I have sought to explain why two industrialized democracies, Britain and France, have sought to privatize state assets. Beyond policy concerns, the decision to transfer state ownership to private hands also raises important substantive issues in political economy. First, in the process of privatizing and in its capacity as the guardian of the "family silver," the state acts as a bad fiduciary agent by selling the winners and keeping the losers. Second, privatization involves a politically forged decision to shape the configuration of markets not so much by relinquishing control, but rather by foregoing instruments of direct in favor of indirect control.

### Selling the Family Silver: The Champions and the Lemons

Cynics argue that privatization is nothing more than just sound and fury. Pierre Bérégovoy, the former Prime Minister, epitomizes the cynic view: "[T]he opposition demands that we privatize enterprises in which the State is the primary shareholder. If they are losers, who will buy them? . . . And if they are winners, why should we privatize them?"[12] To the contrary, cynics are wrong in claiming that governments cannot sell the lemons, and they simply will not sell the champions.[13] The findings here suggest that financially healthy corporations operating in sectors with strong demand growth are likely candidates for privatization. Indeed, the case of oil in both Britain and France confirms this claim. Both BNOC and Elf Aquitaine were profitable SOEs facing a relatively strong demand. Similarly, the inclusion of mostly profitable SOEs in Balladur's program in 1993 that were not included in 1986, such as Renault, further reinforces the point. Telecommunications, on the other hand, provides the exception that actually strengthens this claim; not every winner is up for sale. Despite exemplary performance in a sector with growing demand, FT remains under state ownership. Similarly, not all losers are "safe." After lengthy negotiations, the French treasury managed to sell the ailing CGCT. Moreover, the British government sold ailing SOEs such as British Airways and British Steel, although it must be noted that their finances were first turned around under state management. Perhaps this will be the case with current French candidates for sale, such as Aérospatiale and Air France. Nevertheless, the overall record suggest that winners are more likely candidates for privatization than are losers.

Herein lies the irony of privatization: it is a self-fulfilling prophecy. Selling principally champions and leaving lemons to the public sector perpetuates the myth of the inept entrepreneurial state and accentuates the "need" for more sales. The lack of winners and the presence of losers will sustain, and in some instances even exacerbate, the government's borrowing needs.

Faced with adverse budgetary pressures, governments are likely to continue viewing privatization as a viable option. Contrary to those who view privatization as an ideological fad, the findings here suggest that given present adverse fiscal conditions, pressures for more sales will persist.

The key to understanding this paradox lies in party politics and the mechanics of coupling. Being the guardian of the family silver, the state maintains a portfolio of assets that includes both winners and losers. Sound financial advice would probably suggest to "get rid of the bad apples," to minimize losses. In this case, however, in order to keep privatization floating above other options in the policy stream and consequently facilitate coupling, the state acts as a bad fiduciary agent because it discriminates against itself by maximizing losses and minimizing benefits—that is, by selling winners and keeping losers. Because policy windows are temporary, establishing a precedent and demonstrating early success is crucial. To do that, the governing party chooses to sell precisely those SOEs that are the exact opposite of what official rhetoric claims the public sector to be. Privatization is more likely to be successful when: (1) it is easiest to implement and (2) it will attract the strongest private interest. SOEs that operate in sectors already exposed to competition and those that are financially healthy and face strong demand growth fit this description. They avoid sticky regulatory issues, present fewer valuation problems, and are more likely to widen share ownership by attracting higher numbers of small investors. They are precisely, however, the companies that might generate the most income, and consequently benefits, for the state; if they are such good investments for private entrepreneurs, why aren't they good enough for the state? Success feeds off itself and is used as additional justification for further sales. SOEs that operate as monopolies may follow, depending on a country's historical experience with state ownership and the ideology of the governing party. Viewed in this way, policy choice becomes a question of momentum, which makes the role of the governing party in pushing (or not pushing) for privatization even more crucial.

State Ownership and Control

Does privatization aim to roll back the frontiers of the state? Does it signify, as its supporters maintain, the retreat of the state? Far from rolling back the frontiers of the state, the findings suggest that political influence is likely to continue, not because privatization has been derailed from its original objectives, but because maintaining some form of political influence was part of its original design. In this sense, privatization is a politically forged decision to shape the configuration of markets by foregoing direct control (ownership) in favor of indirect control (hybrid and regulation).[14] The form and intensity of political control, however, vary across sectors and countries.[15] Still, the decision to sell involves more. The ability of SOEs in certain countries to deliver the goods and services they promised as well as to provide a public service—at a substantial cost, to be sure—supplies a rationale for maintaining some or perhaps adjusting the ownership composition of others. These ideas pose a challenge to reformulate the state-versus-market debate and reassess the utility of state ownership in search of novel forms of economic organization that will ultimately serve the public interest.

Privatization entails a divorce of ownership and control. Although public ownership was initially proposed as a means of increasing worker control of the means of production, SOEs later became an instrument of capturing the "commanding heights" of the economy. Since World War II, for many politicians state ownership was the most visible manifestation of a deliberate attempt to subordinate markets to state control. Although privatization reverses this relationship, it does not aim at strengthening one at the expense of the other; it merely substitutes a direct and very visible instrument of control for indirect and less visible ones.

The new approach in Britain contains two elements. First, although the remaining state shares have subsequently been or are scheduled to be sold, the laws enabling privatization called, at least until 1984, for hybrid solutions. In both Britoil and BT, the state continued to be the largest shareholder, albeit in minority position. Such hybrid arrangements include considerable scope for continuing government influence while they have the added benefit of taking the companies off the government's books. Although the government has given up control of BT's daily operations, it is hard to imagine a hybrid or even a private BT at the brink of bankruptcy. Moreover, it is difficult to see how loans to enterprises in which the state was the sole or majority owner could be perceived in capital markets as being guaranteed by the Treasury but loans to hybrids could not. If state ownership does not matter, why not pursue total divestiture? Granted, the number of hybrids in Britain is by now virtually nil, but why wasn't such a policy pursued from the beginning? The answer is that hybrids are, at least partially, designed to give private investors a sense of confidence based on the rationale that the state will not let enterprises in which it has a large stake fail. The state may no longer be the sole owner, but it remains the largest stakeholder. Mixed enterprises, however, necessitate that the state be viewed as a shareholder "just like the others." As I argued in part 2, the British have historically not viewed the role of the state in such terms. Besides, Conservative ideology in the 1980s precluded using state ownership in this way. Consequently, the creation of hybrids was temporary and politically expedient. Once Conservatives gained confidence and experience from previous sales, they sold the remaining shares. Indeed, a large portion of the remaining government shares in BT, one of the last and largest hybrids, were sold off in 1991 and 1993. Second, Conservatives in Britain appear eager to adopt a framework of regulated, privately owned utilities. Government control by regulation illustrates the desire, on the one hand, to shed the political liability of being perceived by the public as being responsible for both economic performance and accountability without, on the other hand, giving up total control. The state still plays a role in protecting the consumer and enforcing the rules of the game.

Although the French case differs somewhat, the conclusion is the same. The participation of many SOEs in the stable nuclei reveal Chirac's and Balladur's determination to exercise influence in the newly privatized companies in the form of proxy rather than direct ownership. Moreover, the presence of state financial institutions as shareholders is a clever way of providing SOEs with access to state capital without high public visibility. Whereas the French state is no longer the sole or even the principal owner in these companies, it remains a financially important partner. What emerges, therefore, is the realization that the new institutional arrangements in both countries do not preclude state intervention. They simply substitute a direct instrument of control—ownership—for indirect ones—hybrid, proxy ownership, and regulation.

The issue of privatization also involves a redefinition of the public interest and a reorientation of the concept of public service. Enterprises were first brought into the public sector partly on the belief that only state ownership could safeguard the public interest in certain industries. Nevertheless, it quickly became obvious that the public interest was not only ambiguous, but also politically expedient. This is particularly true of SOEs charged with providing a public service, such as telecommunications and railroads. The twin objectives of commercial viability and social responsibility were not clearly distinguishable, despite numerous attempts to differentiate between them. It is not surprising, therefore, that privatization reflects a calculated political decision to separate the two and emphasize commercial objectives while it redefines social responsibilities. In some instances, the debate is framed as an either-or dilemma. The decision to privatize BT, for example, aimed in part at steering the SOE toward more commercial objectives, such as profitability. It was as if BT could not fulfill its commercial mission without being absolved of some social responsibilities. Increasing international competition further reinforced this conviction, although total removal of social responsibility was judged to be counterproductive. Ensuring BT's compliance with certain obligations, such as maintaining sometimes unprofitable rural services, was entrusted to Oftel, a new regulatory authority. Paradoxically, this separation of ownership forced the government to make its public service obligations more explicit by formalizing monitoring and compliance systems, such as Oftel.

In other countries, however, such as France, public service and commercial viability are viewed as complementary rather than conflicting goals. In these cases, state ownership still has an important role to play. The debate over FT illustrates the point. The question that has plagued successive French governments has been how to maintain a financially healthy telecommunications authority in the face of keen international competition without sacrificing social responsibility.[16] In other words, the question is one of balance, not sacrifice. The decision to liberalize telecommunications—that is, change FT's status to an SOE, reduce statutory barriers to entry in many services, create a regulatory authority, and embark on a major internal reorganization—show that the road to competitiveness and social responsibility does not necessarily entail private ownership.

Moreover, in cases in which the state has a stronger tradition of providing public services, pressures to privatize are less likely to build. The different ways in which Britain and France treat their railroads demonstrate the point. First, there may be constitutional constraints that may inhibit sales in certain sectors. Although it does not specifically mention railroads, the preamble to the 1945 French Constitution by way of incorporation into the 1958 Constitution precluded thoughts of privatizing SOEs that may have been construed as providing a public service. In addition, the Socialist government's announcement that access to rail constitutes part of every French citizen's "right to transport" further legitimized state ownership and made it even more difficult for Chirac's coalition to justify a sale. Finally, the railroads in France have assumed a developmental role in the postwar period that contrasts sharply with the British view. The deliberate differentiation between social and commercial criteria in estimating returns on new projects reveals the French state's explicit sensitivity to noncommercial objectives. Moreover, the development of the TGV network throughout France shows that SNCF is used as an instrument of regional development. Constructing the northeastern route, for example, was made a priority because of social and political goals. In fact, the French state quite explicitly imposes these obligations on SNCF that extend the company's mission beyond its commercial viability, and in return the state undertakes the responsibility to compensate SNCF by granting it a certain degree of monopoly, subsidizing some routes, and providing considerable capital for investments.[17]

The blatant use of SNCF for developmental aims and generous state subsidies contrasts sharply with BR's predicament. Faced with a Treasury determined to reduce its public service payment to the railroads, BR was forced in the 1980s to concentrate on improving its short-term finances at the expense of long-term investment. It is precisely the weakness of a public service tradition that has enabled the British rail community to entertain thoughts of privatizing BR. This point helps explain the differences in rail policy between the two countries; the British have not sold BR intact because they can't,[18] whereas the French have not privatized SNCF because they don't want to.

### A Caveat

Finally, a caveat is appropriate to the argument. The model presented here deals only with domestic factors affecting the policy process. External factors—in this case, the integration of Europe—may affect privatization in significant ways. Because of the time frame, the analysis did not find that the EU played an important role in indirectly bringing privatization about. The EU of the 1980s, however, is different from that of the 1990s in regard to national political commitment to foster integration. It is therefore possible that supranational authorities may indirectly keep the issue of privatization alive, although SOEs in theory and in practice are fully compatible with EU principles.

First, the ability to successfully carry out privatization in one country provides others with a "real world" example that the policy is not only technically feasible, but also potentially politically rewarding.[19] The British experience is a case in point. Second, one country may lobby the EU to punish another, accusing the latter of "unfair" competition. French competitors to British steel, for example, are state-owned. Britain can request that the EU Commissioner on Competition exert pressure on the French government to curb steel subsidies to its SOEs on the rationale that they discriminate against British steel producers.[20] The need to rationalize or improve efficiency may bring the issue of privatization to the top of the agenda. Third, the issue may be brought up indirectly by the EU itself. An EU directive issued in the summer of 1991 called for publishing all subsidies to industrial SOEs. The purpose was to identify which SOEs and to what extent they were subsidized "unfairly." This requirement was opposed by the French and Italian governments, among others, who argued that it constituted privileged commercial information. The playing field, however, has changed, and national governments on this matter are accountable to a supranational authority. Facing increasing difficulties with injecting capital to SOEs at will, national governments have to look for alternative funding arrangements. This may partially explain the French state's eagerness in recent years to reduce its ownership by encouraging companies, particularly state banks, to buy shares in other SOEs. Hence, as EU powers vis-à-vis national governments are being strengthened, the purpose and usefulness of state ownership may have to be reexamined.

Finally, the goal of a single European market may weaken one of the most important rationales for state ownership: the notion of public service.

The public service mission of SOEs, particularly public utilities, has been traditionally defined in national terms—that is, governments have bestowed public service obligations to certain SOEs, such as universal service, in return for subsidies, a certain degree of monopoly, and the like. The goal of a single European market, however, is to tear down national barriers, which means that a national government may not be able to deny entry to foreign competitors on the basis of the SOE providing a public service to that country alone. This does not necessarily imply privatization, but it certainly calls for a redefinition of the notion of public service that may be compatible along European, not just national, lines.[21] There is no reason why public-service operators would necessarily have to be either public or private—in France, for example, water services have been in private hands for some time. But the debate over public service keeps the issue of the utility of state ownership high on the government's agenda, and consequently it helps focus attention on the option of privatization as a viable alternative.

### Conclusion

Privatization involves a restructuring of the economy. Led by parties of the Right, pressured by high government borrowing needs, and supported by privatization-minded policy communities, governments in Britain and in France have sought to reshape the configuration of their mixed economies. Repudiating state ownership, the British are rediscovering their liberal past. By doing so, they seem to be moving closer to the U.S. model, which tolerates little or no state ownership and relies primarily on regulation as a method of state control. The trader and the sovereign, to return to Adam Smith, seem indeed incompatible characters in Britain.

In contrast, the French have tried to sell SOEs, primarily in manufacturing sectors, banking, and insurance. Ownership in infrastructural industries remains unaltered and in some cases, such as water, in private hands. Yet, the network of interlocking corporate ownership among public and private industrial firms, banks, and insurance companies introduced by the two Center-Right coalitions in stable nuclei and pursued in slightly different form by the Socialists suggests a pattern of reforms that bear a German semblance. This type of "mutual ownership" that is designed to foster institutional stability and promote long-term investment may indeed turn out to be a "novel" form of French economic organization.[22] The state is (re)discovering its role as one among many actors in a mixed economy. The latter search for a "new" state role will certainly go a long way toward reconciling Adam Smith's incompatible characters. The sovereign and the trader in France may yet turn out to be the best of partners.

# Notes

## Chapter 1

1. Quoted in Raymond Duch, *Privatizing the Economy: Telecommunications Policy in Comparative Perspective* (Ann Arbor: University of Michigan Press, 1991), 11.

2. State-owned enterprises (SOEs) are defined here as those in which the state holds majority ownership. I have chosen the term *state-owned* instead of *public* enterprises to avoid confusion with publicly owned companies, whose shares are owned by private individuals.

3. See, for example, Raymond Vernon, ed., *The Promise of Privatization* (New York: Council on Foreign Relations, 1988); William Glade, ed., *Privatization of Public Enterprises in Latin America* (San Fransisco: ICS for the International Center for Economic Growth, 1991); and V. V. Ramanadham, ed., *Privatisation in Developing Countries* (London and New York: Routledge, 1989).

4. This is an estimate supplied by the Reason Foundation and cited in the *Economist,* 13 June 1992, 3.

5. Rodney Lord, ed., *Privatisation Yearbook 1992* (London: Privatisation International, 1992), 7.

6. Vernon, *The Promise of Privatization,* 2.

7. Oliver Letwin, "International Experience in the Politics of Privatization," in Michael A. Walker, ed., *Privatization: Tactics and Techniques* (Vancouver, BC: The Fraser Institute, 1988), 61.

8. James Mitchell, "Britain: Privatisation as a Myth?" in J. J. Richardson, ed., *Privatisation and Deregulation in Canada and Britain* (Hants, U.K.: Dartmouth for the Institute for Research on Public Policy, 1990), 32.

9. Cento Veljanovski, *Selling the State: Privatisation in Britain* (London: Weidenfeld and Nicolson, 1987).

10. Dennis Gayle and Jonathan Goodrich, eds., *Privatization and Deregulation in Global Perspective* (New York: Quorum Books, 1990).

11. John Kay and David Thompson, "Privatisation: A Policy in Search of a Rationale," *Economic Journal* 96 (1986): 19.

12. George J. Stigler, *The Citizen and the State* (Chicago: University of Chicago Press, 1975), xi.

13. Charles E. Lindblom, *Politics and Markets: The World's Political Economic Systems* (New York: Basic Books, 1977).

14. Sir Peter Parker, "Foreword," in John Redwood and John Hatch, *Controlling Public Industries* (Oxford: Basil Blackwell, 1982), vi.

15. David Heald, *Public Expenditure: Its Defense and Reform* (Oxford: Robertson, 1983), 298.

16. Ariane Berthoin Antal, "Comparing Notes and Learning from Experience," in Meiholf Dierkes, Hans N. Weiler, and Ariane Berthoin Antal, eds., *Comparative Policy Research: Learning from Experience* (New York: St. Martin's, 1987), 506.

17. Although Lundqvist adopts a much broader definition, I found his discussion on this point very enlightening. See Lennart J. Lundqvist, "Privatization: Towards a Concept for Comparative Policy Analysis," *Journal of Public Policy* 8 (1988): 1–19.

18. John Vickers and Vincent Wright, "The Politics of Industrial Privatisation in Western Europe: An Overview," *West European Politics* 11:4 (1988): 2.

19. Ibid., 3.

20. John W. Kingdon, *Agendas, Alternatives and Public Policies* (New York: Harper Collins, 1984).

21. The garbage can model was originally developed by Michael Cohen, James March, and Johan Olsen, "A Garbage Can Model of Organizational Choice," *Administrative Science Quarterly* 17 (1972): 1–25.

22. Paul A. Sabatier, "Toward Better Theories of the Policy Process," *PS: Political Science and Politics* 24 (1991): 147–56.

23. The term *technical feasibility* is used in this paper narrowly to refer only to economic and financial criteria of SOE salability. Kingdon uses it more broadly to refer to general policy instruments, but I use his terminology to avoid conceptual confusion.

24. Peter A. Hall, "Conclusion: The Politics of Keynesian Ideas," in Peter A. Hall, ed., *The Political Power of Economic Ideas: Keynesianism across Nations* (Princeton: Princeton University Press, 1989), 373–74.

25. Richard Rose, "Inheritance Before Choice," *Journal of Theoretical Politics* 2 (1990): 263–91; and Margaret Weir, "Ideas and the Politics of Bounded Innovation," in Sven Steinmo, Kathleen Thelen, and Frank Longstreth, eds., *Structuring Politics: Historical Institutionalism in Comparative Analysis* (Cambridge: Cambridge University Press, 1992), 188–216.

26. Arnold J. Heidenheimer, Hugh Heclo, and Carolyn Teich Adams, *Comparative Public Policy*, 3d ed. (New York: St. Martin's, 1990).

27. Francis G. Castles, "The Dynamics of Policy Change: What Happened to the English-Speaking Nations in the 1980s," *European Journal for Political Research* 18 (1990): 491–513.

28. Kingdon, *Agendas*, 204.

29. Although I make historical allusions to inform the state of the current privatization debate, I conduct a detailed investigation of the contemporary period: since 1974 in Britain and since 1981 in France. This difference is due to historical circumstances. Whereas privatizing legislation in Britain was for the most part enacted following Thatcher's election to power in 1979, privatization in France did not begin

until Chirac's victory in the 1986 legislative elections. Because I seek to examine the entire policy formation process, I begin the systematic investigation in 1974 in Britain and 1981 in France. The choice was precipitated by the fact that these dates mark a political rupture with the past. In both instances, incumbent parties were defeated. In addition, the time frame enables me to examine the agenda-setting process for a time period equal for both countries, roughly five years before each privatizing leader came to power. For the need to conduct historically informed comparative research, see Heidenheimer, Heclo, and Adams, *Comparative Public Policy*, 3; Antal, "Comparing Notes," 507–8; and Douglas E. Ashford, ed., *History and Context in Comparative Public Policy* (Pittsburgh: University of Pittsburgh Press, 1992). For examples of such studies, see Peter J. Katzenstein, *Small States in World Markets* (Ithaca, NY: Cornell University Press, 1985); Katzenstein, ed., *Between Power and Plenty: Foreign Economic Policies of Advanced Industrial States* (Madison: University of Wisconsin Press, 1978); and Peter A. Hall, *Governing the Economy: The Politics of State Intervention in Britain and France* (Oxford: Oxford University Press, 1986).

30. Adam Przeworski and Henri Teune, *The Logic of Comparative Inquiry* (New York: Wiley, 1970). For an excellent discussion of problems associated with the selection of cases, see Barbara Geddes, "How the Cases You Choose Affect the Answers You Get: Selection Bias in Comparative Politics," *Political Analysis* 2 (1990): 131–50.

31. Katzenstein, *Small States*, 22.

32. Stephen Krasner, "United States Commercial and Monetary Policy: Unraveling the Paradox of External Strength and Internal Weakness," in Peter J. Katzenstein, ed., *Between Power and Plenty: Foreign Economic Policies of Advanced Industrialized States* (Madison: Wisconsin University Press, 1978), 52.

33. See, for example, Malcolm Gillis, "The Role of State Enterprises in Economic Development," *Social Research* 47 (1980): 248–89; and Thomas J. Trebat, *Brazil's State-Owned Enterprises* (Cambridge: Cambridge University Press, 1983), chap. 3.

34. Thomas J. Biersteker, "Reducing the Role of the State in the Economy: A Conceptual Exploration of IMF and World Bank Prescriptions," *International Studies Quarterly* 34 (1990): 477–92.

35. David Heald, "The United Kingdom: Privatisation and its Political Context," *West European Politics* 11:4 (1988): 31–48; and Jill Hills, "Neo-Conservative Regimes and Convergence in Telecommunications Policy," *European Journal of Political Research* 17 (1989): 95–113.

36. See, for example, Christopher S. Allen, "Meso-Corporatism or Collective Privatization? Sub-National Industrial Policies in the Federal Republic of Germany," unpublished manuscript, The University of Georgia, 1992; and Josef Esser, "Symbolic Privatisation: The Politics of Privatisation in West Germany," *West European Politics* 11:4 (1988): 61–73.

37. Gary P. Freeman, "National Styles and Policy Sectors: Explaining Structured Variation," *Journal of Public Policy* 5 (1985): 467–96.

38. The current French prime minister, Edouard Balladur, has announced an ambitious privatization program that includes additional sectors of possible overlap,

such as airlines, automobiles, and steel. These companies, however, have not yet been sold as of the time of this writing.

39. Kingdon, *Agendas,* 220.

40. Telecommunications here refers to telephone, telegraph, and data transmission networks and excludes audiovisuals—that is, radio and television.

41. Eli M. Noam, "The Public Telecommunications Network: A Concept in Transition," *Journal of Communication* 37:1 (1987): 33–34. This does not suggest that maintaining a solid industrial base is not important. For an argument emphasizing the importance of manufacturing, see Stephen S. Cohen and John Zysman, *Manufacturing Matters: The Myth of the Post-Industrial Economy* (New York: Basic, 1987).

42. Veljanovski, *Selling the State,* 187.

43. Heald, "United Kingdom," 37.

44. John Moore, "British Privatization: Taking Capitalism to the People," *Harvard Business Review* (January–February 1992): 116.

45. In November 1993, the House of Commons finally adopted the Railways Act, which envisioned major structural changes and a peculiar form of privatization. I will elaborate on this Act in chapter 4.

## Chapter 2

1. Patrick Dunleavy, "Explaining the Privatization Boom: Public Choice versus Radical Approaches," *Public Administration* 64 (1986): 13–34.

2. The foundations and assumptions of public choice are carefully laid out by Anthony Downs, *An Economic Theory of Democracy* (New York: Harper and Row, 1957). For a thorough review of recent works, see Dennis C. Mueller, *Public Choice II* (Cambridge: Cambridge University Press, 1989).

3. Stuart Butler, "Changing the Political Dynamics of Government," *Proceedings of the Academy of Political Science* 36:3 (1987): 4–13.

4. Gary S. Becker, "A Theory of Competition among Pressure Groups for Political Influence," *Quarterly Journal of Economics* 98 (1983): 371–400.

5. William A. Niskanen, Jr., *Bureaucracy and Representative Government* (Chicago: Aldine-Atherton, 1971).

6. Madsen Pirie, *Privatization* (Hants, U.K.: Wildwood House, 1988), 52.

7. Ibid., 49.

8. Samuel Brittan, "The Politics and Economics of Privatisation," *Political Quarterly* 55 (1984): 110.

9. Yair Aharoni, "The United Kingdom: Transforming Attitudes," in Raymond Vernon, ed., *The Promise of Privatization* (New York: Council on Foreign Relations, 1988), 45–46; Kay and Thompson, "Privatisation," 18–31; and Brittan, "Politics and Economics of Privatisation": 119.

10. Dunleavy, "Explaining the Privatization Boom," 18.

11. Butler, "Changing the Political Dynamics"; Madsen Pirie, "Principles of Privatization," in Michael A. Walker, ed., *Privatization: Tactics and Techniques* (Vancouver, BC: Fraser Institute, 1988), 3–14.

12. Dunleavy, "Explaining the Privatization Boom," 18.

13. Louis De Alessi, "Property Rights and Privatization," *Proceedings of the American Academy of Political Science* 36:3 (1987): 26.

14. Ibid.

15. For an elaboration of the concept of contestability, see Aidan R. Vining and David L. Weimer, "Government Supply and Government Production Failure: A Framework Based on Contestability," *Journal of Public Policy* 10 (1990): 1–22.

16. George Yarrow, "Does Ownership Matter?" in Cento Veljanovski, ed., *Privatisation and Competition: A Market Prospectus* (London: Institute of Economic Affairs, 1989), 52–69.

17. For thorough reviews, see John Vickers and George Yarrow, *Privatization: An Economic Analysis* (Cambridge: MIT Press, 1988), chap. 2; George Yarrow, "Privatization in Theory and Practice," *Economic Policy* 2 (1986): 324–77; Robert Millward, "The Comparative Performance of Public and Private Ownership," in John Kay, Colin Mayer, and David Thompson, eds., *Privatisation and Regulation: The UK Experience* (Oxford: Clarendon, 1986), 119–44; and Antony Moussios, " 'Hybrid' Status, Regulation, and Performance: An Empirical Analysis of the Denationalization of British Telecom" (DPA diss., University of Georgia, 1994).

18. Michael Beesley and Stephen Littlechild, "Privatisation: Principles, Problems and Priorities," *Lloyd's Bank Review* 149 (July 1983): 1–20.

19. Richard Pryke, "The Comparative Performance of Public and Private Enterprise," *Fiscal Studies* 3:2 (1982): 68–81.

20. D. W. Caves and L. R. Christensen, "The Relative Efficiency of Public and Private Firms in a Competitive Environment: The Case of Canadian Railroads," *Journal of Political Economy* 88 (1980): 958–76.

21. Douglas Sikorsky, "Public Enterprise (PE): How Is it Different from the Private Sector," *Annals of Public and Co-operative Economy* 57 (1986): 477–511.

22. Duch, *Privatizing the Economy*.

23. John B. Goodman and Gary W. Loveman, "Does Privatization Serve the Public Interest?" *Harvard Business Review* (November–December 1991): 35–36.

24. Vickers and Yarrow, *Privatization,* 43; Kay, Mayer, and Thompson, *Privatisation and Regulation,* 16.

25. Vernon, *Promise of Privatization.*

26. Fariborz Ghadar, "Oil: The Power of an Industry," in Raymond Vernon, ed., *The Promise of Privatization* (New York: Council on Foreign Relations, 1988), 231–53.

27. Colin Mayer, "Public Ownership: Concepts and Applications," in Dieter Helm, ed., *The Economic Borders of the State* (Oxford: Oxford University Press, 1989), 251–74.

28. John Kay, "The Privatization of British Telecom," in David Steel and David Heald, eds., *Privatizing Public Enterprises: Options and Dilemmas* (London: Royal Society of Public Administration, 1984), 77–85.

29. Raymond Vernon and Yair Aharoni, eds., *State-Owned Enterprises in the Western Economies* (New York: St. Martin's, 1981), 9. For an elaboration of this argument, see Edward Tufte, *Political Control of the Economy* (Princeton: Princeton

University Press, 1978); Douglas Hibbs, "Political Parties and Macroeconomic Policy," *American Political Science Review* 71 (1977): 1467–87; Francis G. Castles, "The Impact of Parties on Public Expenditure," in Peter Flora and Arnold Heidenheimer, eds., *The Development of Welfare States in Europe and America* (New Brunswick, NJ: Transaction Books, 1981); Francis G. Castles, ed., *The Impact of Parties: Politics and Policies in Capitalist Democratic States* (London and Beverly Hills: Sage, 1982); and André Blais, Donald Blake, and Stéphane Dion, "Do Parties Make a Difference? Parties and the Size of Government in Liberal Democracies," *American Journal of Political Science* 37 (1993): 40–62.

30. Dennis Swann, *The Retreat of the State: Deregulation and Privatization in the UK and the US* (Ann Arbor: University of Michigan Press, 1988).

31. Ibid, 236.

32. David Heald, "Privatisation: Analysing its Appeal and Limitations," *Fiscal Studies* 5:1 (1984): 36–46; and Aharoni, "United Kingdom."

33. Jacques Bourdon, Jean-Maxime Pontier, and Jean-Claude Ricci, "Les Privatisations en France," in Charles Debbasch, ed., *Les Privatisations en Europe,* (Paris: CNRS, 1989), 118–42.

34. Ezra N. Suleiman, "The Politics of Privatization in Britain and France," in Ezra N. Suleiman and John Waterbury, eds., *The Political Economy of Public Sector Reform and Privatization* (Boulder, CO: Westview, 1990), 113–36.

35. Deryck Abel, "British Conservatives and State Ownership," *Journal of Politics* 19 (1957): 227–39.

36. Illustrations of this approach can be found in Jeremy Richardson, ed., *Policy Styles in Western Europe* (London: George Allen & Unwin, 1982); Wolfgang Streeck and Philippe Schmitter, eds., *Patterns of Corporatist Policy Making* (Beverly Hills: Sage, 1985); and John R. Freeman, *Democracy and Markets: The Politics of Mixed Economies* (Ithaca, NY: Cornell University Press, 1989).

37. Many scholars generally agree with the proposition that statism most accurately characterizes French policy-making. It is important, however, to note Hayward's observation that the actual style may differ across issues. See Jack Hayward, "Mobilising Private Interests in the Service of Public Ambitions: The Salient Element in the Dual French Policy Style?" in Jeremy Richardson, ed., *Policy Styles in Western Europe* (London: George Allen & Unwin, 1982), 111–40.

38. Duch, *Privatizing the Economy.*

39. Vickers and Wright, "Politics of Industrial Privatisation."

40. Lundqvist, "Privatization."

41. Harvey B. Feigenbaum, "France: From Pragmatic to Tactical Privatization," paper presented at the annual meeting of the American Political Science Association, Chicago, 1992.

42. Kingdon, *Agendas.*

43. Cohen, March, and Olsen, "Garbage Can Model."

44. Ibid., 1.

45. James G. March and Johan P. Olsen, *Rediscovering Institutions: The Organizational Basis of Politics* (New York: Free Press, 1989), chap. 1.

46. The ideas in this paragrapgh are more fully explored in Nikolaos Zahariadis, "Garbage Cans and the Hiring Process," *PS: Political Science and Politics* 27 (1994): 98–99.

47. Cohen, March, and Olsen quoted in Kingdon, *Agendas,* 91.

48. Kingdon, *Agendas,* 90.

49. Ibid, 115. For a full treatment of the issue of problem definition in public policy, see David Dery, *Problem Definition in Policy Analysis* (Lawrence, KS: University Press of Kansas, 1984); and David A. Rochefort and Roger W. Cobb, "Problem Definition, Agenda Access, and Policy Choice," *Policy Studies Journal* 21 (1993): 56–71.

50. Ibid, 153.

51. Ibid, 173.

52. Ibid, 188.

53. Ibid, 153.

54. Ian McAllister and Donley Studlar, "Popular versus Elite Views of Privatization: The Case of Britain," *Journal of Public Policy* 9 (1989): 175.

55. Pirie, "Principles of Privatization," 16.

56. McAllister and Studlar, "Popular versus Elite Views."

57. Elisabeth Dupoirier and Muriel Humbertjean, "Privatisations," in SOFRES, *L'Etat de l'Opinion* (Paris: Seuil, 1988), 33.

58. Kingdon, *Agendas,* 155.

59. Richard Rose, *Politics in England* (Glenview, IL: Scott, Foresman, 1989), 113.

60. The two periods of cohabitation in the Fifth Republic (1986–88 and 1993—present) actually complicated matters somewhat because the President (a Socialist) and the Prime Minister (a Gaullist) come from different ends of the political spectrum. Nevertheless, this complication inhibited the adoption of laws that are clearly supported by the center-right coalition with the majority of seats in the National Assembly.

61. Rose, *Politics in England,* 113.

62. Olivier Duhamel, "The Fifth Republic under François Mitterrand: Evolution and Perspectives," in George Ross, Stanley Hoffmann, and Sylvia Malzacher, eds., *The Mitterrand Experiment* (New York: Oxford University Press, 1987), 148.

63. Kingdon, *Agendas,* 139.

64. Jack Hayward, "The Policy Community Approach to Industrial Policy," in Dankwart A. Rustow and Kenneth Paul Erickson, eds., *Comparative Political Dynamics: Global Research Perspectives* (New York: Harper Collins, 1991), 401.

65. Kingdon, *Agendas,* 140.

66. Kay and Thompson, "Privatisation," 29.

67. Jean-Baptiste Toulouse, Yves Rolland, Jean-Frédéric de Leuste, and Xavier Pillot, *Finances Publiques et Politiques Publiques* (Paris: Economica, 1987), 320.

68. For a discussion regarding the diversity of definitions in various countries, see Yair Aharoni, *The Evolution and Management of State-Owned Enterprises* (Cambridge, MA: Ballinger, 1986), 6–13. For such a discussion focusing on Western

Europe, see Henry Parris, Pierre Pestieau, and Peter Saynor, *Public Enterprise in Western Europe* (London: Croom Helm, 1987), 5–8.

69. R. P. Short, "The Role of Public Enterprises: An International Statistical Comparison," in Robert H. Floyd, Clive S. Gray, and R. P. Short, *Public Enterprise in Mixed Economies* (Washington, DC: IMF, 1984), 184.

70. Aharoni, *Evolution and Management,* 13.

71. Short, "Role of Public Enterprises," 186.

72. Quoted in Kingdon, *Agendas,* 161.

73. Castles, "Dynamics of Policy Change."

74. Note President Nixon's well-known statement: "We are all Keynesians now."

75. Benjamin I. Page, "The Theory of Political Ambiguity," *American Political Science Review* 70 (1976): 742–52.

76. Kingdon, *Agenda,* 215.

77. Kay and Thompson, "Privatisation."

78. Heidrun Abromeit, "British Privatisation Policy," *Parliamentary Affairs* 41 (1988): 68–85.

79. Letwin, "International Experience."

## Chapter 3

1. Rose, "Inheritance before Choice"; see also Nikolaos Zahariadis and Christopher S. Allen, "Ideas, Networks and Policy Streams: Privatization in Britain and Germany," paper presented at the annual meeting of the American Political Science Association, Washington, DC, 1993.

2. The nature of mixed economy defies precise definition, but the discussion here draws inspiration from two works by Andrew Shonfield, *In Defense of the Mixed Economy* (Oxford: Oxford University Press, 1984) and *Modern Capitalism: The Changing Balance of Public and Private Power* (London: Oxford University Press, 1965).

3. Hansard, *House of Commons* 27 April 1990, 358.

4. It should be noted, however, that the government's coal privatization plan announced in October 1992 was withdrawn after widespread protest. To make matters worse, the High Court later ruled that the government acted illegally by ignoring the miners' right to consultation in the case of pit closures. For more details, see *Economist,* 26 December 1992, 77–78.

5. Tom Kemp, *Industrialization in Nineteenth-Century Europe* (London and New York: Pergamon, 1985), chap. 2.

6. Initially the entire statement from which this phrase is extracted was adopted as the Third Clause of the Constitution. With minor modifications, it became Clause IV at the 1929 Party Conference. For a history of nationalization proposals in Britain, see E. Eldon Barry, *Nationalisation in British Politics* (London: Cape, 1965). For a theoretical treatment of SOEs in socialist thought, see Jim Tomlinson, *The Unequal Struggle? British Socialism and the Capitalist Enterprise* (London and New York: Methuen, 1982).

7. For an elaboration of the public corporation model, see Herbert Morrison, *Socialisation and British Transport* (London: Constable, 1933); and William A. Robson, *Nationalized Industry and Public Ownership*, 2d ed. (London: George Allen & Unwin, 1962). For a comparison between it and other government-owned corporate models that were under review at the time, see the thorough treatment provided in John Thurston, *Government Proprietary Corporations in the English-Speaking Countries* (Cambridge: Harvard University Press, 1937).

8. Morrison, *Socialisation and British Transport*, 284.

9. Ibid, 272. Emphasis added.

10. Quoted in Samuel H. Beer, *Modern British Politics* (New York: W. W. Norton, 1982), 190.

11. A thorough review of British postwar nationalization is included in R. Kelf-Cohen, *Twenty Years of Nationalisation* (London: Macmillan, 1969).

12. Beer, *Modern British Politics*, 194–200.

13. Peter A. Hall, *Governing the Economy: The Politics of State Intervention in Britain and France* (New York: Oxford University Press, 1986), 75–76.

14. Clive Jenkins, *Power at the Top* (London: Macgibbon & Kee, 1959), 16.

15. Kelf-Cohen, *Twenty Years of Nationalisation*, 73–74.

16. A thorough account of events is included in Kathleen Burk, *The First Privatisation: The Politicians, the City, and the Denationalisation of Steel* (London: Historian's Press, 1988).

17. Jenkins, *Power at the Top*, 128.

18. A. A. Berle and G. C. Means, *The Modern Corporation and Private Property* (New York: Macmillan, 1932). For the revisionist argument, see Anthony Crosland, *The Conservative Enemy* (London: Schocken, 1962).

19. Kelf-Cohen, *Twenty Years of Nationalisation*, 150.

20. F. W. S. Craig, *British General Election Manifestos, 1957–1987* (Hants, U.K.: Dartmouth, 1990), 120–21.

21. *Times,* 9 October 1971, 6.

22. Martyn Sloman, *Socialising Public Ownership* (London: Macmillan, 1978), 65.

23. Ibid, 65.

24. Hansard, *House of Lords,* 15 February 1971, cols. 360–61.

25. Margaret Thatcher, *The Downing Street Years* (New York: Harper Collins, 1993), 7.

26. The debate on Britain's postwar consensus politics is amply documented in Dennis Kavanagh and P. Morris, *Consensus Politics from Atlee to Thatcher* (Oxford: Basil Blackwell, 1989). For an enlightened analysis of its subsequent demise, see Dennis Kavanagh, *Thatcherism and British Politics: The End of Consensus?* 2d ed. (Oxford: Oxford University Press, 1990).

27. Thatcher, *Downing Street Years,* 676.

28. See Sir Keith Joseph's *Reversing the Trend* (Chester, U.K.: Rose 1975) and *Stranded in the Middle Ground* (London: Centre for Policy Studies, 1976).

29. There is a voluminous literature in Thatcherism. For detailed analysis and

critiques, see the essays in Dennis Kavanagh, *Politics and Personalities* (London: Macmillan, 1990) and Bob Jessop et al., *Thatcherism* (Cambridge: Polity, 1988).

30. The discussion here draws inspiration in parts from David Heald and David Steel, "Privatising Public Enterprises: An Analysis of the Government's Case," *Political Quarterly* 53 (1982): 333–49.

31. Madsen Pirie, "Principles of Privatization," 6.

32. Interview in C-Span, *The Life and Career of Margaret Thatcher* (West Lafayette, IN: Public Affairs Video Archives, March 1991).

33. Quoted in Oliver Letwin, *Privatising the World* (London: Cassell, 1988), 10–11.

34. *Economist,* 27 May 1978, 21.

35. John Moore, "Why Privatise?" in John Kay, Colin Mayer, and David Thompson, eds., *Privatisation and Deregulation: The UK Experience* (Oxford: Clarendon, 1986), 89.

36. Veljanovski, *Selling the State,* 42–44.

37. Quoted in Candace Hertzner, "Keeping the Aspidistra Flying: Thatcherite Privatization and the Creation of the Enterprise Culture," *International Journal of Public Administration* 11 (1988): 632.

38. Quoted in Kavanagh, *Thatcherism,* 220.

39. *Financial Times,* 22 March 1984, 1.

40. Quoted in Hertzner, "Keeping the Aspidistra Flying," 632.

41. C-Span, *The Life and Career of Margaret Thatcher.*

42. Moore, "British Privatization," 115–24.

43. *Times,* 9 November 1985, 40.

44. Ellen M. Pint, "Nationalization and Privatization: A Rational Choice Perspective on Efficiency," *Journal of Public Policy* 10 (1990): 279–80; Veljanovski, *Selling the State,* 95–101; and Dexter Whitfield, *The Welfare State* (London: Pluto, 1992), 199–223. Doing so, however, left the government vulnerable to accusations of selling "the family silver" too cheaply. In a recent report, the Committee of Public Accounts concluded that the sale of water companies shortchanged the taxpayer. Though it did not quantify the loss, it pointed to the companies' combined value of £9.3 billion in 1991, an increase of 79 percent from their flotation value two years earlier. The sale simply proceeded too fast, it concluded, and the Department of Energy's interest in raising the value of privatization proceeds was at odds with its responsibilities to the customers (*Financial Times,* 23 July 1992, 6).

45. Interestingly, however, the percentage of total equity listed in the London Stock Exchange that is held by individual investors has fallen from 50 percent in 1963 to roughly 20 percent in 1992 (*Economist,* 6 November 1993, 79).

46. *Times,* 6 October 1978, 1; and Craig, *British General Election Manifestos,* 296.

47. Veljanovski, *Selling the State,* 67–75.

48. Robert Fraser, eds., *Privatisation: The U.K. Experience and International Trends* (London: Longman, 1988), 37–38, 43.

49. David Thomas, "The Union Response to Denationalisation," in John Kay,

Colin Mayer, and David Thompson, eds., *Privatisation and Deregulation: The UK Experience* (Oxford: Clarendon, 1986), 305.

50. Kavanagh, *Thatcherism,* chap. 6.

51. Stuart Holland, *The Socialist Challenge* (London: Quartet, 1976).

52. Kavanagh, *Thatcherism,* 181.

53. David Thomas, "Public Ownership: Can its Supporters Make a Convincing Case?" *Public Money* 5 (1985): 25–29.

54. Quoted in Veljanovski, *Selling the State,* 70.

55. For details of Bryan Gould's proposal at the 1987 Labour Conference in Brighton, to create "popular socialism," see Colin Hughes and Patrick Wintour, *Labour Rebuilt: The New Model Party* (London: Fourth Estate, 1990), 44–45.

56. Oonagh McDonald, *Own Your Own: Social Ownership Examined,* Fabian Series (London: Unwin, 1989).

57. For details about how some of these Labour proposals came about, see Hughes and Wintour, *Labour Rebuilt,* 131–33. Interestingly, intellectuals closely affiliated with Labour have little to add to regulation. Although they acknowledge that passing tough but temporary regulatory laws is important, they point to underfunding and "capture" problems. Curiously, they don't suggest detailed innovative remedies to these well-documented deficiencies, neither do they explain why regulation should be temporary. See Whitfield, *Welfare State,* 378–79.

58. Veljanovski, *Selling the State,* 62–64.

59. Data on inflation and GDP growth are taken from European Community sources contained in *European Economy* (December 1991), tables 10 and 24.

60. For elaborate discussions of the institutional framework governing state-SOE relations, see Tony Prosser, *Nationalised Industries and Public Control* (Oxford: Basil Blackwell, 1986); and Peter J. Curwen, *Public Enterprise: A Modern Approach* (New York: St. Martin's, 1986).

61. Curwen, *Public Enterprise,* 46–47.

## Chapter 4

1. Anthony Sampson quoted in Gerry Corti and Frank Frazer, *The Nation's Oil: A Story of Control* (London: Graham and Trotman, 1983), 12.

2. D. I. Mackay and G. A. Mackay quoted in Guy Arnold, *Britain's Oil* (London: Hamish Hamilton, 1978), 34; Corti and Frazer, *Nation's Oil.*

3. Arnold, *Britain's Oil,* 34.

4. Ibid, 46. A government-commissioned report estimated that offshore activities at the time were worth an annual amount of £300 million.

5. In a scathing attack on the licensing system, Lord Balogh, who later played a pivotal role in helping to create the British National Oil Corporation (BNOC), complained that the British people were being robbed of their fair share of oil profits. The Arabs obtained 75 percent, and even the Dutch secured 76.5 percent participation in profits. In contrast, "apart from a few leases in which the nationalized industries participate the British public's total gain is only 50.4 percent from tax and royalties."

(Quoted in Arnold, *Britain's Oil,* 51.) Concurring with the general spirit of the charges was the Public Accounts Committee, which, after thorough examination of oil policy, recommended in 1973 changes in taxation and a review of the licensing system.

6. The idea of creating a National Hydrocarbons Corporation to oversee developments in the North Sea was first circulated inside the Labour Party in 1968, but it was shelved as unworkable because of insufficient oil data at the time. By 1973, the idea had gained wide acceptance and was being given serious consideration. Several factors contributed to this change. First, the discovery of new oil fields and constantly upward revisions of North Sea estimates encouraged a braver government approach to oil companies. Second, the creation of Statoil, Norway's oil SOE, provided a real-world example of how to do it. Third, the Public Accounts Committee report, as well as Lord Balogh's charges of the companies' profit manipulation to evade taxes, made the idea of an SOE more palatable. It could be used to secure oil supplies as well as an alternative source of information.

7. Quoted in Arnold, *Britain's Oil,* 362.

8. Corti and Frazer, *Nation's Oil,* 94.

9. *Times,* 21 February 1975, 3.

10. Not all oil companies were opposed to BNOC. Several small independents, such as Tricentrol and the Charterhouse Group, welcomed the new company, hoping that state protection and finance would enable them to exploit fields that would otherwise be out of their reach. The agreement to participate with BNOC and other oil companies in the production of oil in the Thistle field illustrates the point. At a time when other major oil companies were turning down participation agreements, Chevron entered negotiations with BNOC, valuing future benefits that could accrue from early and voluntary participation. In addition, Burmah Oil, which was strapped for cash, was relieved to receive state support.

11. John Redwood, *Going for Broke* (Oxford: Basil Blackwell, 1984), 101.

12. *Times,* 3 February 1976, 17; *Times,* 24 April 1976, 19.

13. *Banker,* May 1977, 88.

14. Quoted in Arnold, *Britain's Oil,* 162.

15. Some commentators, including Philip Shelbourne, BNOC's chair prior to privatization, have recently suggested that setting up BNOC was "an all-party concept" (Philip Shelbourne, "BNOC's Growth and Prospects," *Coal and Energy Quarterly* 30 [1981]: 3). Yet, there is ample contemporary evidence to substantiate the argument that creating the state oil company was very much a politically contentious issue. Conservatives never felt comfortable with the notion of a sovereign entrepreneur, and since BNOC's inception, as I show, they sought to either limit its privileges or abolish the company altogether.

16. *Times,* 10 September 1975, 2.

17. Arnold, *Britain's Oil,* 319, 322–23.

18. Merrie Gilbert Klapp, *The Sovereign Entrepreneur* (Ithaca, NY: Cornell University Press, 1987), 93.

19. Government ownership was reduced from 68.28 percent to 51 percent—the figure includes both Bank of England and government shares. Fraser, *Privatisation,* 52.

20. *Times,* 6 October 1978, 1.

21. *Daily Telegraph,* 11 December 1978, 7.

22. Redwood, *Going for Broke,* 106.

23. *Daily Telegraph,* 28 July 1979, 1. Interestingly, other state managers concurred as well. For example, Sir Denis Rooke, chair of British Gas (BG), agreed that it was unwise to dispose of valuable energy assets. He, too, was feeling the heat as the government was contemplating stripping BG of its monopolistic privileges and disposing of its oil assets in the North Sea.

24. *Daily Telegraph,* 14 August 1979, 17.

25. There were other proposals on the table as well: (1) an advance sale of oil produced by BNOC; (2) an advance sale of oil that was to be received by the government as royalty payments instead of cash; and (3) a sale of holdings in various gas fields and oil fields.

26. *Financial Times,* 14 February 1981, 17.

27. *Daily Telegraph,* 15 September 1979, 1.

28. *Times,* 15 February 1980, 19.

29. *Financial Times,* 14 February 1981, 17.

30. *Times,* 22 April 1980, 17.

31. *Times,* 23 April 1980, 20.

32. *Daily Telegraph,* 15 September 1979, 1.

33. Net profit ratio figures were calculated from information provided in Moody's *International Manual,* various years.

34. The appointment may have also been a calculated move to facilitate Morton's resignation, because David Howell was aware of the long history of disagreement between the two men when they were both working at Midland Bank.

35. *Financial Times,* 26 March 1981, 1.

36. A. W. Baker and G. H. Daniel, "BNOC and Privatisation—The Past and the Future," *Journal of Energy Resources and Law* 1 (1983): 151–52.

37. Colin Robinson, "The Errors of North Sea Policy," *Lloyd's Bank Review* 141 (July 1981): 31.

38. *Financial Times,* 29 January 1982, 38.

39. Fraser, *Privatisation,* 51–56.

40. The early history of the British telco borrows heavily from Duch, *Privatizing the Economy;* and Douglas Pitt, *The Telecommunications Function of the British Post Office: A Case Study of Bureaucratic Adaptation* (Westmead, U.K.: Saxon House, 1980).

41. Pitt, *Telecommunications Function,* 45–46. Nevertheless, despite chronic capital shortages, telecommunications enjoyed moderate success. In 1938, for example, Britain ranked sixth, with 6.74 telephones per 100 inhabitants, out of a sample of twelve industrialized countries. Although it was far behind the leader, the United States, Britain ranked above its arch rivals Germany and France (Louis-Joseph Libois, *Genèse et Croissance des Télécommunications* [Paris: Masson, 1983], 83).

42. Employment increased to 244,700 employees in 1973, a jump of 26.8 percent from 193,000 in 1963, and profitability, measured as gross surplus over revenue, decreased from 45.6 percent to 42.8 percent during the same period (Richard Pryke,

*The Nationalised Industries: Policies and Performance since 1968* [Oxford: Martin Robertson, 1981], 172).

43. *Times,* 18 May 1976, 17.

44. Department of Industry (The Carter Report), *Report of the Post Office Review Committee* Cmnd 6850 (London: HMSO, 1977).

45. *Daily Telegraph,* 10 September 1979, 1.

46. *Times,* 16 December 1977, 4.

47. To alleviate deteriorating labor relations and increase overall profitability, Eric Varley, Secretary of State for Industry, announced in 1977 a temporary reorganization of PO's board, which increased labor's voice. The new board was to include seven unionists, seven managers, and five independent members.

48. *Daily Telegraph,* 22 May 1979, 8.

49. *Daily Telegraph,* 10 September 1979, 1.

50. Ibid.

51. Carter Report, *Report of the Post Office Review Committee,* 18. Using the number of telephones per employee as an indicator, the report compared the United Kingdom unfavorably to Sweden, Japan, and the United States. Britain's 83 telephones per employee were lower than Sweden's (126.4) and Japan's (127) and almost half the 154 of the United States. Although frequently used, this indicator is not without problems. Critics argue that density of penetration—the number of telephones per capita—more adequately reflects the system's overall efficiency. For a discussion of problems associated with several measures and for alternative indicators of performance, see Duch, *Privatizing the Economy,* 31–36, 69–73.

52. See, for example, Pryke, *Nationalised Industries,* and Gareth Locksley, *The EEC Telecommunications Industry* (Brussels: Commission of the European Communities, 1983).

53. *Times,* 4 October 1980, 15.

54. *Financial Times,* 30 November 1981, 11.

55. *Financial Times,* 30 June 1981, 11.

56. Jill Hills, *Deregulating Telecoms* (Westport, CT: Quorum Books, 1986), 122.

57. Douglas Pitt, "An Essentially Contestable Organisation: British Telecom and the Privatisation Debate," in J. J. Richardson, ed., *Privatisation and Deregulation in Canada and Britain* (Hants, U.K.: Dartmouth for the Institute for Research on Public Policy, 1990).

58. Karin Newman, *The Selling of British Telecom* (New York: St. Martin's, 1986), 26.

59. As Pitt ("Coutestable Organisation," 63) astutely observed, "the values which had sustained a public service ethic were uniquely unfitted to the realities of a market environment. They were the 'wrong stuff' for that stage in its life cycle currently being experienced by BT. The 'right stuff' for values suited to a more threatening and challenging environment were the opposite . . . 'Administrative' mores—enshrined in Jefferson's oft quoted view of Post Office officials that they had the self image of the district commissioner rather than that of the modern entrepreneur—should be relinquished in favor of a more competitive 'management' ethos."

60. Ray Forrest and Alan Murie, *Selling the Welfare State: The Privatisation of Public Housing* (London: Routledge, 1988).

61. The figure includes proceeds from BP, British Aerospace, Cable and Wireless, and Amersham International. See table 3.1 for figures of individual sales.

62. British Telecom, *Report and Annual Accounts* (London: BT, 1985). Figures have been recalculated to reflect BT's accounting practices as a private company.

63. Kenneth Dyson, "West European States and the Communications Revolution," *West European Politics* 9 (1986): 10–55.

64. Jeremy Moon, J. J. Richardson, and Paul Smart, "The Privatisation of British Telecom: A Case Study of the Extended Process of Legislation," *European Journal of Political Research* 14 (1986): 339–55."

65. Hills, *Deregulating Telecoms*, 123; *Financial Times*, 12 November 1981, 8; *Financial Times*, 10 March 1982, 25.

66. Department of Industry, *The Future of Telecommunications in Britain* Cmnd 8610 (London: HMSO, 1982).

67. In Henry Ergas and Jun Okayama, eds., *Changing Market Structures in Telecommunications* (Paris: OECD, 1984), 38.

68. These questions were formally raised by David Steel, "Government and the New Hybrids," in David Steel and David Heald, eds., *Privatizing Public Enterprises: Options and Dilemmas* (London: Royal Institute of Public Administration, 1984).

69. One of the many questions that had a direct impact on the appeal of privatization was BT's pricing policy. How could a private BT's prices be regulated against excessive profits? In a government-commissioned report, Stephen Littlechild, an academic economist, argued that BT's monopolistic behavior could be effectively controlled, partially through open competition in services, such as cellular phones and transmission capacity. To further ensure price controls, Littlechild also proposed the RPI-X formula. Prices would be kept below the Retail Price Index by a margin X that was subject to negotiations between Oftel and BT and adjusted periodically.

70. John Moore, "The Success of Privatization," in John Kay, Colin Mayer, and David Thompson, eds., *Privatisation and Deregulation: The UK Experience* (Oxford: Clarendon, 1986), 96.

71. The government objectives are most clearly spelled out in Department of Industry, *Future of Telecommunications*.

72. See, for example, the studies issued by analysts who were intimately involved in the privatization process: Beesley and Littlechild, "Privatisation"; and John Redwood and John Hatch, *Controlling Public Industries* (Oxford: Basil Blackwell, 1982). In a speech delivered in 1983, the first clear articulation of the government's goals in the privatization process, John Moore emphasized efficiency as the overriding concern. See John Moore, "Why Privatize?" in John Kay, Colin Mayer, and David Thompson, eds., *Privatisation and Deregulation: The UK Experience* (Oxford: Clarendon, 1986).

73. Quoted in Pitt, "Contestable Organisation," 60.

74. *Financial Times*, 27 September 1983, 18.

75. Sue Hastings and Hugo Levie, eds., *Privatisation?* (Nottingham: Spokesman, 1983), 9. Weak union opposition to Britoil's sale could be attributed to the weakness of unions in the oil industry.

76. Chris Bulford, "British Telecom," in Hastings and Levie, eds., *Privatisation?* (Nottingham: Spokesman, 1983), 135.

77. A good example is the pamphlet entitled "How selling British Telecom will harm the blind and disabled" sent by BTUC to members of the House of Lords.

78. Bulford, "British Telecom," 135.

79. Moon, Richardson, and Smart, "Privatisation of British Telecom": 345.

80. Hills, *Deregulating Telecoms,* 127.

81. Centre for Policy Studies, *Telecommunications in Britain* (London: Centre for Policy Studies, 1982).

82. For instance, James Pawsey questioned the pricing policy of rural services. Since they were not as profitable as business or international calls were, would they be axed by a profit-motivated BT? On a different note, Timothy Renton had concerns similar to those of unions, namely, the possibility of job losses resulting from privatization. Toby Jessel took up the issue of providing a free directory service for the blind. The bill was subsequently amended to address these concerns.

83. *Financial Times,* 8 February 1983, 10.

84. *Hansard, House of Commons* 29 July 1982, col. 1434.

85. *Financial Times,* 12 February 1983, 17.

86. Michael Palmer and Jeremy Tunstall, *Liberating Telecommunications: Policy-Making in France and Britain* (Oxford: Basil Blackwell, 1990), 209.

87. Hills, *Deregulating Telecoms,* 96–7.

88. Eric Batstone, Anthony Ferrier, and Michael Terry, *Consent and Efficiency: Labour and Management Strategy in the State Enterprise* (Oxford: Basil Blackwell, 1984).

89. Pitt, "Contestable Organisation," 60.

90. *Financial Times,* 6 October 1983, 1.

91. *Financial Times,* 11 November 1983, 1.

92. *Hansard, House of Lords* 16 January 1984, col. 860.

93. Ibid, col. 843.

94. Ibid, col. 863.

95. Newman, *Selling of British Telecom,* 20.

96. Ibid, 26.

97. *Financial Times,* 28 March 1984, 17.

98. Newman, *Selling of British Telecom,* 12.

99. Telecommunications regulation has since been expanded and tightened.

100. *Financial Times,* 27 December 1991, 13. Although part of the official privatization program, I have not examined this sale in detail because it involved selling shares in a private company, not an SOE.

101. The slow and weak response of domestic equipment manufacturers to the liberalization challenge was a major disappointment for the government and has benefited, as some claim, foreign rather than domestic suppliers. See Hills, *Deregulating Telecoms;* Kevin Morgan and Douglas Webber, "Divergent Paths: Political Strategies for Telecommunications in Britain, France and Germany," *West European Politics* 9 (1986): 56–79.

102. Morgan and Webber, "Divergent Paths," 62; Bulford, "British Telecom," 133–34.

103. These issues are addressed to a limited extent by Oftel.

104. Several factors contributed to this state of affairs. First, railroads were subject to keen competition from road transport. Second, BR's largely obsolete tracks and equipment at the time of nationalization put the company in heavy debt right from the start. Finally, political expediency by both Labour and Conservative governments contributed to BR's decline. Expediency generally took three forms: (1) Keep rail prices low as part of broader anti-inflation programs; (2) Suspend modernization efforts to reduce overall public expenditures; and (3) Keep unprofitable routes to appease the general public. BR's early years are lucidly assessed in Terence R. Gourvish, *British Railways: 1948–1973* (Cambridge: Cambridge University Press, 1986).

105. Winston Churchill, for example, declared his support as early as 1918.

106. The remark belongs to John Davies, minister of Industry under Heath, and is quoted in Gourvish, *British Railways,* 581.

107. See, for example, Richard Pryke and John S. Dodgson, *The British Rail Problem* (Boulder, CO: Westview, 1975).

108. Redwood, *Going for Broke,* 114–15.

109. As I mentioned earlier, BR had historically been underfunded. DOT remained similarly skeptical about BR's investment plan, which was projected to cost £1,876 million for the period 1981–85, an average of £375 million a year (Philip S. Bagwell, *End of the Line?* [London: Verso, 1984], 64).

110. Terence R. Gourvish, "British Rail's Business-Led Organization, 1977–1990: Government-Industry Relations in Britain's Public Sector," *Business History Review* 64 (1990): 141.

111. Bagwell, *End of the Line?,* 43.

112. *Hansard, House of Commons* 14 July 1980, col. 1056.

113. British Transport Hotels showed an average profit ratio of 4.7 percent throughout the 1970s, but Sealink and Hovercraft produced mixed results. The real jewel, however, was the Property Board. It showed a net profit of nearly £30 million in 1979–80 while its nonoperational, and hence salable, assets were valued at £180 million in 1980 (Bagwell, *End of the Line?,* 47–51).

114. Bagwell, *End of the Line?,* chap. 4; Michael R. Bonavia, *Twilight of British Rail?* (Newton Abbot, U.K.: David & Charles, 1985), chap. 9.

115. *Transport,* January/February 1990, 16.

116. *Hansard, House of Commons* 20 June 1988, col. 835.

117. As I explained in chapter 2, public opinion polls prior to privatization showed that the public disapproved of these sales for the most part.

118. *Financial Times,* 11 September 1990, 11.

119. *Financial Times,* 8 June 1988, 23; *Financial Times,* 11 September 1990, 11.

120. *Economist,* 30 March 1991, 51.

121. This alternative was proposed in a report issued by the Centre for Policy Studies: Andrew Gritten, *Reviving the Railways: A Victorian Future?* (London: Centre for Policy Studies, 1988).

122. John Redwood, *Signals from a Railway Conference* (London: Centre for Policy Studies, 1988).

123. *Economist,* 30 March 1991, 51.

124. Kenneth Irvine, *The Right Lines* (London: Adam Smith Institute, 1987).

125. *Financial Times,* 12 April 1989, 10.

126. See, for example, the study by John Hibbs, *Transport Without Politics . . . ?* (London: Institute of Economic Affairs, 1982), 33–39.

127. See, for example, Chris Nash, "Paying Subsidy to British Rail: How to Get Value for Money," *Public Money* 5 (1986): 35–40.

128. More recently, however, Sir Robert's successor denied favoring the plc option (*Financial Times,* 14 January 1992, 6).

129. *Financial Times,* 17 October 1989, 10.

130. *Financial Times,* 14 October 1988, 10; *Financial Times,* 20 July 1989, 6.

131. Under private ownership, argued Jimmy Knapp, the rail union's general secretary, customers could see a 100 percent increase in fares and a possible closure of 1,000 miles of line in rural areas. Workers, he concluded, could expect a loss of up to 25,000 jobs (*Financial Times,* 28 June 1989, 14). In some respects, the union position over privatizing railroads is similar to that over privatizing telecommunications. In both cases, unions opposed privatization in principle but were prepared to fight to maintain the companies' monopolistic position in a postprivatization regime. Keeping BR as a discrete unit benefits unions because it not only enhances the chances of the company's commercial survival, but it also permits unions to retain centralized control over pay bargaining.

132. John Kay and Z. A. Silberston, "The New Industrial Policy—Privatization and Competition," *Midland Bank Review* (Spring 1984): 8–16.

133. *Financial Times,* 23/24 January 1993, 6.

134. Department of Transport, *New Opportunities for the Railways—The Privatisation of BR* Cmnd 2012 (London: HMSO, 1993).

135. The parcels business recently posted an operating loss for the fifth consecutive year; losses stand at 32.5 percent of receipts for 1991–92. The freight business fared better because it has been unprofitable for only the last two years; losses stand at 7.1 percent for 1991–92. Although current financial troubles can be partly attributed to the recession, it remains obvious that the parcels service has been consistently unprofitable. Moreover, BR carries a narrow range of freight whose flow is already in jeopardy (*Financial Times,* 15 February 1993, 10). For these reasons, the government decided to break freight operations into several units. Although such restructuring measures might attract some private interest, it is not clear whether the proposed smaller companies will have sufficient size to compete successfully with road transport (*International Railway Journal,* November 1993, 6).

136. These issues have been raised and discussed in a consultation paper published in October 1992 and in reports by user groups, such as Transport 2000. See *Financial Times,* 14 October 1992, 11; Reg Harman, "Railway Privatization: Does it Bring New Opportunities?" *Public Money & Management* 13:1 (1993): 19–25; and *International Railway Journal,* February 1992, 16.

137. According to BR's annual report, the central government's grant for 1991–92 was £892 million. Keenly aware of BR's troubles and the recession, the Department of Transport abandoned plans to eliminate subsidies to the Network SouthEast division and expected they would reach £400 million by 1993. Similarly, instead of a planned reduction in aid to the other subsidized unit, Regional Railways, the Department estimates an increase to £600 million (*International Railway Journal* April 1992, 8).

138. Philip Burns, "Privatization of Railway Passenger Services," *Public Money & Management* 13:1 (1993): 7–9.

139. *International Railway Journal,* September 1992, 12.

140. *Times,* 21 January 1993, 8; *Times,* 23 January 1993, 2.

141. *Times,* 3 February 1993, 5.

142. Philip Snowden, "Privatizing British Rail," *Public Money & Management* 13:4 (1993): 4–5.

143. Profitability figures in this paragraph were calculated from various years of BR's annual reports.

144. Figures in this and the next paragraphs are calculated from data provided in Central Statistical Office, *Annual Abstract of Statistics* (London: HMSO, 1985; 1991).

145. *International Railway Journal,* July 1992, 17.

146. The long delays and financial difficulties of the most successful (to date), privately financed project, the Channel Tunnel, are instructive. For a review of public-private finance schemes in transport and their problems, see the essays in Economic Research Centre, *Public and Private Investment in Transport,* European Conference of Ministers of Transport Roundtable No. 81 (Paris: ECMT, 1990).

147. ECMT, *Statistical Trends in Transport, 1965–1987* (Paris: ECMT, 1990), 99.

148. *Transport,* January/February 1990, 17.

149. D. Hann, "The Process of Government and UK Oil Participation Policy," *Energy Policy* 14 (1986): 253–61.

150. Redwood, *Going for Broke,* 112.

151. Klapp, *The Sovereign Entrepreneur,* 1. Her claim, however, may have been premature because subsequent practice worldwide suggests that the reverse is true. For recent global privatization and liberalization trends in the oil industry, see Ghadar, "Oil"; and Thomas W. Wälde, "Recent Developments in Negotiating International Petroleum Agreements," *Petroleum Economist (International Energy Law)* July 1992, 1–8.

152. *Economist,* 18 June 1977, 119.

153. See, for example, Arnold, *Britain's Oil,* 312.

154. Prosser, *Nationalised Industries;* and Curwen, *Public Enterprise.*

155. This shift has been noted by several analysts. See, for example, Mitchell, "Privatisation as a Myth?" 24; and Suleiman, "Politics of Privatization," 116–117.

156. *Financial Times,* 6 March 1989, 8.

157. *Financial Times,* 11 September 1990, 11; *Economist,* 15 September 1990, 71–72.

158. *Times,* 10 October 1990, 11.

159. Wolfe similarly argues that privatization in Britain was an ad hoc policy. See Joel D. Wolfe, "Reorganizing Interest Representation: A Political Analysis of Privatization in Britain," in Richard E. Faglesong and Joel P. Wolfe, eds., *The Politics of Economic Adjustment: Pluralism, Corporatism, and Privatization* (Westport, CT: Greenwood, 1989).

## Chapter 5

1. This is not to say that there was no opposition to Mitterrand's nationalization program.

2. Fraser, *Privatisation,* 110–12.

3. Organization for Economic Cooperation and Development, *Economic Surveys: France* (Paris: OECD, 1987), 35.

4. John Tuppen, *Chirac's France, 1986–88* (New York: St. Martin's, 1991), 186.

5. In addition to banks and insurance companies, industrial SOEs not previously offered for sale include Aérospatiale and Snecma in the aerospace industry, Air France and Compagnie Générale Maritime in transport, Renault in automobiles, Seita in tobacco, and Usinor-Sacilor in steel. It was hoped that proceeds from these and other sales would raise FFr40 billion in 1993 alone. *New York Times,* 27 May 1993, C1; *Financial Times,* 27 May 1993, 21.

6. Colbertism, as this tradition is known, calls on state agencies to fully utilize state and private resources (through the development and dissemination of technology, credit, and such) in an effort to foster growth beyond that achievable through sole reliance on private initiative. For an elaboration of the role of Colbertism in the French economy, see William Adams, *Restructuring the French Economy* (Washington, DC: Brookings Institution, 1989), 45–46; and Shonfield, *Modern Capitalism,* 73–80.

7. Claire Andrieu, Lucette Le Van, and Antoine Prost, eds., *Les Nationalisations de la Libération* (Paris: Presses de la Fondation Nationale des Sciences Politiques, 1987), 15.

8. Michel Bauer, "The Politics of State-Directed Privatization: The Case of France, 1986–88," *West European Politics* 11:4 (1988): 49–60.

9. Nationalization events have been summarized by Richard Kuisel, *Capitalism and the State in Modern France* (Cambridge: Cambridge University Press, 1981), 202–11, and explored in greater detail in Andrieu, Le Van, and Prost, *Nationalisations.*

10. De Gaulle quoted in "Nationalization in France," *The World Today* 2 (1946): 365.

11. The state took over Société Générale (SG), Crédit Lyonnais (CL), Comptoir National d'Escompte de Paris, and Banque Nationale pour le Commerce et l'Industrie. The latter two were merged in 1966 to form Banque Nationale de Paris (BNP). Mitterrand purchased the remaining shares of BNP, SG, and CL in 1982, and Chirac put all three up for sale in 1986.

12. In some instances, the behavior of certain industrialists during the World War II prompted the state takeover. Unlike Britain, France was occupied by the Nazis. Because some business leaders collaborated with the Germans, their assets were confiscated after the war. The case of Renault, the automobile manufacturer, is the most celebrated example.

13. Maurice Bye, "Nationalization in France," in Mario Einaudi, Maurice Bye, and Ernesto Rossi, *Nationalization in France and Italy* (Ithaca, NY: Cornell University Press, 1955), 81.

14. Adams, *Restructuring the French Economy.*

15. Shonfield, *Modern Capitalism,* 85–86.

16. Ibid, 130–31.

17. See, for example, the excellent studies by Michel Crozier, *The Bureaucratic Phenomenon* (Chicago: University of Chicago Press, 1964); and Ezra N. Suleiman, *Politics, Power, and Bureaucracy in France* (Princeton: Princeton University Press, 1974).

18. The argument against the "state bourgeoisie" is amply illustrated in the works of two members of that elite who are also fervent proponents of privatization. See Edouard Balladur, *Je Crois en l'Homme plus qu'en l'Etat* (Paris: Flammarion, 1987); and Albin Chalandon, *Quitte ou Double* (Paris: Grasset, 1986).

19. Stephen S. Cohen, *Modern Capitalist Planning: The French Model* (Berkeley and Los Angeles: University of California Press, 1977), 195.

20. Hall, *Governing the Economy,* 158; Jack Hayward, *The State and the Market Economy* (New York: New York University Press, 1986), especially chapter 4.

21. It did not specify, however, which sectors belonged to these categories.

22. These developments yielded mixed results. On the positive side, they strengthened the legitimacy of the SOEs' strategic role and helped provide alternative sources of capital outside public expenditure constraints. They also helped establish a successful French presence in several high-tech areas such as military and civil aeronautics, nuclear engineering, and helicopter production. On the negative side, not all national champions were successful. Projects in computers and air transport, for instance, produced several white elephants such as the Plan Calcul and Concorde. Numerous parliamentary and government-sponsored commissions castigated the wisdom of some of these investments and urged a reversal of course.

23. Jean-Pierre Anastassopoulos, Georges Blanc, and Pierre Dussauge, *State-Owned Multinationals* (New York: John Wiley & Sons, 1987), 115–17, 141.

24. Ibid; Harvey B. Feigenbaum, *The Politics of Public Enterprise: Oil and the French State* (Princeton: Princeton University Press, 1985).

25. For an excellent review of state-management relations, see Raymond Vernon, "Linking Managers to Ministers: Dilemma of State-Owned Enterprise," *Journal of Policy Analysis and Management* 4 (1984): 39–55.

26. Christian Stoffaes and Jacques Victtori, *Nationalisations* (Paris: Flammarion, 1977), 143.

27. Hayward, *State and Market Economy,* 92.

28. Hall, *Governing the Economy,* 202.

29. Stoffaes and Victorri, *Nationalisations,* 325–75.

30. Abdelilah Hamdouch, *L'Etat d'Influence: Nationalisations et Privatisations en France* (Paris: CNRS, 1989); Bertrand Jacquillat, "Nationalization and Privatization in Contemporary France," *Government Union Review* 8:4 (1987): 24; Harvey B. Feigenbaum, "Democracy at the Margins: The International System and Policy Change in France," in Richard E. Foglesong and Joel D. Wolfe, eds., *The Politics of Economic Adjustment: Pluralism, Corporatism, and Privatization* (Westport, CT: Greenwood, 1989), 91.

31. Balladur, *Je Crois en l'Homme,* 47. Although this particular ideology was novel to the Gaullists, a strand of it had already been espoused by Giscard's party in the 1970s.

32. Henri Lepage, *Pourquoi la Propriété?* (Paris: Hachette, 1985).

33. Jacques Garello, *A Nos Dirigeants* (Paris: Albatros, 1986), 123–27.

34. Balladur, *Je Crois en l'Homme,* 48.

35. Chalandon, *Quitte ou Double,* 215.

36. Quoted in Chalandon, *Quitte ou Double,* 217. This was precisely Herbert Morrison's concern with public corporations in Britain.

37. Pierre Dupont Gabriel, *L'Etat-Patron, C'est Moi* (Paris: Flammarion, 1985), 235.

38. Chalandon, *Quitte ou Double,* 217.

39. Ibid, 216.

40. Armand Bizaguet, "The French Public Sector and the 1986 to 1988 Privatizations," *International Review of Administrative Sciences* 54 (1988): 559.

41. The reverse problem—that is, Renault's political ties with the French government—became a major issue in 1993 since the two automobile manufacturers decided to set up joint ventures in component buying (excluding truck-making divisions) and quality control "so as to act," according to Renault, "as if the two groups were one company" (*Financial Times,* 24 June 1992, 17). Largely because of Renault's status as an SOE, Swedish shareholders finally rejected the proposed merger despite assurances by the French that they intended to relinquish state control by privatizing Renault as soon as market conditions permitted.

42. Balladur, *Je Crois en l'Homme,* 63.

43. Chalandon, *Quitte ou Double,* chap. 5.

44. Balladur, *Je Crois en l'Homme,* 53–54.

45. Didier Pene, "La Privatisation en France," *L'Actualité Juridique-Droit Administratif* 5 (May 1987): 291.

46. Balladur, *Je Crois en l'Homme,* 33.

47. Ibid.

48. Ibid, chap. 7.

49. *Journal Officiel, Débats Parlementaires: Sénat,* 21 May 1986, 744.

50. Edouard Balladur, *Vers la Liberté* (Paris: La Documentation Française, 1987), 72.

51. *Journal Officiel, Débats Parlementaires: Assemblée Nationale,* 22 April 1986, 211.

52. Bauer, "Politics of State-Directed Privatization": 53.

53. Quoted in *L'Expansion,* 20 January–2 February 1984, 53.

54. Ibid; Alain Griotteray, *Les Privatisations. Oui, Mais . . .* (Paris: Editions Républicaines, 1987), 160–61. Balladur later admitted that Renault was excluded largely for political reasons. Curiously, he also added that Air France was excluded because it retained a certain degree of monopoly at the time, but he neglected to mention that so did CGE and it was sold. See his testimony before the Commission d'Enquête, *Journal Officiel, Assemblée Nationale, Documents* (Auditions) 9th legislature, 1st session 1989–90 (no. 969), 29 October 1989, vol. 1, 17.

55. When Balladur was pressed to answer this question by the special commission, he was reminded that several of his former colleagues had admitted to this rationale. He denied it, saying that he also sold off money-losing concerns, such as Compagnie Générale des Constructions Téléphoniques (CGCT) and TF-1, but not the profitable Air France. Surely, profitability was not the only criterion used to determine the list of *privatisables,* but the fact that so few on that list were unprofitable reinforces rather than refutes the rule (Ibid, 18).

56. Jacquillat, "Nationalization": 32. Nevertheless, the ruling coalition did not escape the criticism that shares were sold at prices lower than should have been the case. A parliamentary committee's report revealed that shares of eleven out of twelve companies were sold at a 21.1 percent average first-day discount—the percentage difference between the sale price and the quotation price the first day—with the maximum being Sogenal's share (80 percent) and the minimum being Société Générale's share (6 percent). Only one company's shares, Suez, sold off shortly after the stock market crashed in October 1987, showed a negative first-day discount—indicating losses for buyers—of 17.7 percent. Similarly, figures from first-quarter quotations confirmed this general pattern. For a more detailed presentation of these and other figures, consult the special commission's report, *Journal Officiel, Assemblée Nationale, Documents* (Rapport), 160–203, especially 161. Although some of these companies were banks and insurance companies and therefore their share prices were more difficult to value, the consistent pattern of undervaluation fueled accusations that were also leveled at Thatcher's government at the time. The state, critics charged, was selling shares at artificially low prices to create the illusion of small shareholder interest and generate momentum in favor of privatization by pointing to success in each successive sale. Based on this evidence, their charges appear justified. Balladur's more recent sales reaffirm this pattern of undervaluation. BNP's first-day discount was 20.4 percent and Rhône-Poulenc's was 12.6 percent (*Le Figaro-Economie,* 13 December 1993, 14).

57. *L'Express,* 27 September 1985, 29.

58. *L'Expansion,* 9/22 October 1987, 178.

59. Both conditions were later breached.

60. Hamdouch, *L'Etat d'Influence,* 206–9.

61. For more information in the composition of stable nuclei since 1993, see the *European,* 11–17 February 1994, 19.

62. Tony Prosser, *The Privatisation of Public Enterprises in Britain and France:*

*The State, Constitutions and Public Policy,* Working Paper no. 88/364 (Florence, Italy: European University Institute, 1988), 52.

63. "Privatization has not changed a single manager named by the RPR," charged the Socialists in 1988 (Parti Socialiste, *Privatisations: Main Basse sur la France* [Paris: PS, n.d.], 27).

64. For more details, see Hamdouch, *L'Etat d'Influence,* 200–1; and Parti Socialiste, *Privatisations,* 26.

65. Bauer, "Politics of State-Directed Privatization," 60.

66. Pene, "Privatisation en France," 296.

67. Prosser, *Privatization of Public Enterprises,* 52.

68. Parti Socialiste, *Privatisations,* 34–35.

69. *Le Monde,* 17 September 1987, 34.

70. *Le Monde,* 28 May 1988, supplement.

71. Stephane Denis, *Le Roman de l'Argent* (Paris: Albin Michel, 1988), 121–36.

72. Parti Socialiste, *Privatisations,* 23. Two academics further pondered: "[N]ationalization, privatization, what changes? The state is always there" (Michel Bauer and Benedicte Bertin-Mourot, *Les 200: Comment Devient-on un Grand Patron?* [Paris: Seuil, 1987], 190–91).

73. *Le Monde,* 9 April 1988, 12.

74. *Financial Times* (Survey: France), 22 June 1992, iv.

75. *New York Times,* 8 April 1991, C2; *Financial Times,* 13 September 1991, 17.

76. *L'Express,* 19 April 1991, 19.

77. For a review of these instruments, see Michel Durupty, *Les Privatisations en France,* Notes et Etudes Documentaires no. 4857 (Paris: La Documentation Française, 1988), 23–29.

78. *Financial Times,* 29 April 1994, 2.

79. *Financial Times,* 16 March 1993, 19.

80. François Platone, "Public Opinion and Electoral Change," in *Developments in French Politics,* in Peter A. Hall, Jack Hayward, and Howard Machin, eds. (New York: St. Martin's, 1990), 75.

81. For a review of this debate among members of the Center-Right coalition before the 1993 legislative elections, see *Le Figaro (Fig-Eco),* 11 February 1993, iii.

82. *Financial Times,* 24 February 1993, 2.

83. The role of foreign investors in some instances, however, can be a double-edged knife. Renault's case illustrates the potential danger. On the one hand, it has been encouraged to seek a foreign partner, Volvo, to pool technical expertise and increase market share. On the other hand, even after privatization, it should "remain a French-owned company" because the labor unions and the general public would not have it any other way, said Louis Schweitzer, Renault's president (*New York Times,* 3 June 1993, C4). Small wonder that Volvo's shareholders finally rejected the proposed merger.

84. *Le Figaro (Fig-Eco),* 19 March 1993, ii.

85. Hayward, *State and Market Economy,* 229.

## Chapter 6

1. This poverty of energy resources, particularly after the oil shocks in the 1970s, accentuated the need to reduce French dependence on mostly imported oil and to diversify into alternative, domestically produced sources of energy. The drive behind the nuclear program has certainly been motivated by this need. Christian Stoffaes, "Industrial Policy in the High-Technology Industries," in William James Adams and Christian Stoffaes, eds., *French Industrial Policy* (Washington, DC: Brookings Institution, 1986), 47.

2. Michael Tanzer cited in Feigenbaum, *Politics of Public Enterprise,* 55.

3. Quoted in N. J. D. Lucas, *Energy in France* (London: Europa, 1979), 11.

4. Feigenbaum, *Politics of Public Enterprise,* 68–69. The company would also be used as a wedge in the major oil company cartel (Stoffaes and Victorri, *Nationalisations,* 67).

5. Nevertheless, Elf managers resented being used as a quasi-diplomatic instrument of cooperation with oil producers. More specifically, they were opposed to state-to-state contracts because these were negotiated largely for political rather than commercial reasons. This friction created a fertile climate for Elf managers to argue for less state control.

6. J. E. Hartshorn cited in Feigenbaum, *Politics of Public Enterprise,* 61.

7. Philippe Simonnot, *Le Complot Pétrolier* (Paris: Alain Moreau, 1976).

8. Elf CEO Albin Chalandon was able to pressure successive French governments into granting Elf more managerial autonomy in the areas of investment and oil contracts. Elf's purchase of Texasgulf in 1981 was the single largest French acquisition in North America at the time. Despite considerable opposition from unions and several members of the Socialist and Communist parties, Chalandon was able to convince then Industry Minister Pierre Dreyfus to approve the acquisition on the rationale that Elf could become a "little French Exxon." Doing so, he maintained, would enhance the government's commitment to independent management and strengthen the corporation's image as a serious commercial operation (*New York Times,* 22 November 1981, section 3, 4). Oil contracts were the other point of friction. Since the first oil shock in 1973, successive French governments negotiated government-to-government contracts with numerous oil-producing countries in an effort to secure external supplies. When one such oil contract with Saudi Arabia was signed in 1974, its terms reflected the prevailing uncertainty of the time. Eight years later, however, the world oil market had changed dramatically. The oil glut of 1982 brought financial difficulties to Elf's refining operations, precipitating annual losses of FFr 3 billion. In addition, the SOE had to spend half its consolidated profits to pay back the acquisition of Texasgulf. For these reasons, company officials complained of high Saudi oil prices which under the terms of the contract exceeded spot prices in 1982. Convinced that the oil glut was more than just a temporary phenomenon—about which, in retrospect, he was right—Chalandon told a panel of journalists that Elf could do away with Saudi oil because 80 percent of corporate needs were covered from other sources (*Le Monde,* 17 June 1983, 34). This line of thought ran contrary to the tenets

of prevailing energy policy, which called for sacrificing for the sake of long-term security and gave state managers occasion to demand more autonomy.

9. *Le Figaro*, 18–19 June 1983, 14. See also Albin Chalandon's personal account of the affair in his book *Quitte ou Double* (Paris: Grasset, 1986).

10. *Le Figaro*, 16 June 1983, 8; *Le Monde*, 17 June 1983, 34.

11. *Le Monde*, 16 June 1983, 38.

12. There are some instances in which the reverse is true.

13. Figures taken from *French Company Handbook* (Paris: International Business Development, 1988).

14. *Financial Times*, 10 November 1983, 3.

15. Chalandon, *Quitte ou Double*, chap. 3.

16. Jean-Maxime Lévêque, *Dénationalisations: Mode d' Emploi* (Paris: Albin Michel, 1985), 64.

17. See, for example, Bertrand Jacquillat, *Désétatiser* (Paris: Robert Laffont, 1985). This was an argument also endorsed by the French employers' peak association, Confédération Nationale du Patronat Français.

18. *Petroleum Economist*, July 1985, 24.

19. *Petroleum Intelligence Weekly*, 11 November 1985, 7.

20. *Petroleum Economist*, May 1986, 175.

21. *Financial Times*, 26 September 1986, 40.

22. *Le Figaro*, 15 July 1986, 1; *Financial Times*, 15 July 1986, 1. "I must be," emphasized Mitterrand in a televised interview, "the guarantor of national independence" (*Le Monde*, 16 July 1986, 6).

23. Interestingly, on 26 September 1986, Balladur fixed the sale price at FFr 305 per share after consulting with the Commission on Privatization, which specified the minimum price to be FFr 300. The price, however, was 10 percent lower than the value quoted in the Bourse the previous day (FFr 335) and 13 percent lower than the price many financial analysts considered reasonable (FFr 350). Not surprisingly, Socialists immediately accused the ruling coalition of "selling the family silver" too cheaply (*Le Monde*, 27 September 1986, 35). Although Balladur justified his decision as reflecting lower prices due to the global oil glut at the time, his political objectives became clearer one month later when he announced that the offer was oversubscribed. Indeed, being able to show strong interest among small investors and employees was critical to Chirac's privatization program, not only because Elf's was the first sale, but also because it would generate momentum for future sales by virtue of success.

24. Although initially the law set the limit of foreign participation at 10 percent, in a slap to Mitterrand, the revised text raised the limit to 20 percent.

25. André Delion and Michel Durupty, "Chronique des Entreprises Publiques," *Revue Française d'Administration Publique* 40 (1986): 746.

26. *Petroleum Economist*, April 1992, 45.

27. This disengagement can also be witnessed by the sale of government shares in Total. It is important to note, however, that even after the sale of shares in Total (a mixed enterprise), the state retained the right to approve the company's senior officials as well as the right to suspend board decisions that may lead to a change of control (*Petroleum Economist*, July 1992, 41).

28. Edouard Balladur, ed., *Colloque "Pour de Nouvelles Privatisations"* (Paris: Association pour le Libéralisme Populaire, 1988), 135.

29. *Le Monde (selection hebdomadaire),* 25–31 March 1993, 12. Le Floch-Prigent was chief of staff (*directeur de cabinet*) during Pierre Dreyfus's tenure as industry minister in the early 1980s.

30. Ibid.

31. *L'Expansion,* 10 November/8 December 1993, 13.

32. *L'Expansion,* 7/20 October 1993, 116.

33. *Le Figaro (Fig-Eco),* 14 December 1993, iv.

34. *L'Expansion,* 7/20 October 1993, 113.

35. *Le Figaro (Fig-Eco),* 23 December 1993, iv.

36. *Le Monde (selection hebdomadaire),* 10 February 1994, 10.

37. Duch, *Privatizing the Economy,* 170.

38. Ibid, 172, 185.

39. Libois, *Genèse et Croissance,* 83.

40. As evidence of such beneficial effects, it was stressed that terminals for Minitel, a videotext service launched in 1978, were manufactured by two French companies, Thomson and Matra.

41. Libois, *Genèse et Croissance,* 241–43.

42. Genevieve Bonnetblanc, *Les Télécommunications Françaises: Quel Statut pour Quel Entreprise?* (Paris: La Documentation Française, 1985), 154.

43. Duch, *Privatizing the Economy,* 176.

44. International Telecommunications Union (ITU), *Common Carrier Statistics* (Geneva: ITU, 1984).

45. PTT is a generic term used worldwide to refer to the ministry responsible for providing postal, telegraph, and telecommunications services.

46. Jean-Michel Quatrepoint, *Histoire Secrète des Dossiers Noirs de la Gauche* (Paris: Alain Moreau, 1986), 274.

47. Ibid, 263.

48. The argument for using nationalization as a way of reinvigorating private multinationals is explored in Anastassopoulos, Blanc, and Dussauge, *State-Owned Multinationals.*

49. The figure drops to 49 percent if we also include equipment produced by subsidiaries of multinationals such as Philips (Quatrepoint, *Histoire Secrète,* 269).

50. Hall, *Governing the Economy,* 209; Henry Ergas cited in Morgan and Webber, "Divergent Paths."

51. *Financial Times,* 14 January 1985, 17.

52. *L'Expansion,* 21 September/4 October 1984, 194–206; Quatrepoint, *Histoire Secrète,* 274.

53. *Financial Times,* 1 February 1985, 12.

54. Jacques Darmon, *Le Grand Dérangement* (Paris: Jean-Claude Lattes, 1985).

55. Ibid, 185.

56. See, for example, Balladur, *Je Crois en l'Homme;* and Chalandon, *Quitte ou Double.*

57. Note Elf's recruitment patterns and problems discussed earlier.

58. *L'Expansion*, 21 September 1984, 206.

59. Figures include profitability ratios for France Télécom but not COGECOM (the holding company of FT's subsidiaries). Care must be exercised when interpreting the figures because FT was a government agency until January 1991. Because of vast differences in accounting procedures, profitability ratios are not comparable to those of SOEs or private firms. Ratios were calculated from company annual reports.

60. By 1992, FT was spending 25 percent of total revenues in investments and 4 percent in research and development relative to BT's 16 percent and 2 percent, respectively (*L'Expansion*, 25 November/8 December 1993, 79).

61. Gérard Longuet, *Télécoms: La Conquête de Nouveaux Espaces* (Paris: Dunod, 1988), 37.

62. Volker Schneider et al., "The Dynamics of Videotext Development in Britain, France and Germany: A Cross-national Comparison," *European Journal of Communications* 6 (1991): 187–212.

63. Interview with the author, April 1991, Washington DC.

64. *European Telecommunications*, 1 July 1986, 5–6; Longuet, *Télécoms*, 67–95.

65. Gilles de Margerie, "L'Integration Services-Equipments en Télécommunications: Le Cas Français," *Revue d'Economie Industrielle* 39 (1987): 198–207.

66. *European Telecommunications*, November 1984, 8–11. Some of the problems associated with the organizational structure of French telecommunications up to 1986 are discussed in Jean Pierre Coustel, "Telecommunications Services in France," *Telecommunications Policy* 10 (1986): 229–44.

67. *Financial Times*, 25 September 1987, 2; *European Telecommunications*, 1 January 1988, 1.

68. *Financial Times*, 18 December 1987, 2.

69. Longuet, *Télécoms*, 85, 101–2.

70. *Financial Times*, 11 March 1987, 3.

71. *Financial Times*, 20 July 1988, 2; *European Telecommunications*, 15 August 1988, 3.

72. Unlike the British case, France had to contend with directives from Brussels in light of European integration in 1992. In a series of such directives, the most famous of which was the 1987 Green Paper, Sir Leon Brittan, former EU Commissioner in charge of competition, prepared the way for a single market in telecommunications, sometimes without seeking the endorsement of member states. Despite resentment, coming not only from France, EU pressure has had an impact on French thinking. It made the need to change FT's status more obvious and more urgent. More recently, the full deregulation of the EU market by 1998 has set in motion yet another push for changing FT's status.

73. Marcel Roulet, "France Telecom: Preparing for More Competition," *Telecommunications Policy* 12 (1988): 110.

74. *L'Expansion*, 2/15 April 1992, 68.

75. Hubert Prévot, *L'Avenir du Service Public de la Poste et des Télécommunications* (Paris: La Documentation Française, 1989).

76. *Financial Times,* 30 October 1989, 4.

77. *Financial Times,* 19 September 1989, 3.

78. *L'Expansion* 4/17 April 1986, 93.

79. Marc Fossier and Marie-Monique Steckel, *France Telecom: An Insider's Guide* (Chicago: Telephony, 1991).

80. *L'Express,* 25 April 1991, 20; *Le Figaro-Economie,* 11 February 1991, 6.

81. *European Telecommunications,* 1 April 1991, 2.

82. The annual levy the state charges FT disappeared at the end of 1993 when the company started paying normal corporate tax. It is estimated that this change would have contributed an additional FFr 6 billion to FT's net profits in 1991 (*Financial Times* [Survey: France] 22 June 1992, iv).

83. Ibid.

84. *Le Figaro-Economie,* 11 February 1991, 4.

85. Ministère des Postes, Télécommunications et Espace, "La Réforme des PTT est Définitivement Adoptée au Parlement," *En Direct* 72 (1990): 1.

86. The protest mode of input is well documented in Frank Wilson, *Interest-Group Politics in France* (Cambridge: Cambridge University Press, 1987).

87. *Le Figaro (Fig-Eco),* 11 February 1993, iii.

88. *European Telecommunications,* 1 August 1993, 2; *Le Monde (selection hebdomadaire),* 29 July 1993, 9.

89. *European Telecommunications,* 15 December 1993, 1.

90. *L'Expansion,* 25 November/3 December 1993, 78.

91. *Le Figaro (Fig-Eco),* 23 December 1993, iv.

92. *European,* 20–26 May 1994, 17.

93. The Franco-Prussian war of 1870–71 aptly highlighted the inadequacy of the French transport system, which contributed to the humiliating French defeat (Kimon A. Doukas, *The French Railroads and the State* [New York: Columbia University Press, 1945], 52).

94. Ibid, 234–35.

95. SNCF, *Rapport d'Activité* (Paris: SNCF, 1983), 13.

96. Faced with a climbing total deficit of FFr 50 billion in 1982, the Socialists undertook the task of improving the SOE's finances by encouraging investment from local government while simultaneously increasing disbursements from central government. In some cases, such as the Channel Tunnel, the state also solicited participation from private investors. Marking a change from previous practice and in stark contrast to the British case, support from the public purse was to cover, in addition to operational costs, SNCF's development costs. Why? The 1983 act states that such subsidies are warranted "because of the essential contribution made by rail transport to the economic and social life of the nation, its role in meeting the right to transport and its advantages in terms of safety and energy" (*Jane's World Railways, 1983–84* [London: Jane's, 1984], 466). In addition, responsibility for financing public transport for passengers rests not only with central government, but also with councils at the regional and department levels. Although funds from subnational sources barely amount to 1 percent in most cases, many localities require the operator to cross-subsidize loss-making routes with funds generated from more profitable ones (Philippe Gamon,

"France," in *Promoting Regional Transport,* Economic Research Centre, ECMT Roundtable no. 81 [Paris: ECMT, 1990]). Overall support, expressed as funds from state and local government as a percentage of total rail revenues and calculated from various SNCF annual reports and issues of *Jane's World Railways,* remained virtually constant under the governments of Mauroy and Fabius at approximately 23 percent. Interestingly, the same level of support was granted by Chirac, although the figure fell slightly in 1988 to 20.9 percent. Only recently has support increased dramatically, from 28.9 percent in 1989 to 30 percent in 1991. Political factors, however, do not explain the percentage increase from 1989 to 1991; rather, subsidies remained constant whereas total rail revenues fell substantially partly due to the recession.

97. Although the board's powers are weak relative to those of SNCF's management, there is direct worker participation in formulating and executing general rail policy.

98. *International Railway Journal,* July 1991, 49.

99. Further reduction in ownership would have required amending the 1937 Nationalization Act, although that was not outside the government's powers had it wanted to pursue this option.

100. Interestingly, only 22.2 percent of SNCF funds were self-financed in 1991 relative to BT's 90 percent at the time of its sale. Consequently, even without an explosive demand growth, it is unlikely that SNCF will experience the acute modernization capital shortages that BT faced in the early 1980s.

101. Balladur, *Vers la Liberté* (Paris: La Documentation Française, 1987), 72.

102. Jean Loyrette, *Dénationaliser: Comment Réussir la Privatisation* (Paris: Dunod, 1986).

103. Michel Durupty, "Existe-t-il un Critère de l'Entreprise Publique?" *La Revue Administrative* 217 (1986): 7–19.

104. Garello, *A Nos Dirigeants,* 164.

105. This is primarily because of the high risk involved and the length of time required for a positive rate of return. There are projects, however, in which joint public-private or exclusively private financing is desirable. For a full treatment of the subject concerning France, see Bernard Gerardin, "France," in *Private and Public Investment in Transport,* Economic Research Centre, ECMT Roundtable no. 81 (Paris: ECMT, 1990).

106. SNCF, *French Railways in 1991* [Annual Report] (Paris: SNCF, 1992), 7. In fact, total investment for the entire duration of the *contrat de plan* (1990–94) envisioned an unprecedented figure of more than FFr 100 billion (including external sources of funds) in 1989 prices (*Contrat de Plan Etat-SNCF, 1990–1994* [Paris: SNCF, 1990], 55).

107. ECMT, *Statistical Trends.*

108. *Director,* October 1990, 56.

109. Ibid, 59.

110. *International Railway Journal,* October 1989, 23; SNCF, *French Railways,* 25.

111. *L'Express,* 28 January 1983, 41.

112. *Financial Times*, 15 April 1987, 22.

113. *International Railway Journal*, October 1989, 24.

114. *Financial Times*, 24 June 1991, 15. For the Socialist view of transport and public service in light of European liberalization, see the interview by the former Transport Minister Jean-Louis Bianco in *Le Figaro (Fig-Eco)*, 3 February 1993, iii.

115. *International Railway Journal*, July 1991, 48; *International Railway Journal*, September 1992, 28.

116. SNCF, *French Railways in 1990* [Annual Report] (Paris: SNCF, 1991), 10.

117. *Director*, October 1990, 59.

118. For more general information about these instruments, see Anne Stevens, *The Government and Politics of France* (New York: St. Martin's, 1992), 180–82; and Henry W. Ehrmann and Martin A. Schain, *Politics in France*, 5th ed. (New York: Harper Collins, 1992), 334–37.

119. Mitterrand used the same provision to pass his controversial nationalization law. Though it was rarely used in the early years of the Fifth Republic, it was used with increased frequency in the 1980s. During 1988–91 (Rocard's tenure as prime minister), it was used twenty-seven times!

120. Feigenbaum, "France," 5; Jeffrey R. Henig, Chris Hamnett and Harvey B. Feigenbaum, "The Politics of Privatization: A Comparative Perspective," *Governance* 1 (1988): 446.

121. The classic treatments of this widely held argument remain the two works by Ezra N. Suleiman, *Elites in French Society* (Princeton: Princeton University Press, 1978); and *Politics, Power*. This does not mean that the French state is not ridden with strife among different departments, only that the state has the "*capacity* for policy initiative, a *potential* for far-sighted planning and a *propensity* to impose its will when it is necessary to attain public objectives" (emphasis in the original) Hayward, *State and Market Economy*, 19. Wilsford further adds that despite considerable strength and tactical advantages vis-à-vis societal actors, the French State remains somewhat vulnerable to direct action, such as protests, demonstrations, and the like (David Wilsford, "Tactical Advantages versus Administrative Heterogeneity: The Strength and Limits of the French State," *Comparative Political Studies* 21 [1988]: 126–168). For a comparison between France and Britain on a similar point, see the work by Douglas E. Ashford, *British Dogmatism and French Pragmatism: Center-Local Relations in the Welfare State* (London: Allen and Unwin, 1982).

122. Note that Balladur's title in 1986 was Minister of Finance, Economy, and Privatization. The word *privatization* was dropped when Socialists returned to power in 1988. Though privatization has been similarly entrusted to one minister in 1993, the label *privatization* in the minister's title has not been reactivated.

123. Abromeit, "British Privatisation Policy," 68–85.

124. For a theoretical treatment of policy diffusion in reference to privatization, see G. John Ikenberry, "The International Spread of Privatization Policies: Inducements, Learning, and 'Policy Bandwagoning,'" in Ezra N. Suleiman and John Waterbury, eds., *The Political Economy of Public Sector Reform and Privatization* (Boulder, CO: Westview, 1990). Some empirical evidence is found in Henig, Hamnett, and Feigenbaum, "Politics of Privatization."

125. Privatization in Britain received extensive coverage in the French popular and academic press. See, for example, *L'Expansion,* 20 January/2 February 1984, 67–75; and Yves Rolland and Patrick Vieillard, "Les Privatisations en Grande Bretagne," in *Dénationalisations: Les Leçons de l'Etranger* (Paris: Economica, 1986). There were also numerous professional conferences sponsored by (mostly conservative) French groups, such as UNIR, where British officials were invited to share their experiences.

126. See the evidence provided in Feigenbaum, "France," 5–6; and Henig, Hamnett, and Feigenbaum, "Politics of Privatization," 458–59.

127. Note that Heald and Steel begin their examination of British privatization in 1982 by ascertaining that there was no official statement of the government's case. This is entirely consistent with similar claims by Abromeit, Kay and Thompson, and others.

## Chapter 7

1. For a thorough treatment of the controversy, consult André Blais, Donald Blake, and Stéphane Dion, "Do Parties Make a Difference? Parties and the Size of Government in Liberal Democracies," *American Journal of Political Science* 37 (1993): 40–62. Francis G. Castles, ed., *The Impact of Parties: Politics and Policies in Capitalist Democratic States* (London and Beverly Hills: Sage, 1982); Brian W. Hogwood, *Trends in British Public Policy: Do Governments Make a Difference?* (Buckingham and Philadelphia: Open University Press, 1992); and Richard Rose, *Do Parties Make a Difference?,* 2d ed. (London: Macmillan, 1984).

2. John Moore, "British Privatization," 116.

3. Some public choice theorists similarly emphasize the need to politically forge supportive coalitions. See, for example, Butler, "Changing the Political Dynamics," 4–13.

4. See, for example, Bertrand Jacquillat, "Nationalization," 21–50.

5. Stone makes a similar point; Deborah Stone, *Policy Paradox and Political Reason* (Boston: Little, Brown, 1988).

6. March and Olsen, *Rediscovering Institutions,* 13.

7. See, for example, Werner Neu, Karl-Heinz Neumann, and Thomas Schnöring, "Trade Patterns, Industry Structure and Industrial Policy in Telecommunications," *Telecommunications Policy* 11 (1987): 31–44.

8. For works that stress the importance of institutions, see Hall, *Governing the Economy;* R. Kent Weaver and Bert A. Rockman, eds., *Do Institutions Matter?* (Washington, DC: Brookings, 1993); and Sven Steinmo, Kathleen Thelen, and Frank Longstreth, eds., *Structuring Politics: Historical Institutionalism in Comparative Analysis* (Cambridge: Cambridge University Press, 1992).

9. For an argument noting the need to integrate sectors and national styles of policy-making into a common framework, see Gary P. Freeman, "National Styles and Policy Sectors," 467–96.

10. For thorough reviews of the debate on the strength and autonomy of the state, see, among others, Katzenstein, *Between Power and Plenty;* Joel S. Migdal, "Strong States, Weak States: Power and Accomodation," in Myron Weiner and Samuel P. Huntington, eds., *Understanding Political Development* (Boston: Little, Brown, 1987); and Eric Nordlinger, *On the Autonomy of the Democratic State* (Cambridge: Harvard University Press, 1981). For a theoretical treatment regarding privatization, see Feigenbaum, "France." For general critiques of this literature, see Gabriel A. Almond, "The Return to the State," *American Political Science Review* 82 (1988): 853–74; and Timothy Mitchell, "The Limits of the State: Beyond Statist Approaches and Their Critics," *American Political Science Review* 85 (1991): 77–96. For a critique of the strong-weak state dichotomy in regards to privatization, see Vivien A. Schmidt, "Patterns of State Intervention: The Case of Industrial Policymaking in France," paper presented at the annual APSA meeting, Chicago, 1992.

11. Richardson, *Policy Styles in Western Europe.*

12. Quoted in Marc Paillet, *Le Grand Inventaire: Socialisme ou Libéralisme?* (Paris: Denoel, 1985), 9.

13. Raymond Vernon, "Introduction: The Promise and the Challenge," in Raymond Vernon, ed., *The Promise of Privatization: A Challenge for American Foreign Policy* (New York: Council on Foreign Relations, 1988), 15.

14. The argument echoes ideas put forth in a different context by Karl Polanyi, *The Great Transformation* (Boston: Beacon, 1957).

15. For a discussion of the various instruments of control after privatization, see Cosmo Graham and Tony Prosser, *Privatizing Public Enterprises: Constitutions, the State, and Regulation in Comparative Perspective* (Oxford: Clarendon, 1991).

16. This does not mean that enterprises that provide a public service must necessarily be state-owned. In fact, as Emile Zuccarelli, former Minister of Post and Telecommunications, points out, water distribution in France has long been in private hands (Emile Zuccarelli, "Service Public: Une Nouvelle Frontière," *Le Monde,* 20 November 1992, 2).

17. This point is amply illustrated in the writings of SNCF's chair and the latest *Contrat de Plan.* See Jacques Fournier, "L'Entreprise Publique, l'Etat et le Service Public," *Projet* 220 (December 1989): 59–63; *Contrat de Plan Etat-SNCF 1990–1994* (Paris: Conseil d'Administration, 1990).

18. The recent talk of BR's "privatization" may in fact be somewhat misleading, because even John Major calls the plans "semi-privatisation," while John McGregor refers to them as "commercialisation." See the *Economist,* 16 January 1993, 53.

19. For a theoretical treatment of the process of "lesson-drawing" across countries, see Richard Rose, *Lesson-Drawing in Public Policy* (Chatham, NJ: Chatham House, 1993).

20. The controversy has been reported in detail by William Pitt, "A Test of Metal," *The Director,* April 1992, 35–38. For the response of Sir Leon Brittan, former European Community commissioner on competition, see William Pitt, "Head to Head in Europe," *The Director,* July 1992, 48–50.

21. This was precisely the argument made by Jean-Louis Bianco, former French Minister of Transport, in his interview to Jacques de Saint-Victor, *Le Figaro (Le*

*Fig-Eco),* 3 February 1993, III. The minister added that on the basis of the "principle of subsidiarity"—that is, EU decisions should be made at the lowest possible level—the privatization of public-service operators is a matter strictly under the competence of national governments. SOEs can serve additional purposes, such as propping up economically depressed regions, that are compatible with the Treaty of Rome. See Lionel Monnier, "Prospective de l'Entreprise Publique dans le Marché Unique," *Annals of Public and Cooperative Economics* 61 (1990): 9–23.

22. Suleiman, "Politics of Privatization," 133.

# Index